Two WPA Outcomes Linked to Each Core Concept

Critical Thinking, Reading, and Writing	Processes
Critical Thinking, Reading, and Writing	
Processes	Composing in Electronic Environments
Critical Thinking, Reading, and Writing	Rhetorical Knowledge
Critical Thinking, Reading, and Writing	Rhetorical Knowledge
Rhetorical Knowledge	Knowledge of Conventions
Rhetorical Knowledge	Critical Thinking, Reading, and Writing
Critical Thinking, Reading, and Writing	Processes
Rhetorical Knowledge	Processes
Knowledge of Conventions	Critical Thinking, Reading, and Writing

The Essentials of Writing
Writing
Ten Core Concepts

Robert P. Yagelski
University at Albany, State University of New York

CENGAGE
Learning

Australia • Brazil • Japan • Korea • Mexico • Singapore • Spain • United Kingdom • United States

CENGAGE
Learning°

The Essentials of Writing:
Ten Core Concepts,
Robert P. Yagelski

Product Director: Monica Eckman

Product Manager: Chris Bennem

Senior Content Developer: Leslie Taggart

Content Developer: Margaret Manos

Product Assistant: Kerry Devito

Media Developer: Janine Tangney

Marketing Brand Manager: Lydia LeStar

Senior Content Project Manager:
Michael Lepera

Art Director: Hannah Wellman

Manufacturing Planner: Betsy Donaghey

Rights Acquisition Specialist: Ann Hoffman

Production Service/ Compositor:
Integra Software Services Pvt. Ltd.

Cover and Text Designer: Bill Reuter

Cover Image: © Jim Barber/Shutterstock.com

For product information and technology assistance, contact us at
Cengage Learning Customer & Sales Support, 1-800-354-9706

For permission to use material from this text or product,
submit all requests online at **www.cengage.com/permissions.**

Further permissions questions can be emailed to
permissionrequest@cengage.com.

Library of Congress Control Number: 2013952194

ISBN-13: 978-1-285-44299-0

ISBN-10: 1-285-44299-7

Cengage Learning
200 First Stamford Place, 4th Floor
Stamford, CT 06902
USA

Cengage Learning is a leading provider of customized learning solutions with office locations around the globe, including Singapore, the United Kingdom, Australia, Mexico, Brazil and Japan. Locate your local office at **international.cengage.com/region.**

Cengage Learning products are represented in Canada by Nelson Education, Ltd.

For your course and learning solutions, visit **www.cengage.com.**

Purchase any of our products at your local college store or at our preferred online store **www.cengagebrain.com.**

Instructors: Please visit **login.cengage.com** and log in to access instructor-specific resources.

Printed in the United States of America
1 2 3 4 5 6 7 17 16 15 14 13

Brief Contents

Contents

Chapter 4   A Student Writer Applies the Core Concepts

Chapter 5   Working with Ideas and Information

Chapter 6   Designing Documents

Chapter 7   Finding Source Material

Chapter 8 Evaluating Sources

Chapter 9 Using Source Material

Chapter 10 Citing Sources Using MLA Style

Chapter 11 Citing Sources Using APA Style

Chapter 12   Avoiding Common Problems In Style, Grammar, and Usage

Preface

Writing is a way to understand and participate in the world around us. It is a vehicle for learning, a way to make sense of our experiences and convey what we learn to others. Writing is a powerful means of individual expression and social interaction that has the capacity to change us. As the National Commission on Writing in America's Schools and Colleges put it, "At its best, writing has helped transform the world."

Composition teachers know all this, of course. They understand the power of writing, and they know that writing well is necessary for students to succeed in college and beyond. But instructors also know that a one-semester course is never quite enough to help students develop the sophisticated skills they will need to write effectively in their college classes and in their lives outside school. Research indicates that students need their entire college careers to develop those skills. First-year writing courses can lay the foundation for that process.

To make the most of the composition course, *The Essentials of Writing: Ten Core Concepts* focuses on the most important skills and knowledge that students must develop to be able to write the kind of sophisticated prose expected in college. It teaches the foundational lessons that students need to develop their competence as writers.

A Focus on Important Aspects of Writing

Research underscores what composition instructors well know: most college students tend to have difficulty with a few crucial aspects of writing:

- addressing an audience effectively
- focusing on a main idea and developing it sufficiently
- organizing texts appropriately
- adopting an appropriate register or "voice" in writing
- supporting assertions or arguments
- identifying and using appropriate sources
- revising effectively
- applying the conventions of academic writing.

For the most part, these difficulties apply across disciplines and forms of writing. Significantly, research reveals that most of these problems arise from three main sources:

- students' lack of understanding of the rhetorical nature of writing
- students' inexperience with different rhetorical tasks across the college curriculum
- students' misunderstanding of how to manage the process of writing.

In other words, these problems arise from a basic misunderstanding of the rhetorical and social nature of writing and inexperience with managing the writing process *in the context of varied rhetorical tasks*, especially the kind of writing tasks typical of academic work in college.

Consequently, *The Essentials of Writing: Ten Core Concepts* rests on three central ideas about writing:

- *Writing is a rhetorical act.* Writing is fundamentally an interaction between a writer and reader within a specific social context. In this sense, writing is always a social activity, and effective writing connects writers and readers in complex and powerful ways.

- *Writing is a way to participate in the conversations that shape our lives.* Through writing, writers and their readers collaborate in knowledge-making and share information and opinions about issues that matter to them. Writing enables us to take part in the many ongoing conversations about important matters that affect how we live and how we understand ourselves and the world we inhabit. In the most basic way, writing is a way to *construct* the world by participating in these complex conversations.

- *Writing is a means of inquiry.* Writing is an intellectual activity that can lead to a deeper understanding of ideas, experiences, and information. It is a means of understanding ourselves and the world we share. Writing can engage students in careful, critical thinking about themselves and the world around them. Writing is a unique and powerful vehicle for learning.

These ideas inform both the content and structure of *The Essentials of Writing: Ten Core Concepts*. As students are guided through various writing tasks and learn to manage the process of writing efficiently, they also gain a fuller understanding of the nature of writing as rhetoric, conversation, and inquiry. In this way, *The Essentials of Writing: Ten Core Concepts* can help composition instructors meet a central challenge in working with student writers: helping students develop a sophisticated understanding of writing and gain experience as writers acting on that understanding.

The Essentials of Writing: Ten Core Concepts emphasizes what is essential in writing at the college level and guides students as they apply that knowledge to various writing tasks. It trains students to think rhetorically and helps them manage the fundamental characteristics of effective academic writing. In this regard, the Ten Core Concepts serve as a framework for understanding writing and a practical, step-by-step guide for negotiating the demands of academic writing tasks.

Ten Core Concepts

The Ten Core Concepts distinguish this textbook from other writing guides. Most composition textbooks try to cover every conceivable aspect of writing in college and beyond, presenting far more material than students could ever grasp and retain in a single semester. That approach ultimately waters down the most important lessons that student writers must learn. *The Essentials of Writing: Ten Core Concepts* is different. It emphasizes what students must really learn to become effective writers.

These Core Concepts are not basic skills, nor are they procedures for completing specific kinds of writing tasks. Rather, they are fundamental insights into the nature of writing that students must enact as they complete varied writing tasks. These Core Concepts boil down what has been learned through research and practice into key ideas about what writing is and how effective writing works. For example, Core Concept #4—"a writer must have something to say"—emphasizes the need for a piece of writing to convey a clear main point or idea. Studies indicate that college writing instructors identify the lack of a clear main idea as one of the most common weaknesses in student writing. This concept helps students understand why effective writing in most genres is characterized by a focus on a main idea; it also helps them understand how the different expectations in different academic disciplines can shape a writer's main idea and how that main idea is presented and developed in specific kinds of texts. Most important, it guides students through a process that enables them to identify, refine, and articulate the main idea of any writing project they are working on. In this way, the Core Concepts can deepen students' understanding of key insights about writing at the same time that students practice applying those insights in their own writing.

The Ten Core Concepts are not prescriptive. They are not step-by-step instructions for writing in specific genres. Instead, they are fundamental but flexible guidelines for writing; they serve as a set of heuristics that students can apply to *any* writing task.

The Structure of *The Essentials of Writing: Ten Core Concepts*

The Essentials of Writing: Ten Core Concepts is organized into twelve chapters. Chapters 1 through 4 introduce students to the essential insights into writing that they must acquire if they are to be able to apply their writing skills effectively in different contexts. In this section, students explore the fundamental ideas about writing described above: writing as rhetoric, as conversation, and as inquiry. Most important, they learn and practice the Ten Core Concepts that form the heart of this textbook. Chapter 2 explains these concepts, using examples to illustrate the lessons as well as exercises to help students understand how to apply the concepts in their own writing. Chapter 3 is an interactive, visual guide students can use to apply the Ten Core Concepts to any piece of writing. Chapter 4 presents a case study of a first-year student writer as she applies the Ten Core Concepts to completing a writing assignment.

The remaining chapters provide students with practical advice about working with source material, conducting research for their various writing projects, and mastering and applying the conventions of written English. Chapter 5 focuses on essential intellectual skills with which many students struggle in college writing, including summary and synthesis. Chapter 6 guides students in understanding an increasingly important aspect of effective writing today: document design. Chapters 7, 8, and 9 provide an up-to-date guide for finding, evaluating, and using source material in an interconnected world characterized by access to overwhelming bodies of information. Chapters 10 and 11 help students understand and apply the guidelines for citing sources recommended by the MLA and the APA. Finally, Chapter 12 helps students craft effective, engaging prose and avoid errors that can weaken their writing. Rather than trying to reproduce a comprehensive handbook, this chapter focuses on the most common problems in student writing, including the formal errors that research shows are typical of college student writing.

Throughout all these chapters students encounter varied examples of effective writing in different genres and different media. They see how other writers, including student writers, meet the challenges of contemporary writing in college and beyond, and they are given varied opportunities to practice what they learn, all the while using the Ten Core Concepts as their framework for writing.

Integrated Coverage of Digital Literacy Practices

The Essentials of Writing: Ten Core Concepts focuses on the contemporary student, who lives in an increasingly technological, globalized age. To write well today requires students to manage many different rhetorical tasks using various technologies, including constantly evolving digital media that have become essential tools for communication. Rather than addressing "digital literacy" as a separate skill or topic, *The Essentials of Writing: Ten Core Concepts* incorporates emerging digital technologies and literacy practices into the advice and practice it provides students. Throughout this textbook, students encounter examples and exercises that reflect various uses of communications technologies, and they receive advice for taking advantage of these technologies to meet the needs of the rhetorical situations within which they are writing.

Finally, *The Essentials of Writing: Ten Core Concepts* is informed by the basic idea that practice is essential in developing writing competence. In a sense, this idea is the 11th Core Concept. Only through sustained, guided practice in writing different kinds of texts for various rhetorical situations can students develop the understanding and ability to write effectively for different purposes. Accordingly, *The Essentials of Writing: Ten Core Concepts* relies in part on the repetition of the Ten Core Concepts to give students the practice they need to make these Concepts part of their repertoire as writers.

Acknowledgments

Writing a new textbook can be a daunting undertaking, but it is made less so by the inherently collaborative nature of the work. This book is not mine; rather, it is the result of the sustained efforts of many people, whose ideas, dedication, and hard work helped make this book a reality. It is impossible to thank them enough.

First, I am extremely grateful to Lyn Uhl for identifying this project as an important one and providing the support necessary to realize the vision that informed this project from the beginning. I am also deeply grateful to Margaret Leslie, the senior editor for this project, whose steady guidance helped keep the project on track and who expertly managed its many different components over many years. Without her and her staff, this book would not be.

My sincerest gratitude goes to Margaret Manos and Leslie Taggart, the development editors for this project, whose insight, patience, good humor, and constant support not only were essential in keeping the project moving forward but also made it possible for me to find the wherewithal to finish the work. The quality of this textbook is in so many ways a result of their dedication and their expert advice. I could not have done it without them, and I feel blessed to have had the opportunity to work closely with them on such a complex project.

I also wish to thank Andy Fogle, of Bethlehem High School in Bethlehem, New York, who helped with the research and development of several chapters, and Tony Atkins, of the University of North Carolina at Greensboro, who not only provided invaluable insight about the treatment of technology throughout the book but also helped develop the chapter on document design.

Janelle Adsit, a teaching assistant in the doctoral program at the State University of New York at Albany, graciously opened her writing classroom to me as I refined the manuscript. She and her students offered exceptional insights that shaped the revision of the manuscript and helped make this a more useful textbook. I sincerely appreciate Janelle's generosity, and I am humbled by her students' willingness to share their ideas with me. Very special thanks to Elizabeth Parisi, a student in Janelle's class, who graciously allowed me to use her essay for this textbook. Her writing and her willingness to share her experiences make this a much better book and will benefit many other students whom she will never meet.

My colleagues and friends in the Capital District Writing Project, including Aaron Thiell, Christopher Mazura, Molly Fanning, Alicia Wein, Christine Dawson, and especially Carol Forman-Pemberton, have been my supporters and teachers for many years now. I rely on them much more than they know, and their influence infuses this textbook.

Many thanks also to artist Stefan Saal, who created the striking chapter-opening images for the book. The many experts at Cengage who helped with the design, production, and marketing of this textbook also deserve a special thanks: Hannah Wellman, Michael Lepera, Samantha Ross Miller, Betsy Donaghey, Lydia LeStar, and Erin Parkins.

This textbook greatly benefited from the advice of many insightful reviewers, including several who class-tested chapters with their composition students. These reviewers' comments and suggestions guided development from the beginning: Rebecca Adams, Housatonic Community College; Janelle Adsit, University at Albany, State University of New York; Forrest Anderson, Catawba College; Ellen Arnold, Coastal Carolina University; Carolyn Ayers, Saint Mary's University; Vicki Besaw, College of Menominee Nation; Subrata Bhowmik, Arizona State University; Courtney Brandt, Western Michigan University; Mark Browning, Johnson County Community College; Mary Burkhart, University of Scranton; Jasmine Case, University of Wisconsin-Eau Claire; Maureen Cahill, Tidewater Community College; Paul Cockeram, Harrisburg Area Community College; Cheri Crenshaw, Dixie State University; Karin Evans, College of DuPage; Tyler Farrell, Marquette University; Steve Fox, Indiana University-Purdue University Indianapolis; Michael Franco, Oklahoma City Community College; John Gides, California State University-Northridge; Shauna Gobble, Northampton Community College; Dorie Goldman, Central Arizona College; Betsy Hall, Illinois College; M. Suzanne Harper, Penn State Worthington Scranton; Melvin Clark Heller, South Texas College; Harold Hellwig, Idaho State University; Anne Helms, Alamance Community College; George Horneker, Arkansas State University; Barbara Howard, Central Bible College; Lisa Klotz, University of Alabama; Danielle Koonce, East Carolina University; Lindsay Lewan, Arapahoe Community College; Yingqin Liu, Cameron University; Stephanie Masson, Northwestern State University; James McWard, Johnson County Community College; Robert Mellin, Purdue University-North Central; Benjamin Minor, Arizona State University; Catherine Moran, Bristol Community College; Jessica Nowacki, Marietta College; Pratul Pathak, California University of Pennsylvania; Patrick Quinn, College of Southern Nevada; Alma Ramirez, Mt. San Jacinto College; Susan Roack, Purdue University-Calumet; Bernd Sauermann, Hopkinsville Community College; Patrick Tompkins, John Tyler Community College; Anthony Viola, Marshall University; and Sue Watley, Stephen F. Austin University. Most important, the members of the advisory board for the project provided essential advice in the latter stages of the project, for which I am especially grateful: Lauryn Angel-Cann, Collin College; Anthony Atkins, University of North Carolina-Wilmington; Laura Carroll, Abilene Christian University; Sarah Gottschall, Prince George's Community College; Karen Jackson, North Carolina Central University; and Shevaun Watson, University of Wisconsin-Eau Claire.

Finally, I must acknowledge the support of my family, without whom I could never have completed this work and whose patience with me and confidence in me sustained me through many challenging moments. My parents—Ron and Joan Yagelski—and my siblings—Mary Cooper, Gary Yagelski, and Dianne Yagelski—support me in ways they never really see, and their presence in my life reinforces my belief in myself. My mother-in-law, Charlotte Hafich, never fails to offer encouragement and check in on my progress; I can never thank her enough for her love and support. My sons, Adam and Aaron, who light up my life in ways they can never realize, are always ready to share and debate ideas with me, and I am energized by their pride in what I do; they help me see the world in ways that shape my writing and keep me going. And most of all, Cheryl, my wife of 31 years and the love of my life, is the best partner any writer could ever hope to have. Her love, constant support, and boundless confidence in me are the foundation that make it possible for me to undertake a task as big as this textbook and see it through. I am so deeply blessed to be able to share this work—and my life—with her. She always provides safe harbor.

About the Author

Robert P. Yagelski is Associate Vice Provost and Director of the Program in Writing and Critical Inquiry at the State University of New York at Albany, where he is also associate professor of English education in the Department of Educational Theory and Practice. He directs the Capital District Writing Project, a site of the National Writing Project, and has worked closely with schools to improve writing instruction at all levels of education. He is the author of numerous articles and books on writing and writing instruction. *Writing: Ten Core Concepts* is his fourth textbook.

1950　　**1970**　　**1990**　　**2010**　　**2030?**

Why We Write

WRITING IS A POWERFUL MEANS of communicating ideas and information across time and space. It enables us to participate in conversations and events that shape our lives and helps us make sense of the world. In fact, writing can change the world. Consider these examples:

- Adam Smith's economic theories, presented in his 1776 book *The Wealth of Nations*, continue to influence government economic policies today, which in turn affect the lives of almost every person on earth.

- *The Art of War*, believed to have been written in the 6th century B.C.E. by Chinese military strategist Sun Tzu, is still widely read by military leaders, politicians, and business leaders.

- Betty Friedan's *The Feminine Mystique*, published in 1963, is considered by many to have begun the women's rights movement that has reshaped American social, cultural, political, and economic life in the past half century.

- Charles Darwin's *On the Origin of Species*, published in 1859, revolutionized scientific thinking about life on earth and laid the foundation for the modern field of biology.

- *Silent Spring*, by Rachel Carson, which was published in 1962, helped spark the modern environmental movement and influenced the creation of laws to protect wildlife and the environment.

- Al Gore's 2006 book *An Inconvenient Truth* and the film based on it convinced millions of people that global climate change is a grave threat to human life that must be addressed by all nations.

- Messages posted on Facebook and Twitter in 2011 helped provoke protests in Egypt and Tunisia that led to new governments in those nations.

These examples dramatically illustrate the capacity of writing to transform our world.

For many college students, however, writing is mostly a requirement. Most students don't seem to mind writing, but few would choose to write the kinds of essays and reports usually assigned in school. Students consider such assignments necessary, but they don't necessarily enjoy them. For many students, writing in school can be tedious and dull. Maybe you feel the same way.

Yet students write all the time, for all kinds of reasons:

- They send text messages, update their Facebook pages, and tweet to stay in touch with friends, share information, let others know what they think, and keep informed about events or issues that matter to them.
- They respond to their favorite blogs or maintain their own blogs.
- They keep journals or diaries.
- They circulate petitions to support causes on their campus or in their town.
- They rap and participate in poetry slams to express their feelings about important issues in their lives.
- They write essays to gain admission to college or graduate school.
- They create resumes to obtain jobs.

Brian Cahn/ZUMA Press/Corbis

Whether they realize it or not, students regularly use writing to live their lives, to accomplish tasks that they have to or choose to do, and to participate in their communities.

If these kinds of writing don't seem as important as, say, a book like *An Inconvenient Truth* or *Silent Spring*, they should. For if a book can be said to have changed the world, the same is true of tweets and texts and blogs and essays and letters written by ordinary people, including students. A job application letter can change your life. A petition can change a policy on your campus that affects hundreds or thousands of students (see "How Students Changed Their University Through Writing"). An essay can inspire your classmates, change their minds about an issue, or move them to take action. And sometimes ordinary kinds of writing can result in extraordinary changes: In Egypt, in February 2011, tweets, email messages, texts, blog posts, and Facebook entries from ordinary citizens played a key role in the protest movement that led to the resignation of Egypt's president, who had ruled that nation for more than three decades. In other words, writing by ordinary citizens helped change the government of that country—a change that has touched the life of every Egyptian and many people outside Egypt.

During the 2010–2011 academic year, the campus of the Massachusetts Institute of Technology (MIT) was the site of a controversy about the school's dining plan, as explained in the following article. The article, which appeared in February 2011 in *The Tech*, a student newspaper at MIT, includes a great deal of information that only MIT students would be familiar with, but it also tells a compelling story of how the students used writing in various media to express their views and challenge a policy that affected them:

DINING IGNITES CAMPUS CONTROVERSY
Despite loud opposition, new plan still slated to start this fall
By Maggie Lloyd

February 1, 2011

Few topics caused as much tension on campus in 2010 as the ever-changing House Dining Plan, scheduled to go into effect in Fall 2011. In March 2010, the Division of Student Life (DSL) formed the House Dining Advisory Group (HDAG), committed to the creation of a new dining plan with the hope to eliminate the $600,000 deficit from House Dining and to offer more options for student dining.

HDAG consisted of presidents and dining chairs from the five dorms with dining halls (Baker, McCormick, Simmons, Next, and the planned Maseeh Hall), DSL staff, the UA Dining Chair, and other relevant MIT faculty, such as housemasters (including the upcoming Maseeh housemasters).

Throughout the spring, an online Idea Bank collected students' opinions on all-you-care-to-eat (AYCE) service, breakfast offerings, food allergies, and other relevant dining topics, while forums across campus invited students to talk about what they wanted directly to members of HDAG.

On May 19, HDAG released its initial recommendations, introducing AYCE dinner and breakfast to all of the dining dorms seven days a week, including Maseeh Hall, set to open in Fall 2011. Costs for the 10, 12, or 14 meals-per-week options were projected to be $2,900, $3,400, and $3,800 per year, respectively, and the number of meals per week was required to be equally split between breakfast and dinner. Maseeh would also offer lunch Monday through Friday. Freshmen would be required to buy the 14-meal plan, while sophomores would be permitted to choose between 12 and 14 meals, and juniors and seniors would decide between any of the three plans. As with the current House Dining Membership, students in the dining hall dorms would be required to participate in this dining plan.

With the exception of a student protest in Lobby 7 during Campus Preview Weekend, the campus remained relatively quiet in terms of dining discussion as the first semester of 2010 came to a close.

(Continued)

UA survey voices students' concerns; the petitions begin

As the class of 2014 arrived at MIT in the fall, conversations about the new dining plan began again, and concerns about the plan's potential impact on dorm culture and high prices were often mentioned. In the first week of October, the UA distributed a survey to all undergraduate dorms, asking for feedback on several student life topics such as printing, Greek life, shuttles, athletics, and dining, receiving 655 responses. Various comments received in the survey about dining ranged from indifferent—"Dining plan doesn't affect me"—to dissatisfied—"New dining plan is too expensive; too much food, most people don't eat that much"—foreshadowing some of the upcoming tension. As *The Tech* reported on October 12, "out of 222 [survey] respondents who said they lived in a dining dorm, only 98 said they had heard or read specific details about the plan. Of those 98 students, only 8 supported the new dining plan."

The survey results sent a spark through campus, igniting the first of several petitions to be distributed by undergraduates last fall. Next House resident Andres A. Romero '14 initiated a petition against the new dining plan, collecting over 200 signatures, mostly from other students living in Next House. He submitted the petition to the UA, insisting that the petition, which was signed by more than 5 percent of the student population, necessitated an emergency meeting of the UA, according to the UA bylaws.

Within the required 96-hour time limit after a petition submission, on October 13, the UA held its emergency meeting. The UA passed 42 U.A.S E1.1, "Bill to Reform HDAG Dining Proposal and Process in Light of Overwhelming Student Opposition," which called for Chancellor Phillip Clay "to intervene by halting" the approval process for the new dining plan. HDAG representatives claimed they were unable to stop this new plan because the Request for Proposal process, in which a dining vendor would be chosen, had already begun. To stop the process would mean starting over, losing months of work, and rushing to find a new plan in time for implementation in the next academic year.

Changes to HDAG membership

As the noise increased on campus, two of the key students involved in the dining conversations resigned from their positions. On October 26, Paula C. Trepman '13, who represented the UA in HDAG, resigned as UA Dining Chair. In her letter of resignation submitted to the UA, a "very frustrated" Trepman claimed "HDAG has this sense of paternalism and feels that it is their job to regulate and ensure that students eat a normal three meals every day."

Andy Wu '12, who served on HDAG as president of Baker House, followed suit. In a November 29 e-mail to Baker House, Wu stated, "HDAG has regularly dismissed my opinion to the point where I have been unable to contribute to any positive changes for Baker residents."

Student representation, in the form of other dorm presidents and dining chairs, still existed within the HDAG despite these absences.

Fact sheets and petitions fly

In an effort to highlight students' options within the new plan, HDAG released organized fact sheets that covered several topics such as pricing, hours, and other specifics within the new dining plan. These documents, which were released in late October and early November, were available on the House Dining Review website designed specifically for HDAG, *http://studentlife.mit.edu/house-dining-review.*

Throughout November, *The Tech's* Letters to the Editor and Opinion pages flip-flopped arguments for and against the new plan, starting with a Nov. 9 letter from the administration (Phillip L. Clay PhD '75, Christine Ortiz, Costantino Colombo, and Daniel E. Hastings PhD '80) itself. Then, housemasters from the dining dorms (John M. Essigmann PhD '76, Suzanne Flynn, Steven R. Hall '80, Dava J. Newman PhD '92, and Charles H. Stewart III) chimed in with their support a week later. "Not every student agrees with the final recommendation, but students were involved every step of the way," the administration's letter argued.

"Two of the three plans for Baker, McCormick, Next, and Simmons are in the range of what their residents report spending on meals for the period covered by the new program," they said, adding, "residential life at MIT has never been static."

In the next issue, Tyler Hunt '04 challenged the housemasters' letter, claiming that the administration "must understand that when half of Next House signs a statement of opposition, that it has designed a program that is profoundly unpalatable." DAPER coaches then submitted their support of the plan, right next to Professor Alexander H. Slocum '82's advice for what the plan should be like.

Increasing student concern raised the volume of dining talk, starting with another petition from Next House residents Hannah L. Pelton '12 and Austin D. Brinson '13 on Nov. 8. This document, signed by 63 percent of Next House residents, was submitted to President Susan J. Hockfield, claiming HDAG's proposed dining plan was "wrong for us, wrong for Next House, and wrong for MIT." The petition claimed that the "expensive" plan would encourage Next House residents to move to dorms without dining halls, "making it more difficult to develop long-standing culture."

That same week, one of HDAG's own student representatives started a similar petition at Baker House. Despite supporting HDAG's proposed plan, HDAG representative Cameron S. McAlpine '13 reasoned that as Baker Dining Chair he needed to "accurately represent the opinions of Baker residents."

Then came the largest petition yet. Keone D. Hon '11 started writing blog posts on the popular missed connections site, *http://isawyou.mit.edu,* calling for a more organized student response. On November 17, Hon's *http://sayno.mit.edu* went live,

(Continued)

claiming that its perceptions of expense, poor economic sustainability, negative impact on dorms, clubs, and FSILGs, and apparent disregard for student opinion were the main reasons for student dissatisfaction with the new plan. Within 24 hours, the petition had more than 1,400 signatures from undergraduates and others affiliated with MIT, more than all other petitions combined. As of December 2010, 1,570 of the 1,838 signees were undergraduates, 568 of whom were from dining dorms.

From petitions to protests

One day later, roughly 25 students participated in a Baker Dining sit-in, bringing their own food to eat in the dining hall. Two freshmen, Burton Conner resident Michael L. Pappas '14 and East Campus resident Christopher W. Tam '14, organized the protest. Newman, the Baker housemaster, and Senior Assistant Dean of Students for Residential Life Henry J. Humphreys were there to discuss students' concerns, allowing for "civil dialogue," as Pappas described, between students and administration.

As students arrived back on campus after Thanksgiving break on Nov. 29, HDAG released an updated version of the House Dining Plan, introducing a "transition plan" for the classes of 2012 and 2013. This plan would cost $2500 for the year, the cheapest yet offered, allowing those students to choose any 7 meals per week. Students are also able to increase their flexibility in the transition plan by choosing any dining combination of breakfast and dinner "at a modest cost," according to the House Dining Review website. Since news about the new dining plan was available to the Class of 2014 before they came to MIT, DSL said that they must participate in the full-fledged campus dining plan.

On December 3, Hon organized students one more time, this time hosting a protest outside the Media Lab as members of the MIT Corporation walked in for a quarterly meeting. Around 20 students attended to distribute copies of the SayNo petition and to talk briefly to Corporation members attending the meeting. This would be the last organized event concerning dining for 2010, as finals began ten days later. For the first time since October, talk about dining came to a hush.

Although the campus-wide battle of words died down over IAP, only time will tell when the noise will return. As *The Tech* reported this January, MIT Corporation member Harbo P. Jensen '74 said that the members of the Corporation "all agreed that … there is a lot of emotion and energy behind this," acknowledging "it's impossible to make everyone happy." Indeed, the past year has shown that it's the unhappy students who are capable of making the most noise.

Source: Lloyd, Maggie. "Dining Ignites Campus Controversy." *The Tech*, online edition. 1 Feb. 2011. Web. 21 Mar. 2011.

Questions for Discussion

1. What kinds of writing did MIT students use to voice their concerns about the university's dining plan? How did these kinds of writing figure into this controversy?

2. Do you think the students could have accomplished their goals without using writing as they did? Why or why not? What advantages (or disadvantages) do you see in the way students used writing in this situation? What alternatives did the students have?

3. Write a brief essay about a time when you used writing to voice a concern, lodge a complaint, or try to change something. Then, in a group of classmates, share your essays. What similarities and differences do you see in the writing that is described in these essays? What conclusions might you draw from these essays about the role of writing in your lives?

As a college student, you will probably do most of your writing for your classes. This textbook will help you learn to manage college writing assignments effectively. But writing well can also help you live your life in ways that extend far beyond the classroom. So in this chapter—and throughout this textbook—we will examine some of the many different situations in which you might be asked to write.

Understanding Writing

This textbook has another important goal: to help you understand what writing is. One reason so many people struggle with writing is that they don't sufficiently understand the nature of writing. They believe writing is a matter of following arcane rules that are often difficult to remember or grasp. They think writing is a matter of inspiration and creativity, which they believe they lack, or they assume they can't write well because they don't have a large enough vocabulary. These beliefs are based on common misconceptions that can lead to frustration and prevent students from becoming successful writers. Yes, writing well *does* require knowing rules, and having a large vocabulary doesn't hurt. But writing is more than rules or inspiration or vocabulary. Writing should be understood in four important ways:

- Writing is a powerful means of expression and communication.
- Writing is a way to participate in ongoing conversations about ideas, events, and issues that matter in our lives.
- Writing is a unique form of thinking that helps us learn.
- Writing is a way to understand ourselves and the world around us.

For students who come to understand writing in these four ways, learning to write effectively can be a much more satisfying and successful process. Abandoning common misconceptions and appreciating the complexity, power, and joy of writing are the first steps to learning to write well and feeling confident about writing. This textbook will introduce you to the most important ideas—the Core Concepts—that you need to know in order to write well. It is also designed to give you practice in the most common forms of writing for a variety of audiences and purposes—in college, in your community, in the workplace, and in your life in general.

Writing in College

Let's face it: Students have to write well if they expect to do well in school. Whether it's a lab report in a biology class, a research paper in a sociology course, a proposal in a business class, or a literary analysis essay in an English course, writing effectively means better learning and better grades. In this regard, writing in college serves three main purposes:

- It is a way for you to demonstrate what you know.
- It helps you learn.
- It enables you to join important conversations about the subjects you are studying.

Write to Demonstrate What You Know

Writing is a way for you to show your instructors what you have learned. An essay exam in history, for example, helps your instructor decide whether you have understood a particular concept (say, manifest destiny) or learned about historical events that are part of the course syllabus. Similarly, your economics professor might assign an essay requiring you to analyze a market trend, such as the popularity of SUVs, to determine whether you and your classmates have grasped certain economic principles. For this reason, college students are asked to write many different kinds of assignments: reports, research papers, analytical essays, arguments, synopses, creative writing like poems, personal narratives, reflective essays, digital stories, multimedia presentations, and more.

Think about a recent essay exam or assignment that you wrote for one of your classes. First, describe the writing you did. What was the assignment? What exactly did you write? What do you think was most important about that piece of writing? What did it reveal about what you know about the subject? What do you think it suggests about you as a writer?

When writing essay exams, reports, or research papers for your classes, keep in mind that you are writing to demonstrate what you have learned. Have confidence that your writing reflects what you know. And remember that your writing can also help you identify what you still need to learn.

Write to Learn

Writing an essay exam or a research paper isn't just a way to demonstrate learning; it is also a means of learning in itself. As you will see in the next chapter, writing is a form of intellectual inquiry, and it is essential to student learning, no matter the subject. To write an ethnographic analysis of a culture for an anthropology class, for example, is to learn not only about that culture but also about ethnography as a way of understanding how we live together. It's true that students can learn a great deal by reading, but writing engages the mind in ways that reading does not. Reading about ethnography can help students understand what ethnography is; writing an ethnographic report about a culture enables students to *apply* that understanding, which can lead to a deeper learning of the subject matter.

This idea that writing is learning can be easy to forget when you are trying to meet deadlines and follow detailed guidelines for an assignment. But if you approach your writing assignments as a way to learn about your subject matter, the process of writing can be more satisfying and can lead to more effective essays. And remember that every writing assignment is also an opportunity to learn about writing itself. The more you write, the better you understand the power and joy of writing and the better able you will be to meet the challenges of writing.

And one last point about the power of writing as a way to learn: The more you write, especially when you write as a way to explore your subject matter, the more you learn about *yourself* as a writer and thinker. Knowing your strengths as a writer enables you to take advantage of them; knowing your weaknesses is essential if you are to improve your writing. That understanding will help you become a better writer.

Describe a writing assignment you did for a college or high school class that was especially challenging for you. Explain why you found the assignment challenging. Now consider what you learned by writing the assignment. What did you learn about the subject matter? What did you learn about writing? What surprised you about doing that assignment? What surprises you now as you look back on it? What do you think you learned about yourself as a writer?

If you approach writing assignments as opportunities to discover new information, explore new ideas, and enhance your understanding of your subject, writing can be more satisfying, and you might find you learned more than you think you learned. You might also find that your writing improves.

Write to Join Academic Conversations

Writing is the primary way that experts in all academic disciplines do their work and share their ideas:

- Mathematics professors may work mostly with numbers and formulas, but they also write articles for other mathematicians about current problems in mathematics.

- Historians study ancient artifacts to help them understand past events, and they share their understanding in the articles and books they write for other historians.

- Scientists might spend long hours in their labs, but they test each other's theories by sharing and debating the results of their experiments in articles they write for scientific journals.

- Scholars in all fields regularly share information and debate ideas by posting messages to professional online forums and blogs.

In all these cases, writing is the main vehicle by which scholars discuss the central questions in their fields. They cannot do their work without it.

Writing for a college class, whether it be psychology or business or chemistry, is a way for students to enter these conversations about the ideas, information, and ways of thinking that define academic fields. Part of what students learn when they write in college, then, is how to use writing as a tool for discovering and sharing knowledge in various academic disciplines. In this sense, writing an assignment for a college class is a process of learning to write like a scholar in that academic discipline. When you are asked to write a research paper in a psychology course or a lab report in a biochemistry class, you are learning to do the kind of intellectual work that psychologists or biochemists do. You are learning to participate in the conversations about important topics in those academic fields. And by doing so you are using writing to expand and deepen your knowledge about those fields as well as about the world in general.

FOCUS   Think Differently About Your Writing

Take two or more assignments you wrote for different college (or high school) classes. For example, take a literary essay you wrote for an English class, a report you did for a biology class, and a research paper for a history class. Briefly describe the similarities and differences that you notice between them. Look at the writing style you used in each paper, the structure of each paper, and the language you used. What stands out about each paper? In what ways are the papers different or similar? How can you explain the similarities and differences you see in these papers? What do you think the similarities and differences between these papers suggest about the writing you are asked to do in college?

Of course, writing in college also serves another purpose: It gives students genuine practice that helps them become better writers, which can benefit them in their lives outside of school as well.

EXERCISE 1A   Read the three excerpts included here. Each excerpt is taken from an article or book in a different academic subject. The first is from a marketing textbook, the second from an education journal, and the third from a scientific journal. After reading the excerpts, compare them by addressing these questions:

- What do you notice about the writing in these three pieces?
- What do you think are the purposes of the writing in each case?
- Are there similarities or differences in the writing style, language, and structure of these excerpts? What might these similarities and/or differences suggest about writing in different disciplines?
- What does your comparison of these three excerpts suggest about writing in general?

What is Marketing?

What does the term *marketing* mean to you? Many people think it means the same thing as personal selling. Others think marketing is the same as personal selling and advertising. Still others believe marketing has something to do with making products available in stores, arranging displays, and maintaining inventories of products for future sales. Actually, marketing includes all of these activities and more.

Marketing has two facets. First, it is a philosophy, an attitude, a perspective, or a management orientation that stresses customer satisfaction. Second, marketing is activities and processes used to implement this philosophy.

Source: From Lamb, Hair, McDaniel. *Essentials of Marketing.* 7 ed. © 2012 South-Western, a part of Cengage Learning, Inc. Reproduced by permission. Www.cengage.com/permissions.

(Continued)

The American Marketing Association's definition of marketing focuses on the second facet. Marketing is the activity, set of institutions, and processes for creating, communicating, delivering, and exchanging offerings that have value for customers, clients, partners, and society at large.

Marketing involves more than just activities performed by a group of people in a defined area or department. In the often-quoted words of David Packard, cofounder of Hewlett-Packard, "Marketing is too important to be left only to the marketing department." Marketing entails processes that focus on delivering value and benefits to customers, not just selling goods, services, and/or ideas. It uses communication, distribution, and pricing strategies to provide customers and their stakeholders with the goods, services, ideas, values, and benefits they desire when and where they want them. It involves building long-term, mutually rewarding relationships when these benefit all parties concerned. Marketing also entails an understanding that organizations have many connected stakeholder "partners," including employees, suppliers, stockholders, distributors, and society at large.

Source: Lamb, Charles, Joseph Hair, and Carl McDaniel. *Essentials of Marketing*. 7 ed. Kentucky: South-Western, Cengage Learning, 2012. Print.

Brain-Based Teaching Strategies for Improving Students' Memory, Learning, and Test-Taking Success

Decades ago, my high school chemistry teacher slowly released hydrogen sulfide (which produces a smell like rotten eggs) from a hidden container he opened just before we entered his classroom. A few minutes after we took our seats and he began his lecture, a foul odor permeated the classroom. We groaned, laughed, looked around for the offending source. To an outside observer entering our class at that time, we would have appeared unfocused and definitely not learning anything. This demonstration, however, literally led me by the nose to follow my teacher's description of the diffusion of gases through other gases. It is likely that during that class I created two or three pathways to the information about gas diffusion that I processed through my senses and ultimately stored in my long-term memory. Since then, that knowledge has been available for me to retrieve by thinking of an egg or by remembering the emotional responses as the class reacted to the odor permeating the room. Once I make the connection, I am able to recall the scientific facts linked to his demonstration.

Event memories, such as the one that was stored that day in chemistry class, are tied to specific emotionally or physically charged events (strong sensory input) and by the emotional intensity of the events to which they are linked. Because the dramatic event powers its way through the neural pathways of the emotionally preactivated limbic system into memory storage, associated scholastic information gets pulled along with it. Recollection of the academic material occurs when the emotionally significant event comes to mind, unconsciously or consciously. To remember the lesson, students can cue up the dramatic event to which it is linked.

Source: Willis, Judy. "Brain-Based Teaching Strategies for Improving Students' Memory, Learning, and Test-Taking Success." *Childhood Education* 83.5 (2007): 310. *Academic OneFile*. Web. 23 Mar. 2011.

Screening For Depression

Depression is the second most common chronic disorder seen by primary care physicians.[1] On average, 12 percent of patients seen in primary care settings have major depression.[2] The degrees of suffering and disability associated with depression are comparable to those in most chronic medical conditions.[3] Fortunately, early identification and proper treatment significantly decrease the negative impact of depression in most patients.[4] Most patients with depression can be effectively treated with pharmacotherapeutic and psychotherapeutic modalities.[5]

Depression occurs in children, adolescents, adults, and the elderly. It manifests as a combination of feelings of sadness, loneliness, irritability, worthlessness, hopelessness, agitation, and guilt, accompanied by an array of physical symptoms.[6] Recognizing depression in patients in a primary care setting may be particularly challenging because patients, especially men, rarely spontaneously describe emotional difficulties. To the contrary, patients with depression who present to a primary care physician often describe somatic symptoms such as fatigue, sleep problems, pain, loss of interest in sexual activity, or multiple, persistent vague symptoms.[7]

References

1 Wells KB. Caring for depression. Cambridge, Mass.: Harvard University Press, 1996.
2 Spitzer RL, Kroenke K, Linzer M, Hahn SR, Williams JB, deGruy FV 3d, et al. Health-related quality of life in primary care patients with mental disorders. Results from the PRIME-MD 1000Study. *JAMA*. 1995;274:1511–17.
3 Hays RD, Wells KB, Sherbourne CD, Rogers W, Spritzer K. Functioning and well-being outcomes of patients with depression compared with chronic general medical illnesses. *Arch Gen Psychiatry*. 1995;52:11–19.
4 Coulehan JL, Schulberg HC, Block MR, Madonia MJ, Rodriguez E. Treating depressed primary care patients improves their physical, mental, and social functioning. *Arch Intern Med*. 1997;157:1113–20.
5 Elkin I, Shea MT, Watkins JT, Imber SD, Sotsky SM, Collins JF, et al., National Institute of Mental Health treatment of Depression Collaborative Research Program. General effectiveness of treatments. *Arch Gen Psychiatry*. 1989;46:971–82.
6 Diagnostic and statistical manual of mental disorders: DSM-IV-TR. 4th ed, text rev. Washington, D.C.: American Psychiatric Association, 2000.
7 Suh T, Gallo JJ. Symptom profiles of depression among general medical service users compared with specialty mental health service users. *Psychol Med*. 1997;27:1051-63.

Source: Sharp, L. K., and M. S. Lipsky. "Screening for Depression across the Lifespan: A Review of Measures for Use in Primary Care Settings." *American Family Physician* 66.6 (2002): 1001–9. Web.

Writing in the Workplace

In almost any job or career you can think of, you will be expected to use writing in some way to do your work. Consider these anecdotes:

- A few years ago, a student planning to attend law school asked me what she could do now to prepare herself for law school. I called an old friend who is a lawyer to ask what I should tell my student. My friend offered two bits of advice: (1) get good grades, and (2) take as many writing courses as possible. Writing, my friend said, was the most important thing lawyers do.

- A college friend of mine has worked for many years as a management trainer for a large insurance company. Almost every aspect of his job involves some kind of writing: training materials, memos, reports, multimedia presentations, and formal email messages. Effective writing is a central reason he is an effective manager.

- One of my colleagues teaches nursing. His students spend a lot of time as interns in hospitals learning how to take a patient's pulse and blood pressure, obtain blood samples, set up IVs, and administer medication. They also learn to write. Writing accurate and thorough reports, my colleague says, is as important as anything else a nurse does. Communicating with doctors and other nurses is one of the most crucial aspects of a nurse's job, and much of it is done through writing. Without good writing skills, he says, nurses could not care for their patients effectively.

These anecdotes underscore the importance of writing in different work environments and illustrate the different ways that writing enables people to do their jobs well. Professionals already recognize this fact. In one recent study, more than 90% of midcareer professionals reported that the "need to write effectively" is a skill "of great importance" in their everyday work.[1] And because the modern workplace is changing rapidly, you are more likely than ever to be expected to communicate effectively in writing in a number of different media, including traditional print reports, proposals, letters, and memos as well as email, PowerPoint, blogs, wikis, and other online or digital formats. This is the nature of the workplace today, one that already places a great premium on communication and especially on writing—and one that is being reshaped by new media. To succeed in the workplace, you must know how to write well.

---

[1] National Commission on Writing. *The Neglected "R": The Need for a Writing Revolution*. New York: The College Board, 2003. 11. Print.

Examine a piece of your own writing that you finished recently. What do you notice about your writing? What strengths or weaknesses do you see? What might this piece of writing suggest about you as a writer? Now think about how you might present yourself as a writer to a potential employer. What would you say to that employer about your writing? What have you learned about writing that might appeal to an employer? What do you still need to improve upon in order to be ready to write for that employer?

Think of any writing assignment as career training. The better you can write, the more likely you are to succeed in your chosen career. Use your college writing assignments to develop your writing skills in preparation for the writing you will do in your future career. And if you have other kinds of writing experience, such as writing for your school newspaper or developing promotional materials for a student organization, put them on your resume.

EXERCISE 1B Talk to a few people you know about the writing they do for their jobs. Try to find people who work in different kinds of jobs. For example, maybe you have a relative who is a salesperson, a friend who is a physical therapist, or a neighbor who manages a restaurant. Ask them to describe any writing they do in their jobs and the media they regularly use, such as websites, email, and social media. Ask them about the challenges they face as writers in their workplaces. Also ask them for advice about preparing for workplace writing. Then write a brief report for your classmates in which you share what you learned from this exercise about workplace writing—or about writing in general.

Writing as a Citizen

The idea that citizens must be educated in order for democracy to work is deeply embedded in American culture. It is known as the Jeffersonian ideal, which imagines a free and thriving society based on a productive, educated citizenry. Today, "educated" also means "literate," and it's hard to imagine being an active part of society without writing. In fact, we write to participate in our society in many different ways, from political campaigns to consumer advocacy. Consider these examples:

> BECAUSE of a growing budget deficit, your state legislature is considering a tuition increase as well as large cuts in funding for state colleges and universities. Members of your college community, including students, have written letters and emails to legislators urging them to vote against the funding cuts and the tuition hike. Some students have written editorials for the school newspaper expressing opposition to the budget cuts. To organize a rally at the state capitol, students use Twitter, Facebook, email, and blogs, all of which provide information about the rally and background information about the proposed state budget.

> A developer has proposed building a giant new retail store near the business district of your town. Some local businesspeople are concerned that businesses on the town's main street will suffer if the new store is built. Residents opposed to the new store have organized a citizens' group and created a Facebook page to advocate for their position. They post information about the proposed store and share opinions about its potential impact on the town. They also write letters to the local newspaper and distribute fliers to local businesses. Other residents, concerned about the town's slow economic growth, have expressed their support for the new store on a blog and in articles and letters they have written for local publications. They also circulate a YouTube video to explain their support for the new store.

> THE owners of a major league sports team in your city have threatened to leave the city if a new stadium is not built to replace the aging stadium that the team currently plays in. The team is popular and important to the city, and many residents support the proposal for a new stadium. Other residents oppose the plan on the grounds that it will increase taxes without creating new jobs. These residents form a community organization to publicize their concerns. They use social media to explain what they believe will be the impact of a new stadium. They also write letters to government officials and send press releases to local TV stations.

These scenarios illustrate how we can use writing to participate directly in important discussions, decisions, and events that affect our lives. Writing is a way for individual citizens to express their opinions and share information; it is a way for citizens to take action as members of their communities. Through writing, whether in a traditional print form such as a letter to an editor or in a new kind of forum such as a blog, citizens can shape the ideas, opinions, and actions of others involved in the situation at hand. In all these instances, writing helps transform the world.

FOCUS Think Differently About Your Writing

Have you ever written a letter to a politician or business leader to express your opinion or voice a concern? Have you ever written a response to a blog or tweeted to share your perspective on an issue or controversy? Have you ever written a letter to the editor of a newspaper or magazine or sent an email message in response to an article or editorial? If so, what prompted you to do so? Why did you choose to write in that situation? To what extent do you think your writing made a difference—to you or to anyone else who might have read what you wrote?

A well-written letter, a carefully crafted blog post, or even a provocative tweet can often be more effective than a phone call to express a concern, request an action, or raise awareness about an issue.

EXERCISE 1C

Think about an issue that concerns you. Maybe there is a controversy on your campus or in your town that affects you somehow. (On my campus, for example, the university president canceled a popular student picnic because of concerns about alcohol abuse and vandalism, which led to an outcry among students and some faculty.) Or you might have a special interest in an issue in your state or in the nation, such as standardized testing in schools or the creation of wind farms in rural or wilderness areas. Now consider how you might best make your opinion heard in public discussions about this issue. Could you write a letter to someone in authority who is involved in the situation, such as a politician or business leader? What about a letter or email to the editor of your local newspaper? A blog post? A Facebook page? A brochure or newsletter? Maybe a formal proposal intended for someone in a position of authority? Decide what kind of writing you think would work best in this situation, and explain why. Then write it.

Alternatively, if you have ever written out of concern about an issue that was important to you, write a brief essay describing that situation and explaining what you wrote. To what extent did your writing in that situation make a difference to you or others involved?

Jesus Keller/Shutterstock.com

Writing to Understand Ourselves

A few years ago, my family planned a surprise party to celebrate my father's 70th birthday. Many friends and relatives would attend, and we wanted to do something special to celebrate my father's life. I decided to create a video that would be a kind of documentary about him. With help from my siblings, I spent several months collecting old photographs and memorabilia, gathering facts about my father's childhood and working life, and interviewing friends and relatives about their experiences with him. Using this material, I created a 20-minute video that focused on the important aspects of his life, including his military service and his family. As I composed that video, certain themes began to emerge about my father. I learned a lot about him that I hadn't previously known. More important, I gained a deep appreciation for the impact he had on many other people. Eventually, I screened the video at the surprise party, but composing it gave me a better understanding of my father and the world he grew up in; it also helped me learn about myself and my relationship with him.

My video about my father's life illustrates how writing can help us understand ourselves and the world around us. Here are two other examples:

> A student of mine was a veteran of military service in Iraq during the most intense fighting there between 2004 and 2006. For one assignment, he wrote a graphic and disturbing essay, in which he struggled to understand what he had experienced in Iraq. His essay revealed that he had deeply conflicted feelings about the war because, in the midst of the horror he witnessed, he also developed very special bonds with his fellow soldiers and witnessed profound acts of love and bravery. His essay was one of the most compelling pieces of writing I have ever received from a student—not because it was about war but because it was such a heartfelt effort by the student to understand some very difficult experiences.

> ONE of my students was hired by the university's office for international students to help write a newsletter. She was a good writer who earned good grades, but she found writing for international students much more challenging than she expected. Her supervisor constantly required her to revise his articles. Little by little, however, she began to see that her problems with these articles had little to do with her writing skill but arose from her lack of familiarity with her audience. The more she learned about the international students and their experiences in the United States, the better she appreciated their needs as readers of the newsletter. Her articles improved, and in the process of writing them, she learned a great deal about the international students on our campus and the challenges they face as students in the United States. She also learned something valuable about writing and about herself as a writer—and a person.

Writing is a powerful way not only to describe but also to examine, reflect on, and understand our thoughts, feelings, opinions, ideas, actions, and experiences. This capacity of writing is one of the most important reasons we write. In many college classes, you may be asked to write assignments that are designed to help you understand yourself and the world around you in the same way that my student's essay helped him understand his experiences in Iraq. But all of the writing you do in college, whether or not it is directly about your own experiences, presents opportunities for you to learn about yourself.

FOCUS   Think Differently About Your Writing

Think about a time you wrote about an experience or issue that was important to you in some way—in a journal, a letter, a school essay, or on Facebook. Why did you choose to write about that experience? What difference did it make to you to write about the experience? What do you think you learned by writing in that situation?

If you approach every writing assignment as an opportunity to learn not only about your subject but also about yourself, you will find that even the most tedious writing assignment can turn out to be a more rewarding experience.

EXERCISE 1D

Write a brief informal essay about an important experience that helped make you the person you are today. Write the essay for an audience of your classmates, and tell your story in a way that conveys to them why the experience was important to you.

Now reflect on your essay. Did you learn anything—about the experience itself or about yourself—as a result of writing your essay? Did writing about your experience change your view of the experience in any way? What did writing this essay teach you about yourself? What did it teach you about writing?

Ten Core Concepts for Effective Writing

2

WHEN I FIRST LEARNED to rock climb, an experienced climber gave me some advice: Always climb with your eyes. That may sound strange, since climbing obviously involves moving your body up a cliff, but it actually makes good sense. The key to climbing a vertical rock face is finding the right holds for your hands and feet, which is not always straightforward. To keep moving safely and efficiently up the cliff, climbers have to link together handholds and footholds. So even before starting up the cliff, climbers examine it carefully and identify a possible route that they can follow to the top. Climbers call this process "seeing the line" up a cliff or a mountain. Once on the cliff, they are always looking ahead to the next handhold or foothold. That simple statement—"always climb with your eyes"—turned out to be some of the best advice about climbing I ever received. It was a way to boil down the complicated act of climbing into a single, simple, basic idea.

This chapter does the same thing with writing: It boils down the complex, powerful, wonderful, and sometimes challenging activity of writing into ten essential ideas, or Core Concepts. There's much more to learn about writing than these concepts, just as in climbing you have to learn more than how to "climb with your eyes." But these concepts are fundamental insights that every writer must learn in order to write effectively. Students who incorporate these insights into their writing process will become better writers, no matter what kind of writing they are doing.

Learning to write effectively also requires developing a certain kind of attitude toward writing. Some climbers talk about "conquering" a mountain, but many climbers reject that way of thinking. For them, the point of climbing is not about defeating a mountain but about respecting it, adapting to it, and experiencing it. That attitude influences their decisions about which routes to follow up a mountain, when to start a climb, when to abandon it. It also affects the meaning of climbing; for them, climbing is about appreciating the experience of being in the mountains and meeting their challenges.

In the same way, the experience of writing can depend a great deal on a writer's attitude toward writing. Students who believe that writing is mostly about following certain rules tend to see writing as a process of learning and applying rules, which can become tedious and diminish the joy of writing. If, on the other hand, you think of writing as a process of discovery, then each writing task can become a way to learn—about your subject, about yourself, and about the world around you. Students who approach writing in this way are open to the possibilities of writing and better able to harness its power. For them, writing isn't primarily about applying rules; it's about understanding and engaging the world and communicating effectively with others.

The ten Core Concepts discussed in this chapter, then, are not rules to learn or directions to follow. They are insights into how to write more effectively. Learning these concepts is a matter of experiencing the variety, complexity, and power of writing so that you can harness that power. Learning to write more effectively is partly a process of learning how to think differently about writing and about yourself as a writer.

This chapter asks you to examine your beliefs about writing and adopt a certain attitude about writing—an attitude that might differ from what you have learned about writing in the past. It encourages you to shift your focus as a writer from remembering and applying rules to exploring your subject, addressing your readers, and accomplishing your rhetorical goals. That shift can change your entire experience as a writer. In learning and applying these Core Concepts, you will, I hope, feel more like a rock climber who is fully engaged in the arduous yet exhilarating act of moving toward a mountain summit.

The Ten Core Concepts for Effective Writing

The ten Core Concepts are based on what research and experience indicate about writing effectively. Each concept is based on a fundamental insight that student writers can learn in order to write well in a variety of situations—in school, in the workplace, and in the community. Understanding these concepts doesn't guarantee that you will always write effectively, but you cannot learn to write effectively without applying these ten essential insights about writing:

1. Writing is a process of discovery and learning.

2. Good writing fits the context.

3. The medium is part of the message.

4. A writer must have something to say.

5. A writer must support claims and assertions.

6. Purpose determines form, style, and organization in writing.

7. Writing is a social activity.

8. Revision is an essential part of writing.

9. There is always a voice in writing, even when there isn't an I.

10. Good writing means more than good grammar.

Core Concept 1: Writing is a process of discovery and learning.

A few years ago, a student in one of my classes decided to write an essay about her relationship with her parents. Writing that essay turned out to be a much more involved—and important—experience than she expected.

In the first draft of her essay, Chelsea, who was 22 years old, described how her relationship with her parents was changing now that she was an adult. Her draft was lighthearted and full of fond memories and funny anecdotes about her parents that revealed how much she enjoyed her new relationship with them. But something was missing from the draft. For one thing, Chelsea mentioned briefly that her parents had recently divorced after more than 20 years of marriage, but she wrote nothing about why they divorced. That seemed strange to Chelsea's classmates, who asked her about the divorce during a workshop of her draft. The more we discussed her draft, the clearer it became that there was a lot more to the story than Chelsea had revealed in her draft.

As Chelsea revised her draft, her essay began to change. It was no longer a lighthearted story about what it was like to have an adult relationship with her parents; it was now a more complicated essay that revealed Chelsea's conflicted feelings about what had happened to her parents' marriage and how it affected her (see "Learning by Writing" on page 26). There was still humor in the essay, but it was bittersweet, tempered by her realization that her changing relationship with her parents was accompanied by loss as well as gain.

Chelsea's essay became a journey of discovery through which she learned a lot about herself, her parents, and the experience she was describing in her essay. She also learned a valuable lesson about writing. When she began the essay, she thought it would be a simple narrative about her changing relationship with her parents. But the process of writing took her deeper into her experience and the complexities of human relationships. It helped Chelsea gain insight into an important period in her life and, maybe, understand something important about relationships (and life) in general.

Writing her essay also enabled Chelsea to communicate something interesting about relationships to her readers, but what she communicated was knowledge and insight that she gained *through the act of writing*, which enabled her to reflect deeply on her experience. This capacity of writing to help writers learn about and understand something is part of what makes writing so powerful—and so important.

Changes

I didn't know how to handle the fact that my parents were actually two separate people who had ceased to exist as one entity, two people who had other interests and other desires besides just solely being parents. With three grown children they felt that it was their time to move on and become separate people. The combination "Momand-dad" that I had once imagined as this real thing suddenly transformed into a Mom and a Dad who were pursuing their own separate lives and their own interests.

And I had to choose. My brother moved out and found an apartment to hide in, away from the crumbling walls of our family. I was torn—torn between moving out and moving on from the only thing I ever knew, from this Momanddad that was suddenly becoming non-existent. *But we can't leave Dad alone.* And so it was decided that I would live with Mom and my sister would live with Dad. How do you choose? Is who you live with the one you side with, because in that case, it would change everything. Changing. Everything was changing.

—excerpt from "Changes" by Chelsea

As Chelsea discovered, writing is more than a step-by-step procedure for organizing ideas into a specific form, such as a five-paragraph essay, a lab report, or a story. Writing effectively requires understanding that you are on a journey of discovery that enables you to understand something and to convey what you discovered to others. That journey sometimes takes you to places that you didn't expect, and it is rarely a straightforward, linear process from start to finish. If you approach a writing task as such a journey, it won't always be easy, but it can be much more satisfying—not to mention more successful.

SIDEBAR   LEARNING BY WRITING

The Irish singer-songwriter Conor O'Brien revealed during an interview that his songwriting has been influenced by postmodern poetry. O'Brien says that he developed a deep appreciation for the poetry of John Ashberry in a college English literature course. "I remember having to write an essay about John Ashberry and I absolutely despised his words," O'Brien said. "I thought they were really elitist. But  then by the end of my essay, I actually fell in love with it and I thought the complete opposite about it.... It was very rhythmic and very beautiful."

Any writing task can be a surprising journey that leads to new learning and insight, no matter what your topic is or what kind of assignment you're working on:

- When you write a narrative about an experience, as Chelsea did, you might understand that experience more fully.

- When you write an analysis of someone else's words or ideas, as singer-songwriter Conor O'Brien did (see "Learning by Writing"), you can develop a deeper appreciation for those words or ideas.

- When you write a blog post about a political campaign, you engage the ideas of others who might disagree with you, which can help you examine the basis for disagreement.

- When you write an argument about a problem, you might understand that problem better so that you are able to see solutions that were invisible to you before you began writing.

- When you write a lab report about an experiment you did for a chemistry class, you might gain a better grasp of the experimental process and the specific research question you were examining.

This kind of discovery and learning is possible because writing engages your intellect in a way that goes beyond reading or listening. If you have ever been so immersed in a writing task that the time seems to fly by, then you have experienced this capacity of writing to engage your mind fully.

What This Means for You as a Writer

- **Approach every writing task with curiosity.** Don't assume you already know exactly what you want to say or where your writing will end up, even when you're writing about something you know very well. Don't expect to know at the beginning exactly how everything will turn out in the finished text. Be open to unexpected possibilities as you work through an assignment. Even when your assignment is very specific and has rigid rules to follow (for example, a chemistry lab report with explicit directions for format or a persuasive essay in which you're required to provide exactly three arguments for and against your position), remember that you can't know everything at the start. That's why you're writing in the first place: to learn something new or deepen your understanding of something you thought you knew.

- **Be patient.** To engage in writing as a process of discovery and learning almost always involves working through several drafts as you explore your subject, gather information, develop ideas, consider your audience, learn more about your subject, and refine what you thought you wanted to say. This process can be messy and even frustrating at times, but it can also be illuminating. Forcing this process into a step-by-step procedure will not only make it more difficult (as you probably already know) but also prevent it from becoming a worthwhile journey of discovery. And it will usually result in less effective writing. But if you approach a writing task as a process of discovery and learning, you might be surprised by where your writing can take you.

- **Don't try to make your writing perfect as you work through an assignment.** Early drafts of any assignment are opportunities to explore your subject and learn more about it.

Avoid the impulse to make everything perfect the first time. Rough drafts are just that: drafts. They can be changed and improved. Sometimes you have to allow yourself to write messy drafts, especially in the early stages of an assignment. You can even temporarily ignore rules of usage and style in your early drafts and focus instead on exploring your subject matter and discovering what you want to say in your piece, as Chelsea did. You will go back later to correct errors, tighten up your sentences, develop ideas, or clarify a point. (See Core Concept #10.)

■ **Allow yourself sufficient time to write.** Writing at the last minute forces students to rush the process and undercut the discovery and learning that writing can lead to. It is also stressful and less enjoyable. Allowing sufficient time to move through the process deliberately will result not only in greater learning but also greater enjoyment—and more effective writing.

Practice This Lesson

Keep an informal journal or a private blog as you work on your next piece of writing. Each time you work on your writing, describe in your journal or blog what you did. If you read something and take notes for your writing, describe that. If you make an outline or jot down some ideas for your introduction, describe that. If you get an idea while taking a shower or riding a bus, describe that. If you share a draft with a friend or roommate, describe that. Also record any questions, concerns, or problems that arise as you work on this piece of writing, and explain how you addressed those questions, concerns, or problems. Describe how you feel as you work on the piece. What seems to be going well and what doesn't? Keep a record of *everything* you do and think as you complete the writing task. Once you're finished with the writing task, go back and review your journal or blog. What does it reveal about how you write? What does it suggest about writing in general? What surprises you about your descriptions of what you did to complete your writing task? What do you think you can learn from this journal about writing? About yourself as a writer?

If possible, interview someone who is a professional writer or who writes regularly in his or her work, and ask that person what he or she does when writing. What steps or activities does the person engage in when completing a writing task? How does this person explain what he or she does when writing? After you finish your interview, describe in a paragraph or two what you learned about writing from this writer, and compare what he or she does to what you do.

Core Concept 2 — Good writing fits the context.

If writing is a journey of discovery, how do we know when that journey produces writing that is good? The answer is: It depends.

Consider the expression, "Today was a very good day." People say this all the time, but what exactly does it mean? A student who earned a good grade on a test could say it was a good day. Someone receiving a raise at work might consider that a good day, but quitting a job could also make for a good day. Winning the lottery would be a very good day for most people. So would getting married. But getting divorced might also be considered a good day. You get the point: What counts as a good day depends on the person and the circumstances.

The same goes for writing. Students generally believe they know what an instructor means by "good writing," but **what counts as good writing can only be determined by examining the specific context of the writing**.

When it comes to writing, *context* is often understood as the *rhetorical situation*, which traditionally includes the writer, the subject of the writing, and the audience (see "The Rhetorical Situation"). These components determine what constitutes effective writing in a given situation. For example, a lab report that earns an A in a biology class might not qualify as a good report in a pharmaceutical company because the biology instructor and the lab supervisor in a pharmacy might have different expectations for lab reports; moreover, the purpose of the writing differs in each case. Writers have to determine the expectations for each writing situation. They must consider their audience and make decisions about content, form, and style that they believe will most effectively meet the expectations of that audience. Good writing is writing that meets the needs of the rhetorical situation—which often means meeting the specific criteria for an assignment (see "Grades vs. Good Writing" on page 32).

FOCUS   The Rhetorical Situation

In classical rhetorical theory, the rhetorical situation is represented as a triangle. The metaphor of a triangle illuminates the relationships among the writer, reader, and subject matter in a particular act of writing. The writer and the audience have a specific relationship to the subject matter in the form of their shared knowledge about the subject, their opinions about it, their respective experiences with it, their stake in it, and so on. In addition, the writer has some kind of relationship to the audience, even if he or she doesn't actually know that audience. For example, a historian writing an article for a professional journal assumes that she

(Continued)

is writing as a member of the community of professional historians, with whom she shares certain values, knowledge, and expectations when it comes to the subject of the article and to history in general. To write well requires understanding your audience and its relationship to your subject—and to you—so that you can adapt your writing appropriately to achieve your goals in that rhetorical situation.

The rhetorical situation is an essential concept that helps writers better understand the social nature of writing and thus create more effective texts. Most instructors use the term to highlight the observable elements of the writing situation, especially the intended audience and the writer's purpose in addressing that audience. (In this textbook, I generally use the term in this basic way.) Some theorists, however, have illuminated how other factors can influence writing within a rhetorical situation. These factors might include the writer's identity (including race, gender, ethnicity, and so on), the cultural context of the writing, the historical moment, and the reader's background, among other such factors. These factors can shape not only what and how a writer writes but also how the writer's text is given meaning within the rhetorical situation.

To write effectively, then, requires assessing the rhetorical situation. Writers should consider four key dimensions of the rhetorical situation to guide their decisions as they complete a writing task:

- **Purpose.** *Why* you are writing helps determine *what* to write and whether your writing is appropriate and effective in a particular context. A high school guidance counselor might praise your college admissions essay because it is clear and well organized, but can that essay really be considered "good" writing if it does not convince the college admissions officer to admit you to the college? And what if you are rejected by one college but accepted by another? Does that make your essay "good writing" or not? Writing can never really be evaluated without considering the writer's purpose: Are you trying to persuade an admissions officer that you are a good student? Are you attempting to solve a problem by analyzing it carefully? Do you want to share an insight about love by telling the story of a relationship? Good writing accomplishes the writer's goals in a specific rhetorical situation.

- **Form or genre.** Each rhetorical situation demands a specific form or genre—that is, a specific kind of writing: an argument, a report, a blog post, a multimedia presentation, a poem. And each form is governed by specific criteria regarding structure and style. A lab report will be written in a formal, objective style, whereas a blog post might have a more informal, provocative style. Writers select the appropriate form for the rhetorical situation and adapt their writing to the expectations of that form. Certain forms of writing are appropriate for specific rhetorical situations, and no one style is appropriate for every kind of writing. Understanding and using various forms for different rhetorical situations is essential for effective writing.

■ **Audience.** Good writing meets the expectations of the intended audience. That college admissions essay is "good" if it resonates with the college admissions officer who reads it. To write effectively, then, requires identifying your audience, analyzing their expectations, and adapting your text to their expectations for that situation. Sometimes that's a straightforward task: You adopt a formal writing style and avoid irrelevant personal tidbits in a job application letter, assuming that such language and information would be considered inappropriate by the person reviewing job applications. Usually, though, analyzing your audience is more complicated, even when you know the audience. That's because there is always a subjective element to writing. Readers can agree on the general characteristics of good writing but disagree on whether a specific piece of writing is good. For example, they might agree that an editorial is well organized and clearly written—characteristics usually associated with good writing—but disagree about whether that editorial is "good" because one reader finds the writer's style too glib whereas another finds it engaging. Readers react to a piece of writing on the basis of their backgrounds, age, gender, experiences, and personal preferences as well as their reasons for reading that piece. Different audiences might judge the same piece of writing very differently. Writers must understand the challenge of anticipating such differences and adapt their writing as best they can to achieve their purposes with their intended audience.

■ **Culture.** The dimensions of context described so far are all shaped by the broader cultural context. *Culture* can be defined as your sense of identity as it relates to your racial and ethnic backgrounds, your religious upbringing (if any), your membership in a particular social class (working class, for example), and the region where you live (for example, central Phoenix versus rural Minnesota or suburban Long Island). Not only does culture shape how readers might react to a text, but it also shapes basic aspects of a rhetorical situation such as the subject matter and language. Consider, for example, how the issue of gender equality might be understood differently by readers from traditional Muslim households as compared to readers with more secular backgrounds. Writers can't be expected to address all the complex nuances of culture that might influence a specific rhetorical situation, but to write effectively requires being sensitive to these nuances and understanding how a factor such as religious background or ethnic identity might shape readers' reactions.

In addition, the rhetorical context for any writing task includes **the medium**, which can significantly affect what and how a writer writes in a given situation (see Core Concept #3).

So the question of whether the writing is "good" is really beside the point. What matters is whether the writer accomplished his or her purposes with a specific audience in a specific rhetorical situation.

Most students understand that producing good writing and getting good grades on writing assignments aren't always the same thing. Usually, instructors have specific criteria for grading student writing based on course goals and their own views about effective writing. Different instructors can have different expectations for writing even in the same course and for the same writing assignments. Getting an A on a specific assignment doesn't necessarily mean that the student is a "good writer"; it means that the student's writing successfully met the criteria for that assignment in the view of the instructor. By the same token, getting a poor grade on an assignment doesn't mean that the student is a poor writer. Students who regularly get good grades in one subject—English, say—are sometimes frustrated when they get lower grades in another—say, psychology. But usually the lower grades mean that the student has not adjusted to the demands of writing in a different subject.

What This Means for You as a Writer

■ **Consider your purpose.** What do you hope to accomplish with a specific piece of writing? Answering that question, even in a general way, can guide your writing and make it more likely that your text is effective for your rhetorical situation. For college writing assignments, avoid the temptation to think of your purpose as getting a good grade. Instead, identify your purpose in terms of the assignment and what the instructor expects you to learn or do. If your instructor doesn't provide such information, try to obtain it so that you have a clear idea of the expectations or guidelines to help determine what counts as good writing for that assignment. Have a clear sense of purpose that matches the expectations for the assignment.

■ **Consider your audience.** The decisions writers make about matters like content, form, and style should be driven by their sense of what will work best for their intended audience. Even when writing for a general audience (for example, when writing a letter to the editor of a newspaper read by thousands of people with very different backgrounds and expectations), try to identify basic characteristics of your audience (e.g., readers of a regional newspaper are likely to be familiar with a local political controversy or be generally supportive of a local industry) and their likely expectations about a given subject. One of the first things you should always do when you begin a piece of writing is think carefully about your audience.

■ **Consider the form of the writing.** Form does matter when it comes to determining whether a piece of writing is effective. The form of your writing will shape your decisions about style, organization, and length as well as the content of a piece. For each writing task, use an appropriate form and identify the standards for organization, style, length, and so on for whatever form of writing you are using.

■ **Study good writing.** Although there is no single definition of "good writing," students can learn a lot by paying attention to what others—including their instructors—consider good writing. What counts as good writing in each of your classes? What is different or similar about how different instructors evaluate their students' writing? What is it about a specific piece of writing that certain readers like or dislike? Exploring such questions can lead to insight into what features of writing readers value in different situations.

Practice This Lesson

Find a short piece of writing that you think is good. (You might select one of the readings included in this textbook.) Share that piece of writing with two or three friends or classmates, and ask them their opinions of it. What do they like or dislike about the piece of writing? What did they find especially effective or ineffective about it? Ask them to explain their opinions as clearly as they can. Then write a brief reflection on what you learned about "good" writing from this activity. In your essay, compare the reactions of your friends or classmates to the piece of writing you chose, and draw your own conclusions about the role of audience in writing.

Core Concept 3   The medium is part of the message.

Good writing depends on context, and that context includes the medium—that is, the tools or technology the writer uses and the venue for the writing. Writing a blog entry about a controversial parking policy on your campus will be different from writing an analysis of that parking policy for a business course or a letter of complaint to the campus parking office. Different media place different demands on writers. Effective writing means adjusting to the medium.

Students today are fortunate to be living in an age of astonishing technological developments that open up countless opportunities for writers. Using widely available technologies, students exchange ideas and information in ways that were unimaginable even a few years ago. They can communicate easily and widely through social media. They can use cell phones to send text messages, take and share photos, or download music and videos. They can participate in online discussions with their professors and classmates without leaving home. They can use computers to produce sophisticated documents that only a decade ago would have required a professional printing service. They can easily create multimedia presentations incorporating sound, image, and text.

These technologies are dramatically changing how we communicate and may be changing the very act of writing itself. When I create a website for one of my classes, I write differently than when I create a printed syllabus for the same class, even though most of the content is the same. I organize the website differently, because students will use it differently from the syllabus. I change some of the content, because my students don't access content on the website in the same way they find it on the syllabus. I include images as well as links to other online resources. Even my writing style changes a bit. In short, the medium changes my writing.

Think about creating a Prezi presentation as compared to, say, writing a report for an economics class. The audience and purpose might be the same, but the form and some content will differ. More to the point, the tools for composing are different. Prezi enables you to create documents that include much more than text. All these factors can influence both *what* and *how* writers write. For example, you will probably use less text in a Prezi presentation, which will affect your decisions about the content of your presentation. In addition, you will likely incorporate images and even audio and video clips into your Prezi document but not in your report. You also adjust your writing style: For the report, you will use a formal academic style and probably complex sentences and lengthy paragraphs, whereas the Prezi presentation will require more concise language, bul-

Cameron Whitman/iStockphoto.com

leted lists, and brief titles for most slides. All these differences might seem obvious, but because writers today often have several choices for the medium they will use, they need to be aware of the ways in which the medium shapes what they write and how they use writing to accomplish a specific purpose.

Although most essays, reports, and research papers assigned in college course still require students to write in conventional print formats, increasingly students are asked or choose to write in other media. More and more students are required by their instructors to participate in online discussions about course topics, use multimedia programs to make presentations, and produce videos instead of traditional papers. In each case, the medium can shape the writing task in important ways. The medium can also affect your relationship to your audience (see "Blogging vs. Writing a Newspaper Column"). Part of your task as writer, then, is to understand how different media might affect your writing and to adapt to the medium you're using.

SIDEBAR   BLOGGING VS. WRITING A NEWSPAPER COLUMN

Political writer Andrew Sullivan writes a popular blog called *The Daily Dish* as well as a column for the *Sunday Times of London*. Each medium, he says, influences his writing style, choice of subject matter, and interactions with his readers. According to Sullivan, blogging "is instantly public. It transforms this most personal and retrospective of forms into a painfully public and immediate one." It also calls for "a colloquial, unfinished tone." Here's part of how he describes the differences between these two kinds of writing:

> A blogger will air a variety of thoughts or facts on any subject in no particular order other than that dictated by the passing of time. A writer will instead use time, synthesizing these thoughts, ordering them, weighing which points count more than others, seeing how his views evolved in the writing process itself, and responding to an editor's perusal of a draft or two. The result is almost always more measured, more satisfying, and more enduring than a blizzard of [blog] posts.

Source: Sullivan, Andrew. "Why I Blog." *The Atlantic*, 1 Nov. 2008. Web. 24 Apr. 2013.

What This Means for You as a Writer

- **Know the medium.** For most college writing assignments, students use computers to write conventional papers or reports. Such assignments place familiar demands on writers when it comes to organization, style, and so on. Other media, such as blogs, wikis, or Prezi, call for different strategies regarding organization, style, and even content. In many cases, what and how you write may be similar in different media, but not always. Be familiar with the characteristics of the medium in order to use it effectively for the task at hand.

- **Choose an appropriate medium.** If given a choice, consider which medium would enable you to create the most effective document for that rhetorical situation. A Prezi presentation with embedded audio and video clips might be the best choice for an assignment in which your audience will be your classmates. For other writing situations, a blog or even a Facebook page might be more effective, depending upon your message and the audience you hope to reach. Consider the medium carefully as you decide how to complete the writing task at hand in order to achieve your intended purpose with your intended audience.

- **Adjust your writing process to the medium.** All writing tasks require planning, developing ideas, drafting, revising, and editing. But those activities can differ depending upon the medium, so effective writers adjust their writing process accordingly. Obviously, you will organize a research paper for a history course differently than you would a blog entry or video script, but sometimes the differences between one medium and another aren't so obvious. For example, many students make the mistake of writing a PowerPoint or Prezi presentation as if it were a conventional report. As a result, they include too much text in the presentation and fail to take advantage of the capabilities of the medium to engage an audience visually. The outcome can be an ineffective document that may be tedious or difficult for an audience to follow. It is more effective to consider the characteristics of the medium *as you are creating your document*.

Review several text messages or tweets that you recently sent or received. Then write a brief style guide for text messaging and/or tweeting. In your style guide, include what you believe are the main rules for writing text messages or tweets to specific audiences and for specific purposes. Include any advice that you think writers should heed when writing texts or tweets. Also include common abbreviations that writers of text messages use. Consider the different ways that people might use texts and tweets. Now compare your style guide to standard academic writing. What are the main differences and similarities between the two? What might the differences suggest about the role of the medium in writing? (Alternatively, write a brief style guide for another medium, such as Facebook or Prezi.)

Core Concept 4   A writer must have something to say.

Having a clear, valid main point or idea is an essential element of effective writing—not only in college but also in the workplace and other settings. In most cases, college instructors expect students to have a clearly defined main point or idea that is appropriate for the assignment, no matter what kind of writing the assignment calls for. (Research shows that college instructors identify the lack of a clearly defined main idea as one of the biggest problems they see in their students' writing.) Readers expect writers to have something to say; as a writer, you should oblige them. (See "So What?" on page 37.)

This is not to say that the main point or idea is always simple or easily boiled down to a one-sentence summary. Much college writing is about complex subjects, and students are often required to delve into several ideas or bodies of information in a single assignment. A 20-page research paper for an information science course about how new digital technologies are affecting the music industry will include many complicated points and key ideas. So will a critique of the major arguments about the existence of God for a philosophy course. But even such involved pieces of writing, if they are to be effective, will be focused on a main idea and will convey a clear main point. That critique of major philosophical arguments about the existence of God, for example, might focus on the central point that all those arguments reflect the human desire to understand why we exist or that many philosophers equivocate when it comes to this basic question.

Remember, though, that you when you're beginning a writing assignment, you won't always know exactly what your main point will be. Sometimes the assignment will determine your main idea or point. For example, in an anthropology class you may be asked to write an essay defining *culture* as anthropologists generally understand that concept. In such a case, you will be expected to convey a main point based on what you are learning in the course about how anthropologists understand culture. Sometimes, however, identifying your main point or idea will be more complicated. A student of mine once wrote a research paper about being a vegetarian. She started

out thinking that she would write about the pros and cons of being a vegetarian to show that vegetarianism is not practical for most people. But as wrote, she learned more about the subject and began to shift her focus to the environmental destruction caused by eating meat. In the end, her main point changed; she argued in favor of a vegetarian diet as an ethical response to the environmental destruction caused by the standard American diet. As she explored her subject, she was guided by a sense of her main idea, which evolved as she wrote. Her final paper had a clearly articulated main point but not the one she started with.

FOCUS So What?

One useful way to help identify and refine your main idea or point in a piece of writing is to ask, So what? Suppose you've written a personal narrative about your first job. So what? Why should readers care about that experience? What's in it for them? What will you say *about* that experience that might matter to others? Answering such questions can help ensure that you are telling your story in a way that conveys a *relevant* main idea or point to your readers. The same applies to just about any kind of writing you will do in college. For an economics class, you might write an analysis of tax cuts as a way to generate jobs. So what? To answer that question requires you to decide whether your analysis is relevant in the field of economics. Why analyze tax cuts now? What makes that topic something that will interest others in the field? Is your main point something that economists would consider relevant and important? Asking this question about your topic also ensures that you are thinking about your audience and connecting your main point or idea to their interests as well.

What This Means for You as a Writer

- **Identify your main idea.** Every kind of writing—even the most formulaic lab report in a biology or chemistry class—should have a main point. However, it is important to distinguish between your *subject* and your main idea or point. The subject of a biology lab report might be osmosis, but the main point might be that osmosis doesn't occur with a certain type of membrane. Similarly, for an American history course, you might write an analysis of the impact of the Civil Rights movement on race relations in the United States. Your subject would be the impact of the Civil Rights movement on race relations, but your main point would be what you have to say *about* that impact on the basis of your analysis—for example, that race relations were changed in specific ways as a result of the Civil Rights movement.

- **Have something relevant to say.** Having something to say is one thing; having something *relevant* to say is another. Whenever you write, you are participating in a conversation (see Core Concept #7), and what counts as relevant or appropriate depends on the nature of that conversation. In college, what counts as relevant usually depends on the academic subject. For example, in an analysis of the social importance of hip hop music for a sociology class, you might conclude that hip hop's popularity reflects discontent among young people of certain social and racial groups. For a paper in a music appreciation class, by contrast, you might argue that certain musical qualities, such as rhythm, account for hip hop's popularity, an argument that might be considered irrelevant in a sociology course. Part of what makes writing effective is not only having something to say but also knowing what is relevant or appropriate to say in a specific context.

- **Make sure that your main idea or point is clear to your readers.** Don't assume that because something is clear to you, it will also be clear to your readers. Sometimes, students can become so deeply immersed in their writing that they lose perspective. They think they have made their points clearly, but their readers may have trouble seeing the main idea. This is especially true when the assignment is complicated and lengthy. So it's important to revise with your audience in mind to make sure your main idea comes through clearly.

- **Don't try to say too much.** A clear main idea is partly a result of what the writer *doesn't* say. Including too many ideas or too much information in a piece of writing can obscure the main point, even if the ideas and information are relevant. Because most college writing assignments address complicated subjects, it can sometimes be a challenge for students to decide what to include in their writing. It's important to decide whether an idea or piece of information is *essential* in an assignment. If not, consider removing it.

Practice This Lesson

Post a draft of an assignment you are working on to your Facebook page or to an online forum for sharing documents, such as GoogleDocs. Ask your friends to summarize the main idea of your paper. Compare their summaries to your own sense of your main idea. Do their summaries match your idea? If not, consider revising your draft so that your main idea is clear to other readers.

Core Concept 5 — A writer must support claims and assertions.

"Winters are warmer than they used to be around here."

"Most drivers don't obey speed limits."

"The average person doesn't pay attention to politics."

In casual conversation, we usually don't expect people making statements like these to provide supporting arguments or facts to prove the point. In most college writing, however, appropriate support for claims and assertions is essential.

As we saw in Chapter 1, a central purpose of writing in college is to understand and participate in conversations about the topics and questions that define each academic discipline. To participate in those conversations requires knowing how to make a case for a particular point of view and support conclusions about a relevant topic. In other words, not only must writers have something relevant to say, but they must also be able to back up what they say.

Students sometimes fail to support their ideas or assertions effectively because they are unfamiliar with the expectations for doing so in a specific academic subject. The important point to remember is that *all* academic disciplines have such standards, though different disciplines might have different conventions regarding what counts as appropriate support or evidence for a claim or assertion:

- In an English literature class, you might cite passages from a poem or quote from critical reviews of that poem to support a claim about the work of a particular poet. Your claim would be more or less persuasive depending upon whether readers consider those passages or quotations to be sufficient support for your claim.

- In economics, some kinds of statistical information carry more weight than other kinds when drawing conclusions about economic trends or developments.

- In a biochemistry lab, data from experiments might be the main evidence for conclusions or claims.

In each case, an important element of effective writing is using evidence that is considered appropriate and persuasive by readers familiar with that discipline. The same holds true outside of school, though the standards for supporting your statements tend to be less well defined and less rigorous in most popular writing than in academic or workplace writing.

FOCUS   Supporting a Claim

The need for writers to support their claims or assertions applies to any kind of writing, including newspaper and magazine articles, business proposals, legal documents, government reports, petitions, blogs, and many other kinds of documents. The following examples

(Continued)

are taken from various sources: a government report on higher education, an excerpt from a book on women and careers, and a newspaper column about fair pay for baseball stadium vendors. As you read them, notice how each writer backs up his or her statements, and consider how that support affects your reaction as a reader:

There is a troubling and persistent gap between the college attendance and graduation rates of low-income Americans and their more affluent peers. Similar gaps characterize the college attendance rates—and especially the college completion rates—of the nation's growing population of racial and ethnic minorities. While about one-third of whites have obtained bachelor's degrees by age 25–29, for example, just 18 percent of blacks and 10 percent of Latinos in the same age cohort have earned degrees by that time.

Source: U.S. Department of Education. *A Test of Leadership: Charting the Future of Higher Education.* 2006: 1. Print.

. . . .

When I arrived at college in the fall of 1987, my classmates of both genders seemed equally focused on academics. I don't remember thinking about my future career differently from the male students. I also don't remember any conversations about someday balancing work and children. My friends and I assumed that we would have both. Men and women competed openly and aggressively with one another in classes, activities, and job interviews. Just two generations removed from my grandmother, the playing field seemed to be level.

But more than twenty years after my college generation, the world has not evolved nearly as much as I believed it would. Almost all of my male classmates work in professional settings. Some of my female classmates work full-time or part-time outside the home, and just as many are stay-at-home mothers and volunteers like my mom. This mirrors the national trend. In comparison to their male counterparts, highly trained women are scaling back and dropping out of the workforce in record numbers. In turn, these diverging numbers teach institutions and mentors to invest more in men, who are statistically more likely to stay.

Source: Sandberg, Cheryl. *Lean In: Women, Work, and the Will to Lead.* New York: Knopf, 2013. 14. Print.

. . . .

The Angels are one of the richest and most successful franchises in Major League Baseball—in fact, in all pro sports.

They're valued by Forbes at $554 million (up 6% from a year ago), carry the fourth-largest player payroll in the major leagues, and at this point in the season rank fifth in per-game attendance. As they're very much in the hunt for their division lead, it's quite possible that lucrative post-season games will be added to the schedule.

So why are they trying to nickel-and-dime their stadium ushers, ticket sellers and janitors?...

The Angel Stadium employees are the worst paid among all California ballpark workers in their job classifications, the SEIU says. Here are some comparisons provided by the union, which also represents some of the workers at the other parks:

Angel Stadium ushers (the lowest paid among the affected employees) earn $11.21 an hour. At Dodger Stadium the rate is $12.77, and at the Oakland Coliseum it's $14.03. Janitors in Anaheim receive $11.50 an hour; at Chavez Ravine it's $12.31, in Oakland $17.50 and at the San Francisco Giants' AT&T Park $15.15. Ticket sellers at Angel Stadium get $13.65 an hour, but at the San Diego Padres' Petco Park they get $16.43.

Source: Hiltzik, Michael. "Angel Baseball, Paying the Little Guy Peanuts." *Los Angeles Times*, 7 Aug. 2011. Web. 25 Apr. 2013.

What This Means for You as a Writer

■ **Provide sufficient support.** First and foremost, make sure you have adequately supported your main points, claims, and assertions. Regardless of your subject or the kind of writing you are doing, readers expect you to make a case for what you have to say. Review your drafts to be sure you have provided the necessary support for your ideas.

■ **Provide relevant and appropriate support.** What counts as appropriate and effective support for a claim depends upon the subject, the academic discipline, and the rhetorical situation. The kind of evidence used to support a claim in a history course, for example, won't necessarily work in a psychology course; similarly, readers of newspaper editorials have different expectations for relevant support than, say, economists who read professional journals. As a writer, part of your task is to understand the expectations for evidence and support for the kind of writing you're doing. You should be able to anticipate readers' expectations so that the support you provide for your claims will be persuasive and appropriate for the rhetorical situation.

■ **Evaluate your sources.** Citing relevant sources to support or illustrate a point is a crucial part of effective academic writing, but not all sources are created equal. A self-help blog might not suffice as an appropriate source in an essay about teen depression for a psychology course, whereas a study published in a professional journal would. Having information from a source to support a claim or assertion is not the same as having information from a credible source. Make sure the sources you cite are not only appropriate for the writing task at hand, the course, and the rhetorical situation but also trustworthy. (Chapters 7 and 8 provide detailed discussions of finding and evaluating sources.)

Practice This Lesson

Compare how the authors of the following two passages support their statements or arguments. The first passage is from a report by an economist examining the impact of poverty on educational achievement. The second is an excerpt from an analysis by an economist about how the American public's misconceptions about economics affect their voting habits. First, write a brief summary of each passage, identifying the main assertions or points in each. Then identify the supporting evidence or arguments for each main point. What kinds of evidence or support does each author use? What sources do they use to support their points? Finally, discuss the differences and similarities in how these authors support their points. How might you explain these similarities and differences?

1   The impact of education on earnings and thus on poverty works largely through the labour market, though education can also contribute to productivity in other areas, such as peasant farming (Orazem, Glewwe & Patrinos, 2007: 5). In the labour market, higher wages for more educated people may result from higher productivity, but also perhaps from the fact that education may act as a signal of ability to employers, enabling the better educated to obtain more lucrative jobs. Middle-income countries—which frequently have well developed markets for more educated labour—are particularly likely to see the benefits of education translated into better jobs and higher wages. In Chile, for instance, between one quarter and one third of household income differences can be explained by the level of education of household heads (Ferreira & Litchfield, 1998, p. 32).

Source: van der Berg, Servaas. *Poverty and Education.* UNESCO. Paris: International Institute for Educational Planning, 2008. 3. Print.

2   Consider the case of immigration policy. Economists are vastly more optimistic about its economic effects than the general public. The Survey of Americans and Economists on the Economy asks respondents to say whether "too many immigrants" is a major, minor, or non-reason why the economy is not doing better than it is. 47% of non-economists think it is a major reason; 80% of economists think it is not a reason at all. Economists have many reasons for their contrarian position: they know that specialization and trade enrich Americans and immigrants alike; there is little evidence that immigration noticeably reduces even the wages of low-skilled Americans; and, since immigrants are largely young males, and most government programs support the old, women, and children, immigrants wind up paying more in taxes than they take in benefits.

    Given what the average voter thinks about the effects of immigration, it is easy to understand why virtually every survey finds that a solid majority of

Americans wants to reduce immigration, and almost no one wants to increase immigration. Unfortunately for both Americans and potential immigrants, there is ample reason to believe that the average voter is mistaken. If policy were based on the facts, we would be debating how much to increase immigration, rather than trying to "get tough" on immigrants who are already here.

Source: Caplan, Brian. "The Myth of the Rational Voter." *Cato Unbound*, 6 Nov. 2006. Web. 25 Apr. 2013.

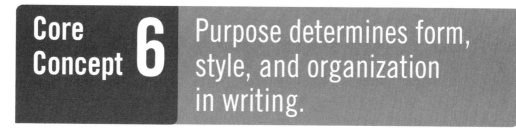

Core Concept 6 Purpose determines form, style, and organization in writing.

A resumé is a carefully structured record of the writer's work history and qualifications; a cover letter for a job application is a statement of the writer's suitability for the job. Each document has familiar conventions regarding content, organization, and style, which the reader (usually a person involved in hiring for the job) expects the writer to follow. A resumé shouldn't be organized in the narrative format that might be used for a report on an internship, nor should a cover letter be written in the informal style and tone of a text message or Facebook post.

The conventional forms of a resumé and cover letter serve very specific purposes for both reader and writer. These forms convey relevant information efficiently within the rhetorical situation. They are functional. That's one reason that they have become standard. Writing an effective resumé and cover letter, then, is partly a matter of knowing how to use a well-established *form* to accomplish a specific purpose (to get a job interview) within a specific rhetorical situation (the job application process). The same is true of *any* kind of writing, including academic writing. Every kind of text—a lab report, a research paper, a personal narrative, a blog entry, a proposal, a review—is governed by general expectations regarding form. (See "What Is *Form* in Writing?") A writer must be familiar with these expectations if a text is to be effective.

FOCUS   What Is *Form* in Writing?

You have probably heard teachers refer to *form* when discussing writing assignments, but what exactly is *form*? Generally, *form* refers to the way a piece of writing is organized as well as to any features that determine the shape or structure of the document, such as subheadings or footnotes. *Form* also includes the introductory and concluding sections of a piece of writing. *Form* is often used interchangeably with *genre*—that is, the kind of writing; for example, you might hear an instructor refer to *narrative* as both a form and a genre of writing. (The Merriam-Webster Dictionary defines *genre* as "a category of artistic, musical, or literary composition characterized by a particular style, form, or content.") Often, terms such as *design* and *layout* are used to describe features of documents that include visual elements, such as graphs or photographs; design and layout can therefore be considered part of the *form* of a document. In many kinds of digital texts—including multimedia documents and online media such as web pages—design, layout, and related components can be as important as the text itself. The alignment of the text or the contrast in font sizes and colors can influence how the text is received. (Chapter 6 discusses these elements of document design.)

For most traditional college writing assignments, *form* is generally used in two ways: (1) to refer to the genre, or the kind of writing, expected for that assignment (research paper, narrative, argument, and so on); and (2) to describe the relevant conventions regarding the format, style, and structure of the document for a specific kind of writing.

Notice that *purpose* is implicit in *form*. A writer uses narrative forms to tell a story, a lab report to present the results of an experiment, or an argument to support a particular point of view about a controversial issue. In this sense, it is helpful to think of the form of a piece of writing as a tool to help you achieve your purpose in a specific rhetorical situation.

For many students, however, the problem isn't learning rules or guidelines for specific kinds of writing, such as lab reports or books reports; the problem is that they learn *only* rules and guidelines for specific kinds of texts without understanding the *purposes* of those rules and guidelines and without considering the rhetorical situation—that is, how their intended readers will read that text. As a result, they tend to approach writing as a matter of creating a certain kind of document rather than adopting a specific form that serves a specific purpose for a specific rhetorical situation. Think again about a resumé. An effective resumé requires more than proper format. It must also include appropriate information about the job applicant that is presented in carefully chosen language. An employer reviews a resumé quickly, looking for specific information to determine whether the writer is a suitable candidate for the job. A resumé is designed to present that information clearly and efficiently. Knowing that, the applicant must select and present relevant information strategically so that the qualifications match the requirements of the job. A successful resumé is one in which the writer uses the form to present his or her qualifications effectively to an employer. Form follows function.

The same principle applies to the writing that students commonly do in college. The format of a lab report in chemistry, for example, enables a reader (the course instructor, other students, or perhaps other chemists) to find relevant information about a lab experiment quickly and easily. A literary analysis essay has less rigid guidelines for format, but readers still expect the writer to follow recognizable conventions when presenting an analysis of a poem or novel. The same is true of analytical writing in philosophy or psychology. The specific forms might differ, but in each case, the form serves certain purposes within the academic discipline. Writers in each discipline learn to use the form to achieve their rhetorical purposes.

Many students focus only on *form* (on the rules and guidelines for a specific kind of text) and neglect *function* (the purpose of the text within the rhetorical situation). Good writers learn the rules and guidelines for the forms of writing they do, whether those forms are business letters or lab reports or blog posts, but they also understand the *purposes* of those forms of writing and apply the rules to accomplish their purposes.

What This Means for You as a Writer

- **Determine the appropriate form for the rhetorical situation.** In many situations, the form will be obvious: a resumé and cover letter for a job application; a lab report for a chemistry class. For most college writing assignments, instructors will specify the form of writing (argument, analysis, review, report, and so on) and provide guidelines for organization, style, length, and so on. When the form of writing isn't clear or specified, assess the rhetorical situation to determine which form would be most appropriate and effective. What is the purpose of the writing? Who is the intended audience? What form of writing would mostly likely reach that audience and communicate your message effectively? Answering these questions will help you decide on the best form of writing for the task at hand. Remember that the form is a rhetorical choice: Select the form that will enable you to accomplish your purpose with your intended audience.

- **Become familiar with the conventions of the form of writing you are doing.** Writers should follow the conventions of well-established forms (e.g., lab reports) to meet their readers' expectations. But *there are no universal rules governing forms or genres of writing that apply to all situations.* In many instances, writers have a great deal of choice regarding organization, style, length, and similar features of a document. Digital texts such as web pages and social media offer writers great flexibility, and even very specialized forms, such as resumés and cover letters, can appear in many acceptable variations of format, style, and even content. As a writer, your task is to learn the basic expectations for a specific form of writing but to *adjust your style and tone according to the specific rhetorical situation and organize your text accordingly.* In most academic disciplines, there are established conventions for form, style, and so on, but sometimes instructors do not make those conventions clear. If you're not sure about those conventions—for example, how to organize an assignment, whether the style must be formal, and so on—ask your instructor and then draft your assignment accordingly.

■ **Pay attention to organization.** How a document is organized is one of the most important elements of form in writing. It is also one of the most challenging for many students. Studies show that college instructors consider the inability to organize texts appropriately to be one of the biggest problems in their students' writing. So it's important to learn how to organize an essay, report, or digital document appropriately for the specific academic subject. In some cases, the format will be provided. For example, lab reports usually require specific sections in a specific sequence; the same is often true of reviews of assigned readings. Following the guidelines for such assignments will essentially organize the report for you. However, other forms allow for more flexibility in organizing the text. Ask your instructor about the expectations for organizing writing assignments, and if possible, find examples of that form or genre to see how they are organized.

Practice This Lesson

Visit a job search website, such as Monster.com, and read several advertisements for jobs that interest you. Then write a resumé and cover letter for two or three such advertisements. (For this exercise, you might write a "fictional" resumé and cover letter, inventing appropriate job experiences and relevant background information, or you can use your own work experience and background.) Alter your resumé and cover letter for each job. Then consider the differences in your resumés and letters. What changes did you make? What remained the same? Why did you make those changes? Now consider what this exercise might suggest about the conventions for the form and style of resumés and cover letters.

NetPhotos/Alamy

Core Concept 7 — Writing is a social activity.

We tend to think of writing as a solitary activity. The image of the writer working alone in a quiet study is a popular one. But this image is incomplete and even misleading. In fact, **writing is an inherently social act in at least three ways:**

- **First, writers write for an audience.** Unless you are writing an entry in a personal diary that you plan never to share with anyone or a note to remind yourself to take out the trash, your writing is almost always intended to be read by someone else. And as we saw earlier, your audience significantly influences what you write, how you write, and even *whether* you write. Whether the audience is a course instructor, classmates, a friend, an employer reviewing job applications, or a larger audience, writers write with their reader or readers in mind, even if they're not always aware of it. In this sense, writing is always a social transaction between writer and reader, a way to connect writers and readers. In addition, the reason for writing something usually arises from a social situation: a paper assigned in a college class; a problem in your town that prompts you to write a letter to the local newspaper; an essay commemorating an important anniversary; a blog post about a current controversy. Writing happens because our interactions with others give us reasons to write. (See "The Rhetorical Situation" on page 29.)

- **Second, writers often involve others in the process of writing.** Writers regularly receive advice or suggestions from trusted readers as they develop a piece of writing. In class students might share drafts with classmates or comment on their classmates' writing. College instructors offer their students suggestions for improving their drafts. Digital media such as blogs enable writers to receive feedback from their readers; wikis allow writers to collaborate directly. In these ways, the act of writing is social rather than solitary. In fact, in business settings and in many other situations outside of school, collaborative writing is the norm, not the exception.

- **Third, the rules, conventions, and forms of writing are socially constructed.** These rules, conventions, and forms have evolved over time as a result of the way people have used writing to communicate, to share ideas and information, to learn, and to accomplish a variety of other purposes. Familiar forms of writing, such as narratives and business letters and research reports, have developed because people needed these forms in order to accomplish specific purposes in writing. Research reports, for example, help make it easier for scientists to share the results of their experiments and to collaborate in answering important scientific questions. Resumés are efficient forms for conveying information about a job candidate's qualifications. By the same token, certain rules for writing style, such as the rule that you shouldn't use the first person in scientific writing, have evolved to fit the purposes of that kind of writing. Even *what* writers choose to write about is shaped by what others have written. The topics considered relevant in, say, a course on business ethics are determined in large part by what others in that field are saying. So both *what* and *how* we write are shaped by social factors.

This idea about the social nature of writing is important because it undercuts the myth that writing ability is innate or exclusively the result of individual effort. This myth leads many students to believe that they don't have the ability to write or that writing is something that they have to figure out exclusively on their own. Neither belief is true. In fact, many social factors shape an act of writing. Individual skill and experience along with effort and motivation do matter, but many other influences outside a writer's individual control affect writing. In this sense, writing ability is as much a function of how writers respond to specific rhetorical situations, which are inherently social, as it is a result of individual skill. Your effectiveness as a writer depends not only on the effort you put into a writing task but also on the way you fit in and respond to the social situations in which you are completing that task. Learning to respond to those situations effectively begins with understanding the social nature of writing.

What This Means for You as a Writer

- **Place your writing in context.** As we saw earlier (Core Concept #2), all writing takes place in a rhetorical context, which shapes what and how the writer writes. Make it a habit to analyze the rhetorical situation for each writing task you have. Students tend to think of writing assignments as a matter of producing a certain kind of text rather than responding to the rhetorical situation. That kind of thinking can lead to ineffective writing because it tends to focus only on the *what* rather than the *why* of the writing task. Focusing instead on the rhetorical situation can help you adapt successfully to the different kinds of writing tasks you are likely to face as a college student; moreover, emphasizing the *purpose* (that is, the *why*) of your writing rather than focusing only on creating a specific kind of text (the *what*) is more likely to engage you in inquiry and learning about your subject (see Core Concept #1).

- **Remember the larger context.** Even when you write for a college course, you are part of larger conversations about important issues in specific academic fields and in the society at large. For example, an analysis of U.S. involvement in the Vietnam War for a history course can be shaped by current debates about the U.S. military efforts in Afghanistan and Iraq. Broader social, cultural, and historical factors can influence what you write, giving it a sense of immediacy and significance. Being aware of these larger contextual forces can lend a sense of relevance to your writing.

- **Seek the input of others.** Even if you do most of your writing by yourself, at some point it will be helpful to get advice or feedback from others. In your writing course, you may be required to share your writing with classmates or to revise in response to your instructor's feedback. But even if you aren't, you can benefit by asking a trusted friend, classmate, or co-worker to read your work-in-progress and consider their reactions to what you've written. Many online sites enable writers to share drafts and ideas and seek advice about their writing. Listening carefully to what others say about your writing can help you decide how to revise to make your writing more effective.

- **Write for your readers.** When you're in the midst of creating a document and perhaps struggling with matters such as organization or style, you can easily forget that you are writing for a reader. Reminding yourself that your text is being created for an audience can often help make the task clearer. Instead of focusing on whether a sentence is correct, for example, consider how a reader might respond to it. That shift in perspective can help you keep the purpose of your writing in view and avoid getting bogged down in rules and procedures. The rules and conventions of writing are important, but following rules and conventions doesn't result in good writing if the writing does not effectively address the intended audience and meet the needs of the rhetorical situation (see Core Concept #10).

Practice This Lesson

Take a piece of writing you did recently, and, in a brief paragraph or two, explore the social aspects of that text:

1. Consider the topic. What made you decide to write about that topic? Was your decision influenced in any way by others? Is the topic of interest to others?

2. Think about your audience. What do you know about that audience? What was your purpose in writing to that audience? What kind of reaction did you hope your writing would provoke?

3. Describe any advice or input you received as you completed this piece of writing. Did you share your drafts with anyone? Did you consult an instructor or post a draft on social media?

4. Examine the broader relevance of what you wrote. Does the analysis focus on subjects that concern people other than your classmates in that course? If so, in what ways? What makes the analysis relevant to your life outside that course? What might make it relevant to others?

5. Consider what your experience with this piece of writing suggests about the social nature of writing.

Core Concept 8 — Revision is an essential part of writing.

The famous American writer Ernest Hemingway once told an interviewer that he revised the ending of his novel *A Farewell to Arms* 39 times. The interviewer asked, "Was there some technical problem there? What was it that had stumped you?" Hemingway replied, "Getting the words right."

"Getting the words right" doesn't mean fixing a "technical problem." It means writing and rewriting until the meaning is clear and the message comes through for the reader. Sometimes that requires tinkering with words and phrases, but often it means much larger changes: adding new material, deleting sentences or paragraphs, moving them from one place to another in the draft, or completely rewriting entire passages. Such rewriting is an integral part of the writing process.

Creating an effective text is rarely so simple that a writer can move from beginning to end in a straight line and then go back to "fix" things. Writing is more often a circuitous, recursive process in which the writer stops and starts, goes back, jumps ahead, changes something, adds or deletes something, starts over, and maybe even writes the ending first (as the best-selling novelist John Irving says he does). It is through this process that writers explore their subjects and make meaning for their readers. Rarely does a writer know at the beginning exactly what his or her text will finally look like or what it will say. The text and its meaning emerge from the process of writing, and revising is central to that process.

Inexperienced writers often make the mistake of believing they can get everything right in a single draft, which they can quickly review to correct minor errors. This belief arises from a lack of practice with the various kinds of sophisticated writing required in college. Eventually students learn that writing an effective text can't be squeezed into a single draft. In most college writing assignments (and most other kinds of writing as well), there are simply too many things going on for a writer to attend to all of them at once. For example, if you are struggling to describe a complicated concept in an analytical essay for a political science course, you are probably not going to be thinking much about spelling and punctuation. By the same token, if you are focused on spelling and punctuation, you are probably not thinking in depth about how to explain that concept.

Most experienced writers divide each writing assignment into manageable tasks. When writing rough drafts, they mostly ignore matters like spelling and punctuation, knowing they can address those matters later, and focus instead on larger matters: Is my paper complete? Are the ideas clearly presented? Are there unnecessary passages that can be eliminated? Is the piece well organized? Have I addressed my intended audience appropriately? Does this piece achieve my rhetorical goals? As they revise each draft, they don't just "fix" mistakes; rather, they pay attention to how well they've covered their subject, how effectively they've addressed their audience, and how successfully they've accomplished their purpose. And they "listen" to their draft to see what meaning begins to emerge from it, learning more about their subject as they write and revising accordingly. Only after they have addressed these larger issues do they focus on improving sentences and correcting errors (see "Revising vs. Editing"). Writers who understand revising in this way usually find writing easier—and their writing becomes more effective.

FOCUS   Revising vs. Editing

Inexperienced writers tend to confuse revising with editing. Revising is the process of working with a draft to make sure it explores the subject adequately, addresses the intended audience effectively, and meets the needs of the rhetorical situation. It is not simply correcting spelling or punctuation errors, adjusting capitalization, and eliminating grammar problems. Those activities are *editing*. Editing means making sure that your writing is correct and that you've followed the appropriate rules for form and usage. It is usually the very last step before a piece of writing is finished.

What This Means for You as a Writer

- **Understand revision as a process of discovery and meaning making.** The British writer E. M. Forster reputedly said, "How do I know what I think until I see what I say?" I take that to mean that Forster never began a piece of writing knowing exactly what he was thinking or what he wanted to say. He found out through the process of writing. His statement can serve as advice for all writers. If you believe that writing is simply a matter of putting down on paper what's already in your head, you'll be frustrated and your writing will never feel right. But approaching writing as a process of discovery opens up possibilities, and revising is how writers find and realize those possibilities. It is the process of making the meaning of writing clear—both to the writer and to readers. (In this sense, this Core Concept is an extension of Core Concept #1.)

- **Don't try to do everything at once.** Approach every writing task as a series of smaller tasks, each of which is more manageable than the whole. Write a *first* draft without trying to make it a *final* draft. Once you have a first draft, work on it in stages, focusing on specific issues or problems in each stage. Start with larger issues, such as whether you have developed your main idea sufficiently or supported your main argument adequately, and then revise for organization or structure. Later, revise to make sure your tone is right for your intended audience, and then attend to your word choice and sentence structure to make sure your sentences are clear. Finally, edit for correctness. Working through a draft in this way will make revision easier and more effective.

- **Leave the editing for last.** Focusing on matters like spelling and punctuation while you're writing a first draft will divert your attention away from your subject and make it harder to focus on the meaning you are trying to convey to your readers. The best way to avoid this problem is to ignore minor errors of spelling, punctuation, grammar, and usage until you are just about finished with your text. At that point, after you have worked through your drafts and developed your ideas sufficiently, you can run your spellchecker, look for punctuation mistakes, attend to usage or grammar problems, and make sure that you have followed the basic rules of standard English. Leaving the editing for last will make your writing go more smoothly.

Practice This Lesson

Using a wiki or a site like GoogleDocs, share a draft of your writing with two or three classmates or friends. Be sure to explain the assignment and purpose of your draft. Ask each person to identify the strengths and weaknesses of your draft and suggest at least one revision for each weakness. Then compare the suggestions for revision provided by your classmates or friends. In what ways do their suggestions overlap? Do they disagree about what needs to be changed in your draft? How might their suggestions help you revise so that your text will achieve your rhetorical purpose? Now consider what their various suggestions might indicate about the process of revision. (You can do this exercise without using a wiki or GoogleDocs by simply having your readers comment on the same copy of your draft.)

Core Concept 9

There is always a voice in writing, even when there isn't an I.

When I was in graduate school, I took a course in sociolinguistics. As someone who knew little about sociolinguistics, I found the assigned readings slow and difficult. But one book by a famous anthropologist named Clifford Geertz stood out. Geertz pioneered a research technique called "thick description," by which he would describe in very rich detail the rituals and common beliefs of a culture in order to understand the culture from an insider's perspective. His research profoundly influenced the fields of anthropology and sociolinguistics. What really struck me about Geertz's work, though, was his writing style. Although his work was scholarly, specialized, and theoretical, it was also engaging to read, even for someone who knew little about anthropology and sociolinguistics. When I praised Geertz's writing during a discussion with my professor, he smiled and acknowledged that students often reacted as I did to Geertz. Geertz's writing, he said, was seductive. His comment surprised me because I had never heard anyone describe academic writing as "seductive." (You can judge for yourself: An excerpt from an essay by Geertz appears in "The Voice of a Scholar.")

My professor was really talking about *voice* in writing. Voice is difficult to define, but it has to do with what we "hear" when we read a text, how the writing "sounds." Voice is partly a technical matter of word choice and sentence structure, but it is also a function of the writer's confidence and authority (or lack of it). It is that nebulous quality that makes a piece of writing distinctive. It's what enables a reader to say, "That sounds like Stephen King." Or Clifford Geertz. As I learned in my sociolinguistics course, it isn't only popular writers like Stephen King whose writing can be said to have a distinctive voice. Even the most conventional scientific research report or philosophical treatise can have a distinctive voice. In fact, a strong, distinctive voice is one of the key elements of effective writing.

FOCUS   The Voice of a Scholar

Here are the opening two paragraphs from "Thick Description: Toward an Interpretive Theory of Culture," by Clifford Geertz, one of the most influential essays ever written in the field of anthropology. As you read, consider which features of Geertz's writing contribute to his voice:

> In her book, *Philosophy in a New Key*, Susanne Langer remarks that certain ideas burst upon the intellectual landscape with a tremendous force. They resolve so many fundamental problems at once that they seem also to promise that they will resolve all fundamental problems, clarify all obscure issues. Everyone snaps them up as the open sesame of some new positive science, the conceptual center-point around which

a comprehensive system of analysis can be built. The sudden vogue of such a *grande idee*, crowding out almost everything else for a while, is due, she says, "to the fact that all sensitive and active minds turn at once to exploiting it. We try it in every connection, for every purpose, experiment with possible stretches of its strict meaning, with generalizations and derivatives."

After we have become familiar with the new idea, however, after it has become part of our general stock of theoretical concepts, our expectations are brought more into balance with its actual uses, and its excessive popularity is ended. A few zealots persist in the old key-to-the-universe view of it; but less driven thinkers settle down after a while to the problems the idea has really generated. They try to apply it and extend it where it applies and where it is capable of extension; and they desist where it does not apply or cannot be extended. It becomes, if it was, in truth, a seminal idea in the first place, a permanent and enduring part of our intellectual armory. But it no longer has the grandiose, all-promising scope, the infinite versatility of apparent application, it once had.

Source: Geertz, Clifford. "Thick Description: Toward an Interpretive Theory of Culture." *The Interpretation of Cultures: Selected Essays.* New York: Basic Books, 1973. 3. Print.

Many students believe that academic writing is supposed to be dull and "voice-less." But they're confusing voice with style or tone (see "Voice vs. Tone"). A scientific paper might be written in an objective style, but that doesn't mean it will have no voice. Moreover, college instructors usually expect students' writing to have voice, even when they don't allow students to use the first person in course writing assignments. Being aware that you have a voice in your writing and that voice is an element of effective writing is an important step toward developing your own voice in writing.

FOCUS Voice vs. Tone

Trying to define voice in writing is like trying to describe the color blue: you can't quite say exactly what it is, but you know it when you see. Still, it's important to be able to talk about voice, because it is a key element of effective writing. It's also important to understand how voice differs from other aspects of writing, especially *tone*. If *voice* is the writer's personality that a reader "hears" in a text, then *tone* might be described as the writer's attitude in a text. The tone of a text might be emotional (angry, enthusiastic, melancholy), measured (such as in an essay in which the author wants to seem reasonable on a controversial topic), or objective or neutral (as in a scientific report). Tone is kind of like your tone of voice when speaking: you can be upset, sad, happy, uncertain, or concerned, and the tone of your voice (how loud or soft it is, how you inflect your speech, how you emphasize certain words—for example, stretching

(Continued)

out *told* in a statement like this: "I *told* you not to go outside in the rain!") reflects that mood. In writing, tone is created through word choice, sentence structure, imagery, and similar devices that convey to a reader the writer's attitude. Voice in writing, by contrast, is like the sound of your spoken voice: deep, high-pitched, nasal. It is the quality that makes your voice distinctly your own, no matter what tone you might take. In some ways, tone and voice overlap, but voice is a more fundamental characteristic of a writer, whereas tone changes depending upon the subject and the writer's feelings about it. Consider how you would describe Clifford Geertz's voice as compared to his tone (see "The Voice of a Scholar" on page 52).

What This Means for You as a Writer

- **Recognize and develop your own writerly voice.** Part of every writer's challenge is to refine his or her voice and use it effectively. The first step is to recognize that you always have a voice in writing, even in academic writing. Many of the exercises in this textbook will help you develop and strengthen your voice. It takes practice. Listen for the voice in the assigned texts in your classes. Try to get a sense of what makes them distinctive. Listen for your own voice in your writing as well. When revising a draft, pay attention to the "sound" of the writing—not only to make sure your writing is clear and understandable but also to give it the "sound" of confidence and authority. Adjust your style and tone so that they are appropriate for the kind of writing you are doing (for example, avoiding vivid descriptive language in a lab report), but always strive to write with a strong voice. A strong voice is more likely to make your writing effective.

- **Remember that *all* writing has voice.** Although you might have been taught that some kinds of academic writing, such as lab reports or science research papers, should be "objective" and therefore do not have a voice, the truth is that good writing will always have voice. That does not mean you should use "creative" language in every kind of writing you do. It *does* mean that you should follow the appropriate conventions for style and tone and use them as effectively as you can to bring out your own distinctive voice.

- **Don't fake it.** If you are unsure of your main idea or if you are confused about the assignment you are working on, your writerly voice is likely to reflect that. Often when students are unfamiliar with a subject or learning something for the first time, they try to "sound" academic by writing convoluted sentences, using inflated language, or substituting wordy phrases for more common words (for example, using "due to the fact that" instead of "because"). Such strategies usually make the writing less clear and weaken the writer's voice. And it's usually easy for an instructor to see that students are "padding" their writing because they aren't sure they have anything valid to say or they're confused about the assignment or subject (as Calvin does in the comic strip). So one way to have a strong, effective voice is to explore your subject sufficiently (Core Concept #1), do appropriate research if necessary (Core Concept #5), and have a clear sense of your main idea or argument (see Core Concept #4).

Practice This Lesson

Compare the three excerpts below. Each excerpt is the introductory passage from an academic article published in a scholarly journal. How would you describe the voice in each passage? What differences and similarities do you see in the voices of these passages? What specific features of the writing do you think accounts for the voice in each passage (e.g., word choice, sentence structure, use of first or third person, and so on)? Which do you like best? Why? What do you think your reaction to these passages suggests about voice in writing?

1. Writing represents a unique mode of learning—not merely valuable, not merely special, but unique. That will be my contention in this paper. The thesis is straightforward. Writing serves learning uniquely because writing as process-and-product possesses a cluster of attributes that correspond uniquely to certain powerful learning strategies.

   Although the notion is clearly debatable, it is scarcely a private belief. Some of the most distinguished contemporary psychologists have at least implied such a role for writing as heuristic. Lev Vygotsky, A. R. Luria, and Jerome Bruner, for example, have all pointed out that higher cognitive functions, such as analysis and synthesis, seem to develop most fully only with the support system of verbal language—particularly, it seems, of written language. Some of their arguments and evidence will be incorporated here.

   Here I have a prior purpose: to describe as tellingly as possible *how* writing uniquely corresponds to certain powerful learning strategies. Making such a case for the uniqueness of writing should logically and theoretically involve establishing many contrasts, distinctions between (1) writing and all other verbal languaging processes—listening, reading, and especially talking; (2) writing and all other forms of composing, such as composing a painting, a symphony, a dance, a film, a building; and (3) composing in words and composing in the two other major graphic symbol systems of mathematical equations and scientific formulae. For the purposes of this paper, the task is simpler, since most students

   (Continued)

are not permitted by most curricula to discover the values of composing, say, in dance, or even in film; and most students are not sophisticated enough to create, to originate formulations, using the highly abstruse symbol system of equations and formulae.

Source: Emig, Janet. "Writing as a Mode of Learning." *College Composition and Communication* 28.2 (1977): 122. Print.

2 Over the past two decades, the presence of computers in schools has increased rapidly. While schools had one computer for every 125 students in 1983, they had one for every 9 students in 1995, one for every 6 students in 1998, and one for every 4.2 students in 2001 (Glennan & Melmed, 1996; Market Data Retrieval, 1999, 2001). Today, some states, such as South Dakota, report a student to computer ratio of 2:1 (Bennett, 2002).

Just as the availability of computers in schools has increased, their use has also increased. A national survey of teachers indicates that in 1998, 50 percent of K–12 teachers had students use word processors, 36 percent had them use CD ROMS, and 29 percent had them use the World Wide Web (Becker, 1999). More recent national data indicates that 75 percent of elementary school-aged students and 85 percent of middle and high school-aged students use a computer in school (U.S. Department of Commerce, 2002). Today, the most common educational use of computers by students is for word processing (Becker, 1999; inTASC, 2003). Given that, it is logical to ask: Do computers have a positive effect on students' writing process and quality of writing they produce?

As is described more fully below, the study presented here employs meta-analytic techniques, commonly used in fields of medicine and economics, to integrate the findings of studies conducted between 1992–2002. This research synthesis allows educators, administrators, policymakers, and others to more fully capitalize on the most recent findings regarding the impact of word processing on students' writing.

Source: Goldberg, Amie, Michael Russell, and Abigail Cook, "The Effect of Computers on Student Writing: A Meta-analysis of Studies from 1992 to 2002." *The Journal of Technology, Learning, and Assessment* 2.1 (2003): 3. Print.

3 Cognitive, or executive, control refers to the ability to coordinate thought and action and direct it toward obtaining goals. It is needed to overcome local considerations, plan and orchestrate complex sequences of behavior, and prioritize goals and sub-goals. Simply stated, you do not need executive control to grab a beer, but you will need it to finish college.

Executive control contrasts with automatic forms of brain processing. Many of our behaviors are direct reactions to our immediate environment that do not tax executive control. If someone throws a baseball toward our face, we reflexively duck out of the way. We have not necessarily willed this behavior; it seems as if our body reacts and then our mind "catches up" and realizes what has happened. Evolution has wired many of these reflexive, automatic processes into our nervous systems. However, others can be acquired through practice because learning mechanisms gradually and thoroughly stamp in highly familiar behaviors.

For example, consider a daily walk to work. If the route is highly familiar and if traffic is light, our mind can wander. Before we know it, we may have gone a considerable distance and negotiated street crossings and turns with little awareness of having done so. In these cases, the control of our behavior occurs in a "bottom-up" fashion: it is determined largely by the nature of the sensory stimuli and their strong associations with certain behavioral responses. In neural terms, they are dependent on the correct sensory conditions triggering activity in well-established neural pathways.

Source: Miller, E. K., and J. D. Wallis. "Executive Function and Higher Order Cognition: Definition and Neural Substrates." *Encyclopedia of Neuroscience*. Vol. 4. 2009. Print.

Core Concept 10 — Good writing means more than good grammar.

When I was a brand-new professor of English, I submitted a grant proposal in which I misspelled the name of Christopher Columbus in the very first sentence. (I spelled it "Columbis.") I learned of the error only after one of the members of the review committee told me about it. It was extremely embarrassing, but it wasn't disastrous. My proposal was selected as a finalist for the grant competition. The reviewers obviously saw the error, but they nevertheless selected my proposal. Why? Despite such a blatant error, they considered the proposal good enough to make the first cut in the grant competition. The error didn't mean that the writing was poor.

I sometimes tell this story to illustrate the point that a correct paper isn't necessarily an effective one—or that an incorrect paper isn't necessarily *ineffective*. Following the rules and conventions of standard written English is important, but good writing is much more than good grammar. A perfectly correct essay can also be a perfectly lousy piece of writing if it does not fulfill the expectations of the task and meet the needs of the intended audience. An error-free history paper won't earn a good grade if it does not meet the instructor's guidelines for historical analysis or if it includes erroneous information and unsupported assertions. By the same token, a brilliant historical analysis that also includes numerous misspelled words, punctuation errors, inappropriate word choice, and convoluted sentences is not likely to earn an A+. Those errors will probably distract your instructor and might even suggest that you were unwilling to devote adequate time and attention to the assignment. For better or worse, "grammar," good or bad, makes an impression upon readers, even if it is only one element of effective writing.

As Chapter 12 explains, student writers tend to make the same errors, and for most students, errors of spelling, punctuation, and usage are not a very serious problem. Nevertheless, many students spend too much time worrying about correctness and far too little time attending to larger issues that make writing effective. As this chapter makes clear, effective writing encompasses many things, "good grammar" among them. It is essential that you apply the rules of usage and follow the conventions of written English, because those rules are part of what makes writing effective. However, if you learn the rules and conventions of standard written English but little else about writing, you will most likely not be a very good writer.

What This Means for You as a Writer

- **Learn and apply the appropriate rules for standard written English.** By the time they reach college, most students know most of what they need to know about the rules for correct writing. They may not always be able to explain those rules, but they have learned many of them intuitively. So recognize that you already know a great deal about the rules for correct writing, but also be aware of what you don't know. When you're unsure about a matter of usage or punctuation, consult your instructor, your campus writing center, an online writing resource, or a textbook such as this one.

- **Recognize that few rules apply in every instance.** Many of the rules for correct writing are clear and well established, but some aren't. There is often disagreement among grammarians and writing teachers about specific points of usage and style. As a writer, you have to be aware that such differences occur and that the rhetorical context determines what rules apply. Learn the accepted conventions for the kind of writing you are doing. Remember, too, that these conventions can change from one academic subject to another, so make it a point to become familiar with the conventions for writing in the different courses you take.

- **Always edit your writing for correctness.** Don't be obsessive about minor errors as you're working through early drafts of a piece of writing (see Core Concept #8), but make sure you edit before submitting your work. It usually doesn't take very long to review your finished drafts for minor errors, to reread them for clarity, and to make corrections to words or sentences, and it doesn't take much effort to run the spellchecker on your word processing program. Editing for minor problems and ensuring that you have followed the conventions of standard English should become a regular part of your writing process.

- **Focus on the errors you regularly make.** Identify the mistakes you regularly make, and review the appropriate rule for each one. For example, maybe you often forget to include a comma after an introductory clause (e.g., "When he woke up the next morning, his wallet and keys were missing."). If you're not sure about the rule, talk to your writing instructor or someone at your campus writing center, or review Chapter 12 of this textbook. Studies show that most students tend to make the same kinds of minor errors. If you focus attention on the errors you tend to make, you will learn to look for these errors when you edit your assignments. Eventually, most of those errors will disappear from your writing.

2

Practice This Lesson

Make a list of the five most common errors of spelling, punctuation, or usage that you tend to make. For each one, consult Chapter 12 to identify the appropriate rule. (You may have to review several past writing assignments to develop this list of common errors.) Use this list when you edit your future writing assignments.

The Ten Core Concepts in Action

WRITING GROWS OUT OF A NEED to answer a question, make a decision, or solve a problem. For college students, that need is usually created by course assignments—but not always. Sometimes it grows out of a situation that calls for writing of some kind:

- a problem on your campus that affects you
- a newspaper editorial that you want to respond to
- an event that raises questions for members of your community
- an important anniversary that evokes memories you want to share with others
- a controversial online video that you want to comment on
- a project that you believe might improve your workplace

In each of these examples, circumstances prompt you to create a document intended for a specific audience for a specific purpose. In other words, the need to write grows out of a rhetorical situation (see page 29 in Chapter 2). Sometimes, too, writing grows out of a writer's simple desire to understand something better.

Whatever your motivation for writing, this chapter takes you through the process of creating an effective text for your specific rhetorical situation:

- If your assignment specifies a topic and genre, follow the guidelines your instructor has provided and adjust each of the following steps to fit those guidelines.
- If your assignment doesn't specify a topic or genre and gives you free choice about what to write, develop a project that enables you to answer a question, make a decision, or solve a problem on an issue that interests you; develop your project so that it fits your specific rhetorical situation.

This chapter uses the Ten Core Concepts described in Chapter 2 to help you identify a worthy topic, explore that topic thoroughly, and write an effective document on that topic that is appropriate for your rhetorical situation.

Think of this chapter as a guide rather than a set of rigid instructions for completing a writing project. As you work through this chapter, you might find that you do not need to complete each step or that you need to repeat a step.

Konstantin L/Shutterstock.com; slobo/iStockphoto.com; Monkey Business Images/Shutterstock.com

Some steps may take a few moments to complete; others will take much longer. That's OK. Writing is a process of exploration that can lead to insights into complicated issues that matter for you and your readers, and the process will not be exactly the same for every writer or writing task. So use this chapter to learn about your topic and create a project that engages your readers.

Step 1   Discover and explore a topic.

Begin with a Question

Identify something you are wondering about, something that intrigues or puzzles you, something that calls for a decision or solution.

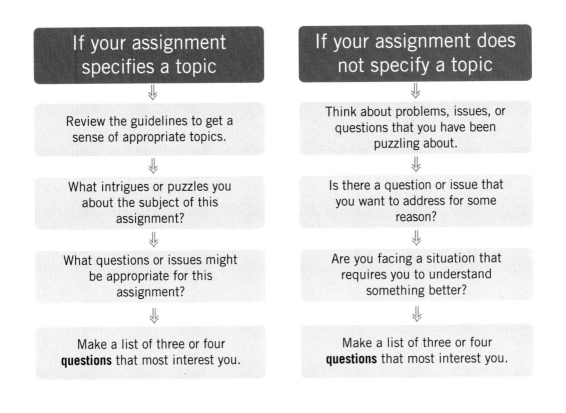

If your assignment specifies a topic	If your assignment does not specify a topic
⇓	⇓
Review the guidelines to get a sense of appropriate topics.	Think about problems, issues, or questions that you have been puzzling about.
⇓	⇓
What intrigues or puzzles you about the subject of this assignment?	Is there a question or issue that you want to address for some reason?
⇓	⇓
What questions or issues might be appropriate for this assignment?	Are you facing a situation that requires you to understand something better?
⇓	⇓
Make a list of three or four **questions** that most interest you.	Make a list of three or four **questions** that most interest you.

Explore Your Questions

Write a brief paragraph for each question, explaining why it might be worth exploring for this project. In each paragraph:

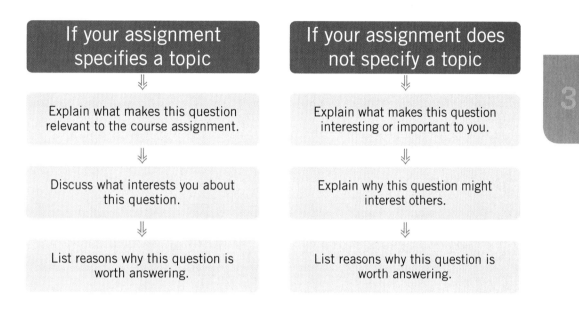

If your assignment specifies a topic	If your assignment does not specify a topic
Explain what makes this question relevant to the course assignment.	Explain what makes this question interesting or important to you.
Discuss what interests you about this question.	Explain why this question might interest others.
List reasons why this question is worth answering.	List reasons why this question is worth answering.

Select a Working Topic

Review your paragraphs and select one of the questions from your list as your working topic for your project. (This question might change as you learn more about your topic, but for now it is the question that will serve as your working topic.)

Identify What You Know About Your Topic

Jot down what you already know about your working topic.

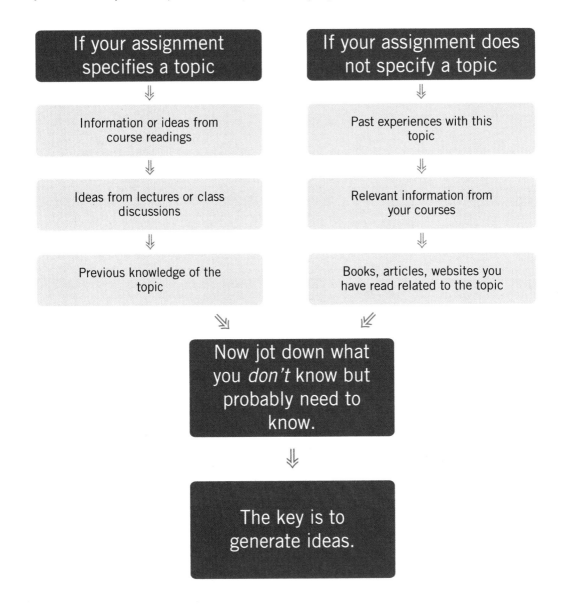

Adjust Your Question

Review your notes to determine whether you should amend your question and working topic.

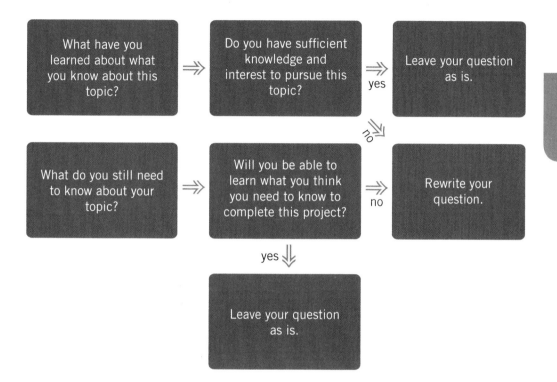

Use Technology to Generate Ideas and Gather Information

Explore your question with digital tools.

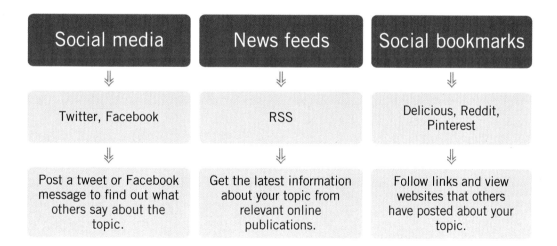

Hearing what others say or think about a topic can help you generate ideas and identify questions you will need to address. These tools provide a fast and easy way to tap into ideas, information, and conversations about your topic.

Write a Discovery Draft

A discovery draft is focused but informal and open-ended writing intended to help you explore your topic. It is not a first or rough draft, nor is it freewriting, in which you just write whatever comes to mind. It is a more purposeful draft to help you generate material you can develop into a complete draft. A discovery draft can be a continuous discussion of your topic, or it can be pieces and fragments, some of which are more developed than others.

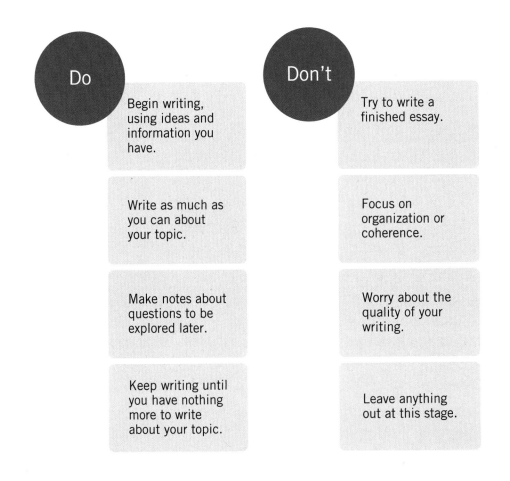

Do

- Begin writing, using ideas and information you have.
- Write as much as you can about your topic.
- Make notes about questions to be explored later.
- Keep writing until you have nothing more to write about your topic.

Don't

- Try to write a finished essay.
- Focus on organization or coherence.
- Worry about the quality of your writing.
- Leave anything out at this stage.

You will eventually use your discovery draft to develop a complete draft of your project, but for now you are exploring your topic and identifying possibilities.

Step 2   Examine the rhetorical context.

Identify Your Audience

Briefly describe the intended audience for your project.

Describe who you expect or hope will read your project.

If your assignment specifies an audience, describe that audience.	If you have no assignment, identify the audience you would most like to reach.

⇊

Be as specific as possible.

If your assignment does not specify an audience, assume that your instructor and/or your classmates are your audience.	If your intended audience is general (e.g., readers of a national newspaper like *USA Today* or people interested in politics), say so. If you are writing for a more specialized audience (e.g., students on your campus, people who snowboard, or video gamers), identify that audience as clearly as you can.

⇊

Explore your audience.

Jot down your sense of your instructor's expectations for this assignment. Refer to the assignment guidelines to understand additional audience expectations for the assignment.	Anticipate what your intended audience might know about your topic. Write down what you think they will expect from your project. Consider relevant special circumstances (e.g., video gamers will likely be familiar with online gaming sites).

Consider the Context

Examine how the specific circumstances under which you are writing might influence your project.

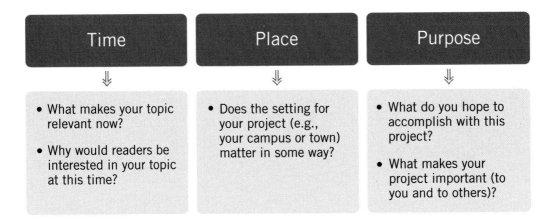

Time
- What makes your topic relevant now?
- Why would readers be interested in your topic at this time?

Place
- Does the setting for your project (e.g., your campus or town) matter in some way?

Purpose
- What do you hope to accomplish with this project?
- What makes your project important (to you and to others)?

Review Your Question

Adjust the question you developed for Step #1 in view of what you have learned about your audience and the context for your project.

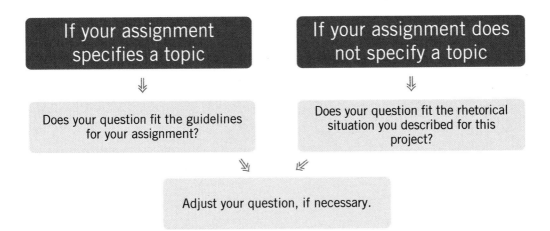

If your assignment specifies a topic

Does your question fit the guidelines for your assignment?

If your assignment does not specify a topic

Does your question fit the rhetorical situation you described for this project?

Adjust your question, if necessary.

Develop Your Discovery Draft

Review your discovery draft in light of what you have learned about your audience and your rhetorical situation.

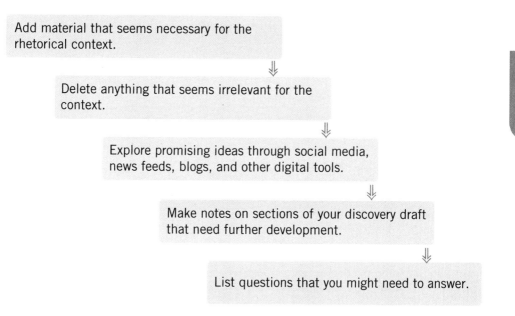

Add material that seems necessary for the rhetorical context.

Delete anything that seems irrelevant for the context.

Explore promising ideas through social media, news feeds, blogs, and other digital tools.

Make notes on sections of your discovery draft that need further development.

List questions that you might need to answer.

Remember that at this point you are still exploring your topic in a way that will make it effective for your audience.

Step 3 Select an appropriate medium.

Most college assignments call for conventional academic essays, which are usually submitted either electronically (as a Word or PDF file) or in hard copy. In such cases, the medium is traditional print text, and you should follow appropriate conventions for standard academic writing. (Assignments that call for conventional writing for non-academic forums, such as newspapers, magazines, or newsletters, might follow slightly different conventions but are still print texts.) However, writers today have access to many different media, including digital and online media.

Select a Medium

Identify a medium that would be appropriate for your rhetorical context.

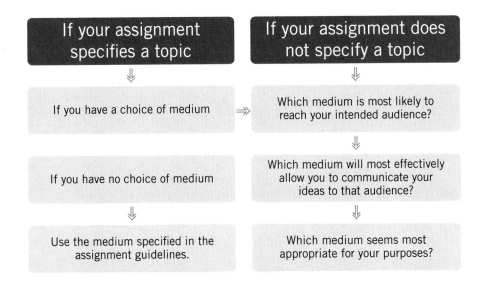

A traditional print text (an essay, report, proposal, research paper) might be the best way to achieve your rhetorical purpose, but consider other media through which you can present your ideas:

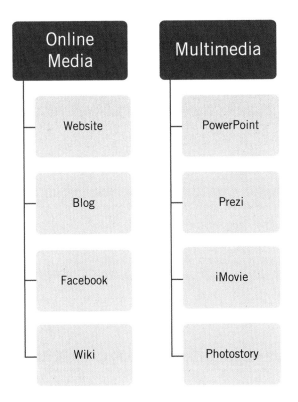

Consider How the Medium Might Shape Your Project

Your choice of medium can significantly affect the way you present your ideas to your audience.

Structure	• Does this medium require you to organize your project in a specific way? • What options for structuring your project does this medium provide?
Length	• Does this medium place any length restrictions on your project? (For example, an essay written to be read aloud on the radio may need to be shorter than a traditional print essay.) • If so, will these restrictions compromise the depth of your exploration of your topic?
Image and sound	• Does this medium enable you to incorporate sound and/or visual elements? • If so, what kinds of images and/or sound are appropriate? • How will you incorporate these elements?
Style	• What are the expectations for writing style in this medium? • Will you have to adopt any specific stylistic conventions for this medium? (For example, blogs usually call for shorter sections, or "chunks," of texts to help readers scroll more easily through the post.)

Return to your Discovery Draft to make notes about how your choice of medium might affect the development of your project.

Step 4 | Have something to say.

At this point, you have a topic, but you must determine what you will *say* about that topic. What will be the main point of your project?

Revisit Your Main Question

Reread your Discovery Draft, and then return to the question you developed for Step #1:

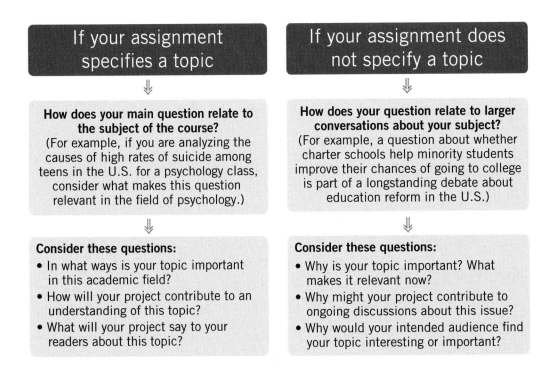

If your assignment specifies a topic

⇓

How does your main question relate to the subject of the course?
(For example, if you are analyzing the causes of high rates of suicide among teens in the U.S. for a psychology class, consider what makes this question relevant in the field of psychology.)

⇓

Consider these questions:
- In what ways is your topic important in this academic field?
- How will your project contribute to an understanding of this topic?
- What will your project say to your readers about this topic?

If your assignment does not specify a topic

⇓

How does your question relate to larger conversations about your subject?
(For example, a question about whether charter schools help minority students improve their chances of going to college is part of a longstanding debate about education reform in the U.S.)

⇓

Consider these questions:
- Why is your topic important? What makes it relevant now?
- Why might your project contribute to ongoing discussions about this issue?
- Why would your intended audience find your topic interesting or important?

Write a Guiding Thesis Statement

On the basis of your notes from Step 1, write a brief paragraph explaining your main point and the purpose of your project as you understand it at this point. Include your main question and a brief explanation of why it is important to your intended audience.

This paragraph is your Guiding Thesis Statement, a working summary of the main idea for your project. Your Guiding Thesis Statement may change as you develop your project, but you can use it to guide your work as you explore your topic.

Revise your Guiding Thesis Statement as often as necessary as you gain a clearer sense of the main point of your project.

Review Your Discovery Draft

Use your Guiding Thesis Statement to review your discovery draft:

Identify ideas, issues, or questions that seem important to your main point as described in your Guiding Thesis Statement:
- Which sections of your discovery draft seem especially important to your main point?
- Which sections need more development, given your main point?

⇓

Identify gaps in your Discovery Draft:
- Does anything seem to be missing that is relevant to your main point?
- What questions about your topic remain to be addressed?
- What more do you need to know about your topic to address the main point described in your Guiding Thesis Statement?

⇓

Consider the Rhetorical Situation:
- Is your main point relevant to your intended audience?
- Does your Discovery Draft present your main point in a way that addresses your intended audience?
- What might be missing from your draft that your audience will expect?

Revise Your Guiding Thesis Statement

On the basis of your review of your Discovery Draft, revise your Guiding Thesis Statement so that it clearly explains the nature and purpose of your project and accounts for audience expectations. You now have a working statement of the main point of your project.

Step 5 Back up what you say.

Most college writing assignments require students to support their claims, assertions, and positions. Even in narrative writing, writers provide support (often in the form of anecdotes or descriptions rather than factual evidence) for the ideas or events they describe. As you develop your project and learn about your topic, be sure to support your main points or claims.

Remember: At this point in the process, you are still exploring your topic, developing your ideas, and gathering information. "Backing up what you say" is as much a process of learning and exploring as it is a matter of identifying evidence or support, so be open to possibilities.

Begin by referring back to your Guiding Thesis Statement to remind yourself of your main question and the main purpose of your project.

Identify Your Main Claims or Assertions

On the basis of your Guiding Thesis Statement, identify and explore the major points you will make in support of your main point.

List your major claims or assertions.

List any claims or assertions that seem relevant at this stage.

Be as specific as possible, knowing you will adjust your list as you explore your topic.

Explore each claim or assertion.

Write a sentence explaining why each claim is relevant to your main point.

Write a sentence describing what you need to know to support each claim or assertion.

Prioritize your list of claims or assertions.

Which claims or assertions seem most important?

Which claims or assertions might be secondary to other claims or assertions?

Identify potential sources.

What kinds of information or evidence do you need to support your claims or assertions?

Where might you find the information or evidence you need? (See Chapter 7.)

Begin exploring each claim.

Develop your ideas for each major claim or assertion.

Find information or evidence to support each claim or assertion.

Review Your Discovery Draft

Return to your Discovery Draft and make sure it includes the major claims and assertions you have identified.

Write a Complete Draft

At this point, you should be ready to write a draft of your project. If so, write as complete a draft as you can based on what you have learned so far about your topic and using the information you have gathered for this exercise. Use your Discovery Draft as the basis for your complete draft, or simply refer to your Discovery Draft for ideas to be included in your complete draft.

If you are ready to write a draft

Keep in mind that this is a rough draft.

Make your draft as complete as possible, but don't worry about making it polished.

If you are not ready to write a draft

Write whatever portions of your draft that you feel ready to write.

Continue exploring your topic, and move on to Step 6.

Step 6   Establish a form and structure for your project.

The form of your project should present your ideas and information clearly and effectively to your intended audience. In deciding on an appropriate form for your project, consider the following aspects.

Genre	• Follow the conventions governing form for the genre (argument, analysis, narrative) in which you are writing. • Parts II, III, and IV of this textbook will guide you in developing a proper form for specific genres.

Medium	• The medium can shape the form and even the content of your project. • Multimedia and online projects will influence how you structure your project.

Rhetorical situation	• The form of a project will be shaped in part by your sense of your intended audience. • The form will also be influenced by your sense of the purpose of your project.

If you have already written your rough draft, use this exercise to determine whether your draft is organized effectively.

Identify the Main Parts of Your Project

Review your rough draft or use your Discovery Draft as well as your notes to make a list of the main sections or components of your project.

Develop an Outline

Use your list to create a basic outline for your project.

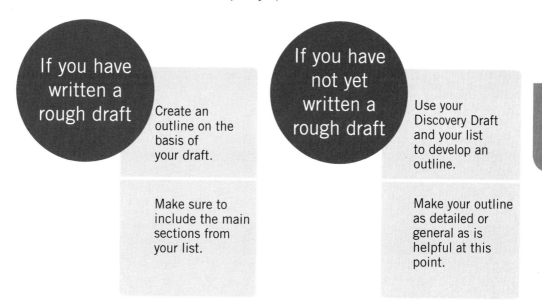

If you have written a rough draft

Create an outline on the basis of your draft.

Make sure to include the main sections from your list.

If you have not yet written a rough draft

Use your Discovery Draft and your list to develop an outline.

Make your outline as detailed or general as is helpful at this point.

Refine Your Outline

Review your outline to determine whether it effectively meets the needs of your rhetorical situation.

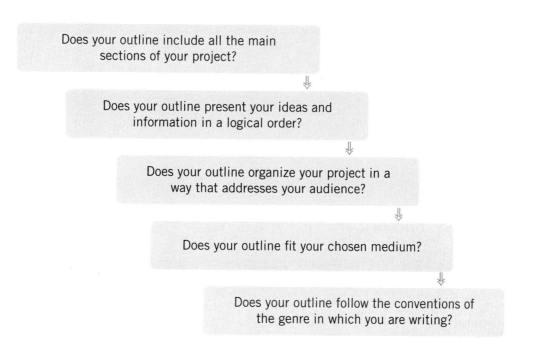

Does your outline include all the main sections of your project?

Does your outline present your ideas and information in a logical order?

Does your outline organize your project in a way that addresses your audience?

Does your outline fit your chosen medium?

Does your outline follow the conventions of the genre in which you are writing?

Write or Revise Your Draft

Using your outline as a guide, write a rough draft of your project or revise the rough draft you have already written to strengthen the structure of your project.

Step 7   Get feedback.

Even writers who work alone are writing in a social context, and their writing is ultimately influenced by others. So it makes sense at this point to involve others in the process to help you determine whether your draft is effective and to identify potential problems to address in your revisions. The goal is to get a sense of whether your project is achieving its purpose with readers and to help you decide which revisions to make.

It helps to have one or more trusted readers—a friend, roommate, co-worker, or classmate—who can respond to your draft. Your course instructor might specify a procedure for sharing your draft with classmates. If so, use that procedure. You can also supplement your instructor's procedure and obtain additional advice for revising your essay.

Use technology to help get the feedback you need.

> Post your draft on a blog or Facebook to invite responses.

⇓

> Use a wiki or GoogleDocs to enable trusted readers to offer reactions and suggestions.

⇓

> Join a web-based discussion forum that is relevant to your topic to seek comments.

Ask Your Readers to Respond to Your Draft

Use the following sets of questions to guide your readers' responses.

Topic	• Is the topic interesting and relevant? • Is the purpose of the project clear? Is it worthwhile? • Is the main point or idea clear? Does the writer have something to say? • Does the draft sufficiently explore the topic? Is anything missing? • Are the main claims or assertions adequately supported?
Medium and Form	• Does the medium work for this topic? Does it address the intended audience effectively? Does the writer take advantage of the capabilities of the medium? • Is the project organized effectively? • Does the introduction sufficiently introduce the topic and main ideas? Does it draw readers into the project? • Does the conclusion adequately sum up the project? Does it emphasize the writer's main ideas?
Style	• Is the writing generally clear and readable? • Are there passages that are confusing or difficult to follow? • Are there any problems with usage or grammar that impede meaning? • Does the writer's voice come through clearly and effectively?

In addition, ask your readers to jot down any other questions they have about your draft. **Remember** that the more specific your readers' comments, the more useful they are likely to be, so ask your readers to elaborate on their responses to specific sections of your draft.

Identify Common Themes in Your Readers' Responses

If you had more than one person read your draft, look for similarities in their responses.

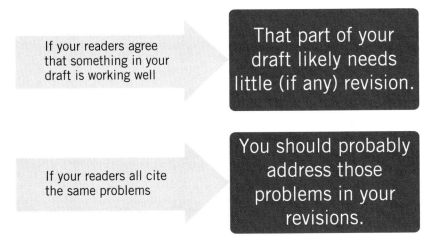

If your readers agree that something in your draft is working well → That part of your draft likely needs little (if any) revision.

If your readers all cite the same problems → You should probably address those problems in your revisions.

If you had only one reader respond to your draft, pay special attention to that reader's strongest reactions.

Review Disagreements Among Your Readers

Different readers might have different reactions to your project. Such disagreements might indicate sections of your draft that need revision. Consider disagreements among your readers as you decide upon specific revisions.

If your readers disagree about specific aspects of your draft	• Review the readers' comments to understand their disagreements. • Consider each reader's perspective about that part of your draft. • Review that part of your draft carefully, and consider each reader's suggestions for revising it.
If you agree with one reader and disagree with others	• Consider why you agree or disagree. • Review the relevant sections of your draft to see whether your readers' comments might have changed your mind. • If possible, ask readers to explain or clarify their reactions.

On the basis of your review of your readers' responses to your draft, make notes about possible revisions you should make.

Remember that *you* must decide which revisions are best, based on your assessment of the rhetorical situation and your own purposes for your project.

Step 8   Revise.

Revision is part of the process of discovery and learning. It is also a rhetorical process by which you craft your project so that it effectively addresses your intended audience and achieves your rhetorical purposes. As you revise, keep in mind that you will continue to learn about your topic even as you improve your draft.

As you proceed, refer to your notes for Step #7 as well as to your Guiding Thesis Statement to decide on specific revisions.

Focus First on Content

Review your draft to determine whether you have sufficiently developed your ideas and effectively made your main point.

Main idea	• Do you have something to say in this project? • Does your point come through clearly? • Is the relevance of your topic evident?
Focus	• Does your project stay focused on your main idea? • Do you get off track at any point? If so, should you rewrite or eliminate those sections?
Development	• Have you developed your ideas sufficiently? Do any sections of your outline need further development? • Have you presented enough information to support your claims or assertions? • Have you gone into too much detail in any sections? If so, should you condense or eliminate those sections?

Focus Next on Form

Reread your revised draft from beginning to end to determine whether you need to reorganize it or strengthen its form or structure (refer to your outline and your notes from Step #6).

Organization	• Have you presented your ideas in a sensible order? • Should any section be moved so your ideas are more logically presented to your readers? • Can any sections be combined to make your project tighter?
Transitions	• Do you make clear transitions between the main sections of your project? • Do your transitions help your readers follow your discussion? • Are any transitions confusing or missing?
Medium	• Have you followed the conventions for your medium? • If you are working in a digital medium, have you structured your project so readers/viewers can follow it easily? • For multimedia projects, have you placed visual or audio elements effectively?

Consider Your Rhetorical Situation

Review your revised draft to be sure you have addressed your intended audience effectively and fulfilled the needs of your rhetorical situation. Use the questions from Step #2 to guide your review of your draft. Revise your draft to address any issues related to your rhetorical situation.

Revisit Your Introduction and Conclusion

Return to your introduction and conclusion to make sure they effectively introduce and conclude your project in view of your rhetorical situation.

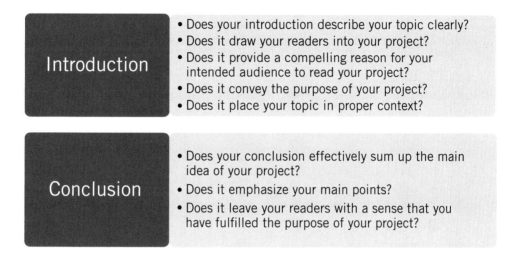

Introduction
- Does your introduction describe your topic clearly?
- Does it draw your readers into your project?
- Does it provide a compelling reason for your intended audience to read your project?
- Does it convey the purpose of your project?
- Does it place your topic in proper context?

Conclusion
- Does your conclusion effectively sum up the main idea of your project?
- Does it emphasize your main points?
- Does it leave your readers with a sense that you have fulfilled the purpose of your project?

At this point, you should have a revised draft that is close to finished. All the main pieces should be in place: a focused, sufficiently developed project that presents your main ideas effectively and clearly to your intended audience; a sound structure; an engaging introduction; and an effective conclusion.

Step 9 Strengthen your voice.

No matter the rhetorical situation, effective writing has a strong voice that reflects the writer's command of his or her subject matter. Your voice will give your readers confidence that your project is worth reading.

Consider Your Rhetorical Context

Review the rhetorical context for your project to gain a better sense of how your voice might meet the expectations of your readers and help you achieve your purpose. Review your draft to identify passages where you might adjust your voice to fit your rhetorical situation.

Are there any specific expectations or restrictions regarding voice, tone, and writing style in this rhetorical context? (For example, a business proposal should not be written in a conversational style.)

Do your voice, tone, and writing style fit the form or genre of your project? (For example, a lab report should have an objective voice and formal writing style.)

Does your draft speak with a voice that fits your rhetorical context? If not, what changes should you make so your voice and writing style fit the rhetorical context?

Consider Whether You Should Use the First Person

Determine whether the use of first person is appropriate for this project:

If first person is appropriate → Decide whether using the first person will make your project more effective. → If so, revise accordingly.

If first person is inappropriate → Review your draft to eliminate any uses of "I."

Strengthen Your Voice

Reread your draft to "listen to" your voice, and consider the following questions to guide your revisions.

> Does your voice sound authoritative and confident? Does it convey a sense that your project is valid and worthwhile?

> Is your voice consistent throughout your project? If not, where is it weakest? What changes might make it stronger in those sections?

At this stage, assume that your project is complete and appropriately structured and try to ignore those aspects of your project as you review your draft for voice and style.

Step 10 Make it correct.

Edit your draft for clarity and correctness.

Make your sentences clear.	• Revise sentences that are unclear. • Eliminate wordiness. • Restructure sentences that are difficult to follow. • Refer to Chapter 5 for advice on style.
Use sources correctly.	• Integrate source material smoothly into your prose (see Chapter 9). • Check quotations for accuracy. • Make sure sources are cited correctly (see Chapters 10 and 11). • Format your bibliography correctly (if appropriate).
Correct errors.	• Correct errors of usage and punctuation. • Refer to Chapter 12 for guidance in correcting errors.

A Student Writer Applies the Core Concepts

ELIZABETH PARISI was a first-year student at the State University of New York at Albany when she wrote the following essay for her introductory writing course. As a psychology major with a minor in philosophy and as someone who had taken advanced English courses in high school, Elizabeth well understood the importance of writing. When she received an assignment requiring an "analytical argument that will complicate and critique a common conception or construction of literacy, writing, or writers," she didn't have any trouble coming up with an idea for her paper.

Elizabeth Parisi

Step 1 Discover and explore a topic.

Begin with a Question

Elizabeth's essay began with her own experience as a student writer in a state where standardized tests seemed to influence how her high school teachers taught writing. As a high school student, she took honors and Advanced Placement (AP) English courses as well as several elective courses in English because of her interest in writing. But she noticed important differences in those courses. The advanced courses focused on more sophisticated writing skills, especially the ability to analyze a rhetorical situation and write an appropriate piece for a specific audience. By contrast, the elective courses seemed to focus on preparing students to write for the standardized tests required by New York State. She didn't enjoy those courses, but she had assumed that they prepared her for college. Now, as a first-year college student, she wasn't so sure. She wondered:

> *Did the emphasis on preparing students for standardized tests that I endured as a student actually prepare me for college writing?*

Wavebreakmedia/Shutterstock.com, Carla Donofrio/Shutterstock.com

She suspected not, but she was interested in learning more. Because these experiences were so recent and important to her and because this topic seemed to fit her assignment so well, Elizabeth felt confident that she could pursue it.

Explore the Question

Elizabeth's instructor, Janelle, asked her students to explore ideas for their essays in a series of short, informal writing exercises that she called "checkpoints." In one such checkpoint, Elizabeth wrote about her concerns regarding the emphasis her high school teachers had placed on correctness in writing. Here's part of what she wrote in that checkpoint:

> When teachers will read text solely to scrutinize proper punctuation and grammar, they will come across errors routinely expected. Students then assume that the teacher doesn't care about what they write because teachers only correct punctuation and grammar. When you think about language, "good writing" is not measured by how well you convey the essence of your message, but rather the number of punctuation errors you have.

Janelle encouraged Elizabeth to explore these ideas further.

Eventually, Janelle asked her students to write an informal proposal describing a potential topic for the assignment. Here's the proposal Elizabeth submitted:

> My topic for my analytical paper is how writing in academic disciplines is too focused on grammatical error and "teaching to the test." I want my readers to know that there is more to writing than punctuation. You have to have a voice in your writing for it to be effective. I would also like to address the fact that teaching according to a test doesn't allow students to learn anything other than how to take the test. I want to be able to show that the Regents Exams are not as successful as they were designed to be. Life does *not* give you tests or hand out specific instructions. You have to learn what works and doesn't work for you. I would like to use research to show the pros and cons of being taught according to a test like the Regents. I predict that research will show that giving kids more than grammatical corrections—like allowing them to have a voice—will make them much better writers.

Even in this brief proposal, Elizabeth was already beginning to delve into her questions about the impact of "teaching to the test." She identified several issues that she might investigate in her paper—including the importance of voice in writing and the pros and cons of preparing students for standardized tests—and she made a prediction about what she would find in researching her question.

Select a Working Topic

Through this process of exploration, Elizabeth quickly identified a working topic: *the impact of standardized tests on high school students' preparation for college-level writing.* This topic is rich with possibilities and presented Elizabeth with several subtopics to investigate, including how writing is taught in schools, the effects of education policies (such as mandated tests), the impact of those policies on students' readiness for college, and the nature of writing ability. Although these issues are related, Elizabeth couldn't cover all of them adequately in a single essay. Eventually she would have to focus on a main idea that she could develop sufficiently in her paper. At this stage of the process, though, she remained open to possibilities and allowed her curiosity about the topic to guide her exploration.

Identify What You Know About Your Topic

Most of what Elizabeth knew about her topic was based on her own experience as a student writer. For example, she knew that "teaching to the test" had become more common in the high school she attended, and she was aware that state and federal education policies (such as the Common Core State Standards) are part of the reason for this new emphasis on standardized tests. She also had taken several different kinds of English courses at her high school, including honors courses and regular-level courses; as a result, she knew that there were differences in how writing was taught in those courses. These experiences were an important starting point for her exploration of her topic. Elizabeth also read some articles about standardized testing and new education policies that place greater emphasis on standardized tests. As soon as she decided on this topic, she began looking for other source material.

Adjust Your Question

On the basis of her preliminary exploration, Elizabeth planned to address the following question:

> Does an emphasis on preparing students for standardized tests in high school prepare students adequately for college-level writing?

Use Technology to Generate Ideas and Gather Information

Because Elizabeth's experience as a student writer is common, she could use social media to share her developing ideas with her friends, many of whom might have opinions about the issues she was exploring. Also, the increasing emphasis on standardized testing had become controversial in New York, where Elizabeth attended school, as well as in other states; as a result, many social media sites had been established where students, parents, and educators share their views and, in some cases, discuss strategies for resisting the trend toward more testing. Elizabeth was able to gather information and ideas for her paper by following some of these discussions.

Write a Discovery Draft

Because of her keen interest in her topic and the information she had already gathered, Elizabeth was able to write a Discovery Draft that included some of the key ideas that would become important in her paper. She says, "Once I obtained a substantial amount of information, I began to write a very rough draft, starting with a pretty solid introduction and then using material from the articles I wished to use." Her Discovery Draft was only a partial draft, but it was a good starting point for a complete rough draft. Here's what it looked like:

DISCOVERY DRAFT

In New York State, students are required to take a series of Regents Exams in order to graduate from high school, a result of the No Child Left Behind policy enforced by former President George Bush and his administration. However, this approach which attempts to provide students the tools to graduate high school and ultimately be well prepared for their college career may actually be hindering whether students are properly equipped for college. Due to the strict regulations of New York Education Department, teachers must educate students on how to pass the Regents, rather than the essence of what the subject it truly about; it's as if teachers are training students to take a test correctly. The idea that this paper aims to convey is since students are subjected to this style of learning, they are unprepared for college level writing—they lack the skills to create a sophisticated piece or work. Furthermore, students who are enrolled in college level classes while in high school are more equipped to compose an essay more so than students in standard English courses because they touch on topics and abstract concepts that aren't addressed in a typical classroom.

Arthur Goldstein, a teacher from NYS shared his primary encounters with NYS rigid education system. He explains that if a student cannot pass the Regents, then they can't graduate; with this in mind, he has no other choice but to teach students how to take the test to ensure they pass it and receive a diploma. He realizes the faults to this method because students are not obtaining the skills which are needed for them to succeed in their college career. Students are not able to grasp the core concepts of language and are ultimately depriving them of proper instruction. Statistics provided by 2009 graduates in the article *How Many Passed the Regents Tests and Were Deemed College Ready,* strengthened Goldstein's observations even further. The results had determined less than one-third of New York City's class of 2009 graduates met the state's definition of "college ready" in English based on their Regents scores. This reveals that this current teaching method cannot be used on all students; everyone has different writing strengths and weakness, something which the Regents' Exams do not take into account.

Peter Parisi, a high school house principle, will be speaking to me about the opportunity differences of students enrolled in honors English courses as opposed to typical classes. Questions that will be asked are as follows:

1. What are your current views of standardized testing? Do you feel they fulfill the purpose that they are designed for?

2. What are the differences in curriculum of an AP English course compared to a typical English course?

3. Do you feel students who take AP English courses are well prepared for college?

4. Do you feel students who take regular English classes are well prepared for college?

5. What are the advantages/disadvantages of AP level courses?

6. What are the advantages/disadvantages of standard courses?

Notice that writing her Discovery Draft enabled Elizabeth not only to identify key ideas for her paper but also to determine what kinds of information she needed to find. She says, "As I worked on my draft, I acquired the idea of adding a supporting argument about how AP courses influence a student's future in college. To explore this idea further, I set up an interview with a high school principal named Peter Parisi to understand how he feels about New York's current education policies." Writing the Discovery Draft helped Elizabeth discover ideas she had and information she needed for her project.

Notice, too, that Elizabeth did not worry too much about grammar and style in this Discovery Draft. Her primary concern was to get ideas on paper so she could begin her research and develop a more formal draft. In her later drafts, she would focus on correcting errors and making her sentences clearer.

Step 2 Examine the rhetorical context.

Identify Your Audience

From the very start of this assignment, Elizabeth began to think about her audience. The assignment guidelines indicated that students should assume they would be writing for a broader audience of people interested in literacy and writing, which would include students in the class. Elizabeth also knew that many people who might not necessarily have an interest in writing and literacy would still be interested in her topic because standardized testing had become such a controversial issue affecting students in New York and many other states. From the beginning, she imagined that her audience was a broad group of people with some interest in or concern about education policy.

In addition, Elizabeth imagined that she would be writing to officials at the New York State Education Department who set the policies that led to the standardized tests she was required to take as a high school student. She says, "Originally, I thought of my audience mostly as teachers and other interested people, such as students and parents. But then I thought about the policy-makers at the state. I thought that they should read my argument about how tests were affecting the way kids learn to write."

Although Elizabeth's assignment called for an academic paper, she selected a topic that had wide appeal, and she imagined her audience as one that went beyond her class.

Consider the Context

Time: As already noted, Elizabeth's topic was timely because of recent policies that increased the emphasis on standardized testing in high schools. These policies sparked controversies that were heating up at the time Elizabeth was writing.

Place: New York State, where Elizabeth was a high school student, was in the midst of implementing new policies that affected every student in the state. But what was happening in New York was happening in many other states as well. Although Elizabeth was writing about specific policies in New York, she was also addressing issues that were relevant in other states.

Purpose: As she indicated in her proposal, Elizabeth was keenly interested in showing her readers that there is much more to writing than what students learn when preparing for standardized tests. As someone who had already made the transition from high school to college, she hoped to show how educational trends in her state would not necessarily help other students succeed in college.

Review Your Question

In thinking about the rhetorical context, Elizabeth saw no need to make significant adjustments to her question. She felt confident that her topic was relevant to her intended audience. In addition, her instructor indicated in her comments on Elizabeth's proposal that the topic was "appropriate for the rhetorical situation you're writing within."

Develop Your Discovery Draft

Elizabeth now had a clear sense of the rhetorical context. She returned to her Discovery Draft to develop some of her ideas. One of those ideas was to interview a high school principal, which she did. She says, "During this interview I began to realize that the Regents Exams were only part of the problem; there is also the need for family or community support that a child must have in order to be successful. With this new information, I felt ready to start my second draft." She would develop additional ideas for her project as she progressed through subsequent drafts, but for now her examination of her rhetorical situation enabled her to continue exploring her ideas and prepare to write a complete draft.

Step 3 Select an appropriate medium.

Select a Medium

Like most college assignments, Elizabeth's assignment called for a conventional academic essay to be submitted electronically (as a Word or PDF file) or in hard copy, so she did not have to select a medium for her project. However, she knew that she would have to follow the conventions for standard academic writing.

Consider How the Medium Might Shape Your Project

The structure and style of Elizabeth's paper would be shaped by the conventions of academic writing, as you'll see later. As a student who had taken advanced English classes in high school, she was generally familiar with these conventions and kept them in mind as she proceeded with her project.

Step 4 Have something to say.

As you can tell from Elizabeth's proposal, Elizabeth had a sense of her main point from the beginning. In her proposal, she wrote, "I would also like to address the fact that teaching according to a test doesn't allow students to learn anything other than how to take the test. I want to be able to show that the Regents Exams are not as successful as they were designed to be." That's a good start on a main point or claim.

Revisit Your Main Question

Here's Elizabeth's main question from Step #1:

Does an emphasis on preparing students for standardized tests in high school prepare students adequately for college-level writing?

Notice that the first paragraph of her Discovery Draft began to show how her main question fit into larger issues related to education:

In New York State, students are required to take a series of Regents Exams in order to graduate from high school, a result of the No Child Left Behind policy enforced by former President George Bush and his administration. However, this approach which attempts to provide students the tools to graduate high school and ultimately be well prepared for their college career may actually be hindering whether students are properly equipped for college. Due to the strict regulations of New York Education Department, teachers must educate students on how to pass the Regents, rather than the essence of what the subject it truly about; it's as if teachers are training students to take a test correctly. The idea that this paper aims to convey is since students are subjected to this style of learning, they are unprepared for college level writing—they lack the skills to create a sophisticated piece of work.

Here Elizabeth was beginning to identify what made her topic relevant and why it might matter to her intended audience at that point in time.

Write a Guiding Thesis Statement

Elizabeth could use the first paragraph of her Discovery Draft to develop a Guiding Thesis Statement:

Education policies have resulted in greater use of standardized tests in schools, which has forced teachers to teach to the test. However, although this approach is intended to provide students with the tools to graduate high school and succeed in college, it may actually leave them unprepared for college-level writing.

Review Your Discovery Draft

After reviewing her Discovery Draft, Elizabeth saw a need to expand her Guiding Thesis Statement to include ideas about the kinds of writing skills she believed students should develop as a result of their high school classes.

Revise Your Guiding Thesis Statement

Here's Elizabeth's revised Guiding Thesis Statement:

> Education policies have resulted in greater use of standardized tests in schools, which has forced teachers to teach to the test. However, although this approach is intended to provide students with the tools to graduate high school and succeed in college, it may actually leave them unprepared for college-level writing. Teaching to the test does not help students develop a strong voice in their writing or learn how to connect with their audience through their writing. High school courses that focus on these skills, such as Advanced Placement English, help students learn to write more sophisticated essays.

This was a statement of the main point she would make in her essay. However, as she conducted research and learned more about her topic, she might have to refine or adjust this statement.

Step 5   Back up what you say.

Almost as soon as she identified her topic for her assignment, Elizabeth began to think about gathering information to support her developing position on the issue of teaching to the test. She says, "I knew I had to do a lot of research because I needed a lot of supporting data to convince my audience." Notice that Elizabeth's research was shaped by her sense of her audience and her rhetorical purpose. As we have seen, Elizabeth had begun her research even before writing her Discovery Draft. She read a few relevant articles and, as a result of writing her Discovery Draft, decided to interview a high school principal to gain a better understanding of some issues relevant to her topic. Now she was ready to engage in a more concerted effort to find relevant information and to explore various perspectives on the issues related to standardized testing and the teaching of writing.

Identify Your Main Claims or Assertions

With her Guiding Thesis Statement, Elizabeth had a good sense of the major claims or assertions she would likely make in her essay, and she could begin looking for information to support those claims and to explore her topic further. Here are the main claims Elizabeth expected to make in her essay:

- State and federal education policies force high school teachers to teach to the test.
- Teaching to the test does not prepare high school students for college-level writing.
- Students who are subjected to a teach-to-the-test approach learn how to write only for standardized tests.
- To write well requires more than being able to use correct grammar; it also means having a voice and connecting with an audience.
- Some high school classes help students develop these skills.

Reviewing this list, Elizabeth realized that she could reorganize the list into two main claims and several supporting claims:

1. Teaching to the test does not prepare high school students for college-level writing.

    a) State and federal education policies force high school teachers to teach to the test.

    b) Students who are subjected to a teach-to-the-test approach learn how to write only for standardized tests.

2. Some high school classes help students develop appropriate skills for college.

    a) To write well requires more than being able to use correct grammar; it also means having a voice and connecting with an audience.

With this list of claims as a guide, Elizabeth used online research tools to find relevant sources. (See Chapter 7 for information about finding sources.) In addition to her interview with a high school principal, Elizabeth found a study of the effect of New York's Regents Exams on student writers; she also found several articles about the controversy surrounding standardized testing.

As she learned more about her topic through her research, she identified other important issues. For example, her interview with the principal helped her realize that some students are so far behind in developing writing skills by the time they enter high school that they would not benefit from courses like Advanced Placement. She also learned about other factors that can affect whether students develop appropriate writing skills. She says, "During this interview, I began to realize that the Regents Exams were only part of the problem; there is also the need for family or community support that a child must have in order to be successful."

Through this process, Elizabeth began to find supporting evidence for each of her claims, but even more importantly, she deepened her understanding of the topic. That understanding would help her develop a more valid argument and a more persuasive paper.

Review Your Discovery Draft

Elizabeth's Discovery Draft already included some of her key claims. As a result of her research, she now had new information to incorporate into that draft. "With all this new information to use in my argument," she says, "I felt ready to start a complete draft."

Write a Complete Draft

Here's the first full draft Elizabeth wrote:

FIRST DRAFT

In New York State, students are required to take a series of Regents Exams in order to graduate from high school, a result of the No Child Left Behind policy enforced by former President George Bush and his administration. However, this approach which attempts to provide students the tools to graduate high school and ultimately

(Continued)

be well prepared for their college career may actually be hindering whether students are properly equipped for college. Due to the strict regulations of New York Education Department, teachers must educate students on how to pass the Regents, instead of the essence of what the subject is truly about; it's as if teachers are training students to take a test correctly. The idea that this paper aims to convey is since students are subjected to this style of learning, they are unprepared for college level writing—they lack the skills to create a sophisticated piece of work. Furthermore, students who are enrolled in college level classes while in high school are able to compose an essay of better quality more frequently than students in normal English courses because they touch on topics and abstract concepts that aren't addressed in a typical classroom.

Arthur Goldstein, a teacher from NYS shared his encounters with the rigid education system. He explains that if a student cannot pass the Regents, then they can't graduate; with this in mind, he has no other choice but to teach students how to take the test to ensure they pass it and receive a diploma. "Regrettably, though the kids worked very hard, writing almost until their hands fell off, the only skill they acquired was passing the English Regents. Because the exam placed more emphasis on communication than structure, I did not stress structure. I knew that when my kids went to college, they would have to take writing tests—tests which would place them in remedial classes." Teachers realize the faults to this method because students are not obtaining the skills which are needed for them to succeed in their college career. Students are not able to grasp the key concepts of language and teachers are ultimately depriving them of proper instruction.

Research has also been conducted in a study called *Talking Back to the Regents*, conducted by Octavia Davis which supports the notion of standardized testing to be severely flawed. In this study, Davis uses her own college students to find out their experience with New York's English Regents examination, and what steps can be put forth to not only to enhance their writing skills, but change their attitude of writing as well. She proposed that her students discussed how they viewed the Regents through open-forum reflective writing in which they would analyze the piece afterward. Only two of the twenty-three students (9%) who participated in the study found that they had a positive outlook of the regent's exam and their writing. (Davis, 364) "I knew it was an easy task but difficult part was taking this seriously. I am telling you if they put anything serious for example current events to 'write to the senator.' I would have been going through with enthusiasm instead of merely looking for the stupid fact that could support my 'stance on vending machines'."(360). Her students emphasized that their responses on the exam resembled what they anticipated would be a passing essay rather than the answer expressing their authentic ideas about the posed question.

Davis's study also demonstrates that this approach to education does not allow the student to be creative or innovative. "Well I started reading and … I remember thinking that going for the band had two sides while going against the band had only one supportive argument…. So I went with the stance that had the most options," said a student in Davis's study (359). Sixty-seven percent of students began their essays with the position that had the most information. More than half of her students assumed that to be successful in terms of the regent's exam they needed to refrain from thinking analytically.(359) This evidence suggests that to obtain a good grade, students feel that they must create an essay which would appeal to the grader, not necessarily an idea which defends the writer's own point of view.

Another objection to the New York State Regents Exams was propose by former assemblymen Steven Sanders, who believed a student's ability should not be determined by a single test. According to the article *Flaws Could Spell Trouble for N.Y. Regents Exams,* "His belief that students entire pre-collegiate careers should not hinge on passing exams… The New York City Democrat suggests that scores on the Regents test should be but one factor among many that local school officials use to decide whether a student should graduate." He recognizes that there is a need for appropriate standards, but to give simply a test which defines their capability to succeed in college does not allow for students to flourish. Every student has different writing abilities, and the regent's generalizes teaching styles rather than adapting to what an individual need to succeed. This reveals that this current teaching method cannot be used on all students; everyone has different writing strengths and weakness, something which the Regents' Exams do not take into account.

I conducted an interview with Peter Parisi, a high school principle, who spoke about the opportunity differences of students enrolled in honors and A.P English courses opposed to typical English classes. Students enrolled in AP courses must obtain an understanding of the curriculum at a faster pace, as well as experience a different level of complexity of assignments. The content in honors and AP classes are more difficult than the Regents, and students must take make it their responsibility to fulfill the requirements of the task. Parisi made note that the more challenging the course curriculum is, the need to obtain the skills to be successful is greater. However, he stresses that prior experience is key to a student's success in writing. "We have juniors in high school reading and writing at a fifth grade level. They would not benefit from taking AP courses because they lack the experience to be learning college-level material. For a student to even consider enrolling in an honors class, they must have the proper level of preparation in the discipline in order to be successful." He views standardized testing as unreliable means of determining if a student is prepared for college level writing, and fails to provide students with the skills and knowledge essential for that discipline. However, students may not be prepared for college for reasons other than Regents Exams.

If students lack the experience to write in a typical English course let alone an AP course, are they destined to fall short of what is expected of them at college? Perhaps if educators examined how elementary students approached reading and writing, they could recognize the problem areas the students face early on rather than at the high school level. Furthermore, a 'home' component can be crucial to whether a child is

(Continued)

successful in the world of academia. A student's level of achievement relies on the support given to them by their family or community; otherwise the child does not see the importance in their education.

Works Cited

Davis, Octavia. "Talking Back to the Regents." *Talking Back to the Regents*. Project Muse, 2012. Web. 4 Mar. 2013.

Goldstein, Arthur. "Students Learn Differently. So Why Test Them All the Same?" *SchoolBook*. WNYC, 2 Feb. 2012. Web. 4 Mar. 2013.

Hoff, David J. "Flaws Could Spell Trouble For N.Y. Regents Exams." *Education Week* 23.10 (2003): 22–27. Education Full Text (H.W. Wilson). Web. 4 Mar. 2013.

Parisi, Peter. Personal interview. 7 Mar. 2013.

Step 6 Establish a form and structure for your project.

Elizabeth's assignment called for a conventional academic paper, but the guidelines for organizing the paper were vague. Like many college instructors, Elizabeth's instructor did not impose a specific structure but rather left it up to students to decide what kind of structure would work best for their individual projects. Elizabeth found this task challenging. She considered the following:

Genre: She was writing what her instructor called an "analytical argument," so she assumed that the best strategy was to organize her paper according to her main claims, incorporating her analysis into her discussion of each claim.

Medium: She would follow the conventions for writing an academic paper, which means that she would present supporting evidence for each claim and cite her sources using MLA style (which her instructor required).

Rhetorical Situation: Elizabeth's primary concern was persuading her audience that her argument about teaching to the test was valid, so she wanted to present her claims in a clear sequence that would make her argument more convincing.

You'll notice that Elizabeth's draft was already generally well organized. She identified her main points and then methodically moved from one main point to the next. Her task now was to decide whether the structure of that draft worked for her rhetorical situation.

Identify the Main Parts of Your Project

As we have seen, Elizabeth began her draft with a clear sense of her main claims. She was making two central claims and several supporting claims. Her list of claims (see Step #5) could serve as a guide to organizing her essay.

Develop an Outline

Normally, Elizabeth does not work from an outline. "It feels restricting when I'm writing a draft," she says. She usually spends a lot of time writing her introduction to make sure she has clearly established her focus and identified the main points she will make. That's what she did in this case. "I started with a pretty solid introduction," she says, which helped her decide how best to organize her draft. With her main claims clearly presented in her introduction, she completed her draft, moving from one main point to the next.

Refine Your Outline

Reviewing her draft, Elizabeth was satisfied with its structure, but she still had questions about whether it was organized effectively. Even after completing her revisions, she says, "I still wonder whether a different way of organizing the paper would make it more convincing for my readers." Notice that Elizabeth's main concern was making sure the structure of her paper fit the needs of her rhetorical situation. Nevertheless, she was unsure about whether she should reorganize her draft at this point.

Write or Revise Your Draft

Although Elizabeth had doubts about the structure of her draft, she did not reorganize it. Instead, she decided to wait to see what her peer reviewers and her instructor would have to say about the paper's structure.

Step 7   Get feedback.

Ask Your Readers to Respond to Your Draft

Elizabeth received feedback on her draft from several classmates as well as from her instructor. The feedback from her classmates was guided by the requirements for the assignment. Her instructor provided students with specific questions to address as they reviewed each other's drafts. But Elizabeth was also eager to see whether her argument was convincing to her peers.

Identify Common Themes in Your Readers' Responses

Elizabeth's classmates generally found her draft to be clear and persuasive. One student praised Elizabeth's use of her own experience to support her claims: "I could relate, because I also took the state tests." The same student also found Elizabeth's evidence to be strong: "Halfway through the analysis I found myself agreeing with your points and examples."

But her classmates also felt that Elizabeth didn't have enough analysis in certain sections of her draft. "My peer editors stressed that I needed to look back at my supporting evidence and elaborate on my views about why the Regents Exams were not a useful tool for students to further their education," she says. This concern would become the focus of her revisions.

Elizabeth's instructor made numerous comments that focused Elizabeth's attention on how to bring her draft into line with the conventions of academic writing, especially the conventions regarding how to support claims:

In New York State, students are required to take a series of Regents Exams in order to graduate from high school, a result of the No Child Left Behind policy enforced by former President George Bush and his administration. However, this approach which attempts to provide students the tools to graduate high school and ultimately be well prepared for their college career may actually be hindering whether students are properly equipped for college. Due to the strict regulations of New York Education Department, teachers must educate students on how to pass the Regents, instead of the essence of what the subject it truly about; it's as if teachers are training students to take a test correctly. The idea that this paper aims to convey is since students are subjected to this style of learning, they are unprepared for college level writing—they lack the skills to create a sophisticated piece or work. Furthermore, students who are enrolled in college level classes while in high school are able to compose an essay of better quality more frequently than students in normal English courses because they touch on topic's and abstract concepts that aren't addressed in a typical classroom.

> *Your central claim is clearly stated.*

Arthur Goldstein, a teacher from NYS shared his encounters with the rigid education system. He explains that if a student cannot pass the Regents, then they can't graduate; with this in mind, he has no other choice but to teach students how to take the test to ensure they pass it and receive a diploma. "Regrettably, though the kids worked very hard, writing almost until their hands fell off, the only skill they acquired was passing the English Regents. Because the exam placed more emphasis on communication than structure, I did not stress structure. I knew that when my kids went to college, they would have to take writing tests—tests which would place them in remedial classes." Teachers realize the faults to this method because students are not obtaining the skills which are needed for them to succeed in their college career. Students are not able to grasp the key concepts of language and teachers are ultimately depriving them of proper instruction.

> *Don't forget to cite your source. This supports your ethos and gives you credibility.*
>
> *What's the central point you want to make in this paragraph? A topic sentence can help your readers understand where you're taking them and how each paragraph relates to the larger argument.*

Research has also been conducted in a study called *Talking Back to the Regents*, conducted by Octavia Davis which supports the notion of standardized testing to be severely flawed. In this study, Davis uses her own college students to find out their experience with New York's English Regents

> *This study supports your argument, but you introduce it in a somewhat awkward way that is hard to follow. It might slow down a reader.*

examination, and what steps can be put forth to not only to enhance their writing skills, but change their attitude of writing as well. She proposed that her students discussed how they viewed the Regents through open-forum reflective writing in which they would analyze the piece afterward. Only two of the twenty-three students (9%) who participated in the study found that they had a positive outlook of the regent's exam and their writing (Davis, 364). "I knew it was an easy task but difficult part was taking this seriously. I am telling you if they put anything serious for example current events to 'write to the senator.' I would have been going through with enthusiasm instead of merely looking for the stupid fact that could support my 'stance on vending machines'."(360). Her students emphasized that their responses on the exam resembled what they anticipated would be a passing essay rather than the answer expressing their authentic ideas about the posed question.

> You need to introduce this quote to clarify who is saying it. A reader might think that the quote is from Davis rather than from one of the students in her study.

> OK, but what does Davis's study mean? You have presented some relevant findings but you need to interpret them and show how they support your point here.

Davis's study also demonstrates that this approach to education does not allow the student to be creative or innovative. "Well I started reading and... I remember thinking that going for the band had two sides while going against the band had only one supportive argument.... So I went with the stance that had the most options," said a student in Davis's study (359). Sixty-seven percent of students began their essays with the position that had the most information. More than half of her students assumed that to be successful in terms of the Regent's exam they needed to refrain from thinking analytically.(359) This evidence suggests that to obtain a good grade, students feel that they must create an essay which would appeal to the grader, not necessarily an idea which defends the writer's own point of view.

> Nice analytical claim. Your logic is clear in this section. Each sentence follows from the one before it. Use this as a model as you work to improve the coherence of your other paragraphs.

Another objection to the New York State Regents Exams was propose by former assemblymen Steven Sanders, who believed a student's ability should not be determined by a single test. According to the article *Flaws Could Spell Trouble for N.Y. Regents Exams,* "His belief that students entire pre-collegiate careers should not hinge on passing Exams... The New York City Democrat suggests that scores on the Regents test should be but one factor among many that local school officials use to decide whether a student should graduate." He recognizes that there is a need for appropriate standards, but to give simply a test which defines their capability to succeed in college does not allow for students to flourish. Every student has different

> Again, don't forget to cite your sources properly.

writing abilities, and the regent's generalizes teaching styles rather than adapting to what an individual need to succeed. This reveals that this current teaching method cannot be used on all students; everyone has different writing strengths and weakness, something which the Regents' Exams do not take into account.

I conducted an interview with Peter Parisi, a high school principle, who spoke about the opportunity differences of students enrolled in honors and A.P English courses opposed to typical English classes. Students enrolled in AP courses must obtain an understanding of the curriculum at a faster pace, as well as experience a different level of complexity of assignments. The content in honors and AP classes are more difficult than the Regents, and students must take make it their responsibility to fulfill the requirements of the task. Parisi made note that the more challenging the course curriculum is, the need to obtain the skills to be successful is greater. However, he stresses that prior experience is key to a student's success in writing. "We have juniors in high school reading and writing at a fifth grade level. They would not benefit from taking AP courses because they lack the experience to be learning college-level material. For a student to even consider enrolling in an honors class, they must have the proper level of preparation in the discipline in order to be successful." He views standardized testing as unreliable means of determining if a student is prepared for college level writing, and fails to provide students with the skills and knowledge essential for that discipline. However, students may not be prepared for college for reasons other than Regents Exams.

If student's lack the experience to write in a typical English course let alone an AP course, are they destined to fall short of what is expected of them at college? Perhaps if educators examined how elementary students approached reading and writing, they could recognize the problem areas the students face early on rather than at the high school level. Furthermore, a 'home' component can be crucial to whether a child is successful in the world of academia. A student's level of achievement relies on the support given to them by their family or community; otherwise the child does not see the importance in their education.

As a reader, I expected a transition here to help me see the connection between this paragraph and the previous one.

It seems to me that you're advocating for a certain kind of difficulty in writing classes. You don't want a more difficult Regents Exam that's utilizing the same modes; you want an entirely different approach. This might be something to make clearer as you refine your argument.

This point is underdeveloped. I wonder if it can be cut.

You seem to end your essay rather abruptly. Have you considered a more forceful way to sum up your argument and reinforce your main point?

As you'll see, Elizabeth would take many of her instructor's comments into account in revising her draft.

Review Disagreements Among Your Readers

There were no significant disagreements among the students who reviewed Elizabeth's draft, but, she says, the "peer reviews were almost like a wake-up call." They helped her see that she was not allowing her own voice to emerge in her draft. This realization led her to decide to incorporate more of her own experience into her essay—specifically, her experience taking both regular and advanced English classes in high school.

Step 8 Revise.

As she progressed with her project, Elizabeth continued to learn more about her topic and refine her argument. Using her classmates' and instructor's comments as a guide, she worked through several revisions, each time addressing more specific issues to strengthen her essay.

Focus First on Content

Elizabeth focused her revisions initially on two main areas: developing her analysis and incorporating her own experiences to support her claims. She says, "I sought to make a connection between my analysis and my own experiences as a high school student. It was when I wrote about my own familiarity with the Regents-level courses and honors courses that I felt I expressed my views about standardized testing most coherently." To address these issues, Elizabeth added material to support her second main claim about the value of advanced English courses in preparing students for college writing. Here are some of the important changes she made to her draft:

- **She added material to the second paragraph:**

    Draft: Arthur Goldstein, a teacher from NYS shared his encounters with the rigid education system. He explains that if a student cannot pass the Regents, then they can't graduate; with this in mind, he has no other choice but to teach students how to take the test to ensure they pass it and receive a diploma. "Regrettably, though the kids worked very hard, writing almost until their hands fell off, the only skill they acquired was passing the English Regents. Because the exam placed more emphasis on communication than structure, I did not stress structure. I knew that when my kids went to college, they would have to take writing tests—tests which would place them in remedial classes." Teachers realize the faults to this method because students are not obtaining the skills which are needed for them to succeed in their college career. Students are not able to grasp the key concepts of language and teachers are ultimately depriving them of proper instruction.

    Without a good transition from the introductory paragraph, this source material is not introduced in a way that will help a reader understand its relevance.

    The discussion that follows the quote highlights the faults of a test-prep "method" but does not explain why these faults matter.

    Revised version: As a college freshman who endured the Regents Exams in high school, I have begun to realize the different expectations of high school teachers and college professors. College professors tend to focus on the content of an essay and how well the writer conveys his or her message, whereas high school teachers emphasize grammar and correctness so that their students are prepared for the state tests. Many teachers recognize that the skills they teach students are not the ones they should prioritize. Arthur Goldstein, a New York teacher, explains that students who cannot pass the Regents Exams in English can't graduate, so he has no choice but to teach students how to take the test. "Regrettably," he says, "though the kids worked very hard, writing almost until their hands fell off, the only skill they acquired was passing the English Regents... I knew that when my kids went to college, they would have to take writing tests—tests which would almost inevitably label them as ESL students and place them in remedial classes"(Goldstein). Because of this emphasis on test preparation, many students are not able to grasp key concepts of language and develop writing skills needed for college. These skills include the ability to connect to an audience and allow your writerly voice to shine through while conveying your message clearly and effectively. Without these skills, students will have difficulty not only in college English courses but also in other fields of study that require writing.

The three sentences added to the beginning of this paragraph provide a better transition from the introduction and also introduce the source material cited in this passage. Notice, too, that Elizabeth refers to her own experience to begin establishing her credibility as someone who understands these issues.

Elizabeth expanded her discussion of the quoted source material to show readers its importance and connect it to her main point. Notice that she added a new final sentence that points explicitly to the problem she wants to highlight.

■ **She developed an important point in the fourth paragraph:**

Draft: Davis's study also demonstrates that this approach to education does not allow the student to be creative or innovative. "Well I started reading and... I remember thinking that going for the band had two sides while going against the band had only one supportive argument.... So I went with the stance that had the most options," said a student in Davis's study (359). Sixty-seven percent of students began their essays with the position that had the most information. More than half of her students assumed that to be successful in terms of the regent's exam they needed to refrain from thinking analytically.(359) This evidence suggests that to obtain a good grade, students feel that they must create an essay which would appeal to the grader, not necessarily an idea which defends the writer's own point of view.

This paragraph presents evidence for Elizabeth's main point that preparing students for standardized tests does not prepare them for college writing. However, she doesn't show explicitly how this study supports that claim. The final sentence begins to do so, but it doesn't go far enough.

Revised version: Davis's study also demonstrates that a test-prep approach does not allow students to be creative or innovative because they must avoid expressing themselves in their writing if they expect to do well on the exams. Another student who participated in Davis's study explains why he selected one side of an issue for an argumentative essay about a proposed state ban on vending machines in schools: "Well I started reading and... I remember

Adding the *because* clause helps explain the problem more clearly and reinforces the point.

thinking that going for the band [sic] had two sides while going against the band [sic] had only one supportive argument…. So I went with the stance that had the most options" (359). Like this student, 67% of the students in the study began their persuasive essays on the exam with the position that had the most information rather than the position they actually supported. More than half of the students assumed that to be successful on the exam they had to refrain from thinking analytically and simply give the test-scorers what they want (359). This evidence suggests that to obtain a good grade, students feel that they must create an essay which would appeal to the test-scorers and not necessarily write an essay in which they defend their own point of view. A good piece of writing encourages readers to open their mind and may even provoke an audience to view an issue differently. This is not what students learn when they learn to write for standardized tests.

These two new sentences explain why learning to write specifically for standardized tests is not a good way to prepare high school students for college writing.

■ **She added material from her own experience to elaborate on a key point:**

Draft: Moreover, there is a significant difference in students' college performance, depending on if they enrolled in English honors and AP English as opposed to a regent's level course. As a former New York State high school student, I was required to take the Regents Exams in order to graduate high school and register in college. However, if did not enroll in honors classes, I cannot be certain that I would be successful in my current college career. Taking honors English allowed me to learn the curriculum at a college-level pace, with topics including rhetoric and analysis. We were taught to focus more on the context of our writing instead of focusing on grammatical errors. I had also participated in a regent's English course as an elective and found myself 'going through the motions' of writing—not feeling connected to the piece I had created. The guidelines set by the Regents were too structured and did not allow for my voice to be heard in the piece I composed. In my honors English course however, we were taught to develop ideas not according to a critical lens format, but by analyzing a piece of literature and expanding on the topic using our personal views.

This paragraph includes important material from Elizabeth's own experience that exposes the flaws in the test-prep approach. But her discussion of her experience doesn't show clearly that there are alternatives to this approach that work.

Revised version: The flaws in writing instruction that is driven by standardized testing are further illuminated by the differences in college performance between students who take high school English honors or Advanced Placement (AP) courses and students who take standard English courses in high school (which are called "Regents-level" courses in New York state). As a high school student, I was required to take the Regents

This revised sentence serves as a better transition from the previous paragraph and also as a topic sentence that establishes the focus of this paragraph.

Exams to graduate; however, if I had not taken advanced classes, I cannot be certain that I would have been prepared for college. Honors English classes enabled me to learn college-level skills. I learned to focus on the rhetorical context of writing rather than exclusively on avoiding grammatical errors. I also took a Regents-level English course as an elective, in which I found myself just going through the motions with no real investment in my writing. In order to get a high score on the so-called "Critical Lens" essay, which is a standard part of the English Regents Exam consisting of five paragraphs, each covering various aspects of the topic, the student has to follow a series of steps in each paragraph in order to compose a "good" essay. The most outrageous requirement concerns the development of the essay, which is graded according to "the extent to which ideas are elaborated using specific and relevant evidence from the text." These guidelines don't allow for the writer's own voice to be heard, forcing the student to focus instead on the texts that are supplied for the exam. In my honors English course, however, we were taught to develop ideas not according to a standard format but by analyzing a piece of literature and exploring the topic from our own informed perspective.

Here Elizabeth explains more clearly the differences between advanced and regular English classes and why those differences are important.

This new material provides a concrete example of the test-prep approach and further reinforces the problems Elizabeth sees with that approach.

Elizabeth made a number of other revisions (which you can see in her finished version on page 110) to elaborate on important points, reinforce her claims, clarify her arguments, condense unnecessarily lengthy passages, and eliminate unnecessary or confusing passages.

Focus Next on Form

Although Elizabeth was still a little uncertain about the structure of her essay, as she reread her draft and her reviewers' comments, she gained confidence that she presented her claims and evidence in a clear and straightforward way. So she saw no need for reorganizing her draft. However, her instructor had noted several missing or weak transitions, which she addressed in her revisions.

Consider Your Rhetorical Situation

Throughout the revision process, Elizabeth considered changes that would make her argument more persuasive for her intended audience. She says, "I was very mindful of the rhetorical situation. I tried to make the issues understandable for a general audience but I wanted my analysis to be sophisticated and I didn't try to dumb down the issues or the argument. I also reviewed my claims to see if I had adequate and appropriate support for my arguments, keeping in mind the expectations of my audience." In her finished essay, you can see numerous adjustments she made to clarify or strengthen a point, always with her readers in mind.

Here's one example of revisions Elizabeth made to address her specific rhetorical situation. In the third paragraph of her draft, she cited an important study to support her main claim about the problem with test-prep writing instruction. However, this paragraph is not clearly written and doesn't explain the study in a way that helps a reader understand its importance to her claim:

> **Draft:** Research has also been conducted in a study called *Talking Back to the Regents*, conducted by Octavia Davis which supports the notion of standardized testing to be severely flawed. In this study, Davis uses her own college students to find out their experience with New York's English Regents examination, and what steps can be put forth to not only to enhance their writing skills, but change their attitude of writing as well. She proposed that her students discussed how they viewed the Regents through open-forum reflective writing in which they would analyze the piece afterward. Only two of the twenty-three students (9%) who participated in the study found that they had a positive outlook of the regent's exam and their writing (Davis, 364). "I knew it was an easy task but difficult part was taking this seriously. I am telling you if they put anything serious for example current events to 'write to the senator.' I would have been going through with enthusiasm instead of merely looking for the stupid fact that could support my 'stance on vending machines'."(360). Her students emphasized that their responses on the exam resembled what they anticipated would be a passing essay rather than the answer expressing their authentic ideas about the posed question.

In her revised version, Elizabeth explained the study more clearly but did not "dumb it down" for her readers. She used quotations more effectively, and she corrected her citations. This version makes more effective use of the study to support her main claim, which helps make her argument more persuasive to her readers:

> **Revised version:** The faults of a test-prep approach to writing instruction have been documented by researchers. In one study, Octavia Davis asked her own college students to write uncensored, unedited reflections on their experiences with New York's English Regents Examination. Only 9% of the students in the study had a positive outlook on the Regents Exam and on their own writing (Davis 364). One student in her study wrote, "I knew it was an easy task but difficult part was taking this seriously. I am telling you if they put anything serious for example current events to 'write to the senator.' I would have been going through with enthusiasm instead of merely looking for the stupid fact that could support my 'stance on vending machines'" (360). (This quotation is reproduced verbatim from the original study.) It is evident that Davis's students wrote exam responses that they believed would result in a passing essay rather than answering the exam questions with their own ideas about the topic. Davis found that "the exam confined most of my students to scripted situations that compelled them to silence their critical voices" (354). This kind of experience, she writes, teaches students "lessons that are contrary to what we may want to teach in first-year [college] writing" (353).

Revisit Your Introduction and Conclusion

Elizabeth was generally satisfied with her introduction, but she made numerous minor revisions to make her sentences more readable, to state her main ideas more clearly, and to place her argument in the context of ongoing developments in education policy.

Draft: In New York State, students are required to take a series of Regents Exams in order to graduate from high school, a result of the No Child Left Behind policy enforced by former President George Bush and his administration. However, this approach which attempts to provide students the tools to graduate high school and ultimately be well prepared for their college career may actually be hindering whether students are properly equipped for college. Due to the strict regulations of New York Education Department, teachers must educate students on how to pass the Regents, instead of the essence of what the subject it truly about; it's as if teachers are training students to take a test correctly. The idea that this paper aims to convey is since students are subjected to this style of learning, they are unprepared for college level writing—they lack the skills to create a sophisticated piece or work. Furthermore, students who are enrolled in college level classes while in high school are able to compose an essay of better quality more frequently than students in normal English courses because they touch on topics and abstract concepts that aren't addressed in a typical classroom.

> Some readers might be unfamiliar with the Regents Exams, which Elizabeth doesn't explain.
>
> This reference is somewhat vague.
>
> Also vague
>
> Elizabeth's statement of her main points isn't as clear as it could be, and she doesn't reinforce the idea that what's happening in her state is part of a nationwide trend.

Revised version: Like many states, New York requires students to take a series of standardized tests, called Regents Exams, in order to graduate from high school, a result of the No Child Left Behind policy developed by former President George W. Bush and passed by Congress in 2002. This test-based approach to education reform, which continues in President Barack Obama's Race to the Top program, attempts to provide students with the tools to graduate high school and to prepare them for college. However, this approach may actually prevent students from being properly equipped for college. Because of the emphasis now placed on standardized tests, teachers in New York State must focus on teaching students how to pass the Regents Exams rather than helping students truly learn the subject. In this paper, I argue that teaching to the test leaves students unprepared for college-level writing. The current push for "college and career readiness," which is part of the national Common Core State Standards movement, may in fact be pushing students away from college and career success.

> This places New York within a national context.
>
> Elizabeth more clearly explains the Regents Exams and the connection between New York State policy and national education policy.
>
> Elizabeth states her main argument more clearly and succinctly.
>
> This new final sentence reinforces her main argument and explicitly connects it to the larger national context.

These careful revisions made Elizabeth's introduction more effective in establishing the focus of her paper and drawing interested readers into her argument.

Elizabeth's conclusion was a different matter. Her instructor commented that her draft ended too abruptly, and Elizabeth knew the conclusion needed work. "I always have trouble with conclusions," she says. As you can see in her finished essay, she added a concluding paragraph that she believed would reinforce her main ideas.

Elizabeth did not make all these revisions at once. Rather, she worked through several drafts, beginning with the larger issues and eventually focusing on more minor issues until she was satisfied that her essay was adequately developed and her argument well supported.

Step 9 Strengthen your voice.

Elizabeth found that the revisions she made to strengthen her argument also strengthened her voice. As she developed her analysis, she says, "I finally used my own voice and emphasized my opinions." Her confidence in her analysis translated into a more confident voice.

Consider Your Rhetorical Context

As she reviewed her draft, Elizabeth felt that the more confident voice that emerged in her revisions helped make her essay better fit her rhetorical situation. She says, "If you have an argument and you don't show yourself within that argument, it's just words. If you use your own voice and reveal your passion, it's more compelling for your readers." Her goal was to convince her readers not only that her argument was sound but also that her own experience and her passion about the topic gave her credibility as a writer. She accomplished that goal in part by adding material based on her own experience and allowing her own views about that experience to come through more clearly.

Consider Whether You Should Use the First Person

You'll notice that Elizabeth avoided using the first person in her Discovery Draft, but as she moved through subsequent drafts, she incorporated the first person where it felt appropriate, especially when describing her own experiences. She believes that her use of the first person gave her essay a more passionate voice and thus made it more effective in conveying her argument to her readers.

Strengthen Your Voice

The most important revision that Elizabeth made to strengthen her voice was adding material about her own experiences and using the first person strategically. She says, "My early drafts were too factual and straightforward and didn't reflect my passion about this problem." That changed, she believes, as a result of her revisions, which she made with her voice in mind.

Step 10 Make it correct.

Elizabeth's early drafts had numerous minor errors of punctuation, spelling, and usage. She also failed to cite her sources properly. Elizabeth addressed these problems in her final set of revisions. Here are some examples:

■ **She introduced quotations more smoothly and succinctly:**

> **Draft:** Research has also been conducted in a study called *Talking Back to the Regents,* conducted by Octavia Davis which supports the notion of standardized testing to be

severely flawed. In this study, Davis uses her own college students to find out their experience with New York's English Regents examination, and what steps can be put forth to not only to enhance their writing skills, but change their attitude of writing as well.

Revised version: The faults of a test-prep approach to writing instruction have been documented by researchers. In one study, Octavia Davis asked her own college students to write uncensored, unedited reflections on their experiences with New York's English Regents Examination.

■ **She corrected punctuation errors.** In this example, she inserts a necessary comma before the word *however* and removes an unnecessary comma after *format*:

Draft: In my honors English course however, we were taught to develop ideas not according to a critical lens format, but by analyzing a piece of literature and expanding on the topic using our personal views.

Revised version: In my honors English course, however, we were taught to develop ideas not according to a standard format but by analyzing a piece of literature and exploring the topic from our own informed perspective.

■ **She used correct MLA citation format:**

Draft: Only two of the twenty-three students (9%) who participated in the study found that they had a positive outlook of the regent's exam and their writing. (Davis, 364)

Revised version: Only 9% of the students in the study had a positive outlook on the Regents Exam and on their own writing (Davis 364).

Here's Elizabeth's finished essay:

FINAL DRAFT

Are We Trying Too Hard or Not Hard Enough?

Like many states, New York requires students to take a series of standardized tests, called Regents Exams, in order to graduate from high school, a result of the No Child Left Behind policy developed by former President George W. Bush and passed by Congress in 2002. This test-based approach to education reform, which continues in President Barack Obama's Race to the Top program, attempts to provide students with the tools to graduate high school and to prepare them for college. However, this approach may actually prevent students from being properly equipped for college. Because of the emphasis now placed on standardized tests, teachers in New York State must focus on teaching students how to pass the Regents Exams rather than helping students truly learn the subject. In this paper, I argue that teaching to the test leaves students unprepared for college-level writing. The current push for "college and career readiness," which is part of the Common Core State Standards movement, may in fact be pushing students away from college and career success.

As a college freshman who endured the Regents Exams in high school, I have begun to realize the different expectations of high school teachers and college professors. College professors tend to focus on the content of an essay and how well the writer conveys his or her message, whereas high school teachers emphasize grammar and correctness so that their students are prepared for the state tests. Many teachers recognize that the skills they teach students are not the ones they should prioritize. Arthur Goldstein, a New York teacher, explains that students who cannot pass the Regents Exams in English can't graduate, so he has no choice but to teach students how to take the test. "Regrettably," he says, "though the kids worked very hard, writing almost until their hands fell off, the only skill they acquired was passing the English Regents... I knew that when my kids went to college, they would have to take writing tests—tests which would almost inevitably label them as ESL students and place them in remedial classes"(Goldstein). Because of this emphasis on test preparation, many students are not able to grasp key concepts of language and develop writing skills needed for college. These skills include the ability to connect to an audience and allow your writerly voice to shine through while conveying your message clearly and effectively. Without these skills, students will have difficulty not only in college English courses but also in other fields of study that require writing.

The faults of a test-prep approach to writing instruction have been documented by researchers. In one study, Octavia Davis asked her own college students to write uncensored, unedited reflections on their experiences with New York's English Regents Examination. Only 9% of the students in the study had a positive outlook on the Regents Exam and on their own writing (Davis 364). One student in her study wrote, "I knew it was an easy task but difficult part was taking this seriously. I am telling you if they put anything serious for example current events to 'write to the senator.' I would have been going through with enthusiasm instead of merely looking for the stupid fact that could support my 'stance on vending machines'"(360). (This quotation is reproduced verbatim from the original study.) It is evident that Davis's students wrote exam responses that they believed would result in a passing essay rather than answering the exam questions with their own ideas about the topic. Davis found that "the exam confined most of my students to scripted situations that compelled them to silence their critical voices" (354). This kind of experience, she writes, teaches students "lessons that are contrary to what we may want to teach in first-year [college] writing" (353).

Davis's study also demonstrates that a test-prep approach does not allow students to be creative or innovative because they must avoid expressing themselves in their writing if they expect to do well on the exams. Another student who participated in Davis's study explains why he selected one side of an issue for an argumentative essay about a proposed state ban on vending machines in schools: "Well I started reading and... I remember thinking that going for the band [sic] had two sides while going against the band [sic] had only one supportive argument.... So I went with the stance that had the most options" (359). Like this student, 67% of the students in the study began their persuasive essays on the exam with the position that had the most

(Continued)

information rather than the position they actually supported. More than half of the students assumed that to be successful on the exam they had to refrain from thinking analytically and simply give the test-scorers what they want (359). This evidence suggests that to obtain a good grade, students feel that they must create an essay that would appeal to the test-scorers and not necessarily write an essay in which they defend their own point of view. A good piece of writing encourages readers to open their minds and may even provoke an audience to view an issue differently. This is not what students learn when they learn to write for standardized tests.

Steven Sanders, a former New York State Assemblyman, believes that "students' entire pre-collegiate careers should not hinge on passing exams" (Hoff). He suggests that "scores on the Regents test should be but one factor among many that local school officials use to decide whether a student should graduate" (Hoff). Sanders recognizes a need for appropriate standards, but he also understands that using a test to define students' writing ability does not allow students to flourish in college. Every student has different writing abilities, but standardized tests encourage generalized teaching styles rather than instruction adapted to students' individual needs.

The flaws in writing instruction that is driven by standardized testing are further illuminated by the differences in college performance between students who take high school English honors or Advanced Placement (AP) courses and students who take standard English courses in high school (which are called "Regents-level" courses in New York State). As a high school student, I was required to take the Regents Exams to graduate; however, if I had not taken advanced classes, I cannot be certain that I would have been prepared for college. Honors English classes enabled me to learn college-level skills. I learned to focus on the rhetorical context of writing rather than exclusively on avoiding grammatical errors. I also took a Regents-level English course as an elective, in which I found myself just going through the motions with no real investment in my writing. In order to get a high score on the so-called "Critical Lens" essay, which is a standard part of the English Regents Exam consisting of five paragraphs, each covering various aspects of the topic, the student has to follow a series of steps in each paragraph in order to compose a "good" essay. The most outrageous requirement concerns the development of the essay, which is graded according to "the extent to which ideas are elaborated using specific and relevant evidence from the text." These guidelines don't allow for the writer's own voice to be heard, forcing the student to focus instead on the texts that are supplied for the exam. In my honors English course, however, we were taught to develop ideas not according to a standard format but by analyzing a piece of literature and exploring the topic from our own informed perspective.

Peter Parisi, a high school principal in Schenectady, New York, agrees that students enrolled in AP courses must develop an understanding of the curriculum at a faster pace and experience a greater level of complexity in their assignments than students in regular courses. According to Parisi, the more challenging the course curriculum is, the greater the need to develop more sophisticated writing skills. He views standardized testing as an unreliable means of determining whether a student is prepared for college-level writing. He also believes that a test-prep approach fails to provide students with the skills and knowledge essential for college writing (Parisi).

There are other reasons besides standardized testing for students' lack of readiness for college-level writing. Some students, for instance, enter high school without the basic skills to succeed even in a typical English course, let alone an AP course. Furthermore, the home environment can be crucial factor in determining whether a child is successful in school. A student's level of achievement relies in part on family and community support. Without such support, a child might not see the importance of their education or develop the ability to further their education.

Standardized tests like the New York State Regents Exams can do more harm than good. Such tests do not guarantee that a student will be successful in college. According to Arthur Goldstein, the exams encourage a curriculum that does not require thoughtful or in-depth knowledge, and studies like Davis's show that students often approach such exams with the idea that they are not writing from their own knowledge and perspective but instead trying to guess how the test-scorer would answer the question. In the end, more standardized testing will not help students prepare for college-level writing. More likely it will mean that more students will struggle as writers.

Works Cited

Davis, Octavia. "Talking Back to the Regents." *Talking Back to the Regents*. Project Muse, 2012. Web. 4 Mar. 2013.

Goldstein, Arthur. "Students Learn Differently. So Why Test Them All the Same?" *Schoolbook*. WNYC, 2 Feb. 2012. Web. 4 Mar. 2013.

Hoff, David J. "Flaws Could Spell Trouble for N.Y. Regents Exams." *Education Week* 23.10 (2003): 22–27. Education Full Text (H.W. Wilson). Web. 4 Mar. 2013.

Parisi, Peter. Telephone interview. 7 Mar. 2013.

The story of Elizabeth's essay illustrates the importance of the Ten Core Concepts in effective college writing and demonstrates how a writer can apply those concepts to create a piece of writing that fits her rhetorical situation. Through this process, Elizabeth learned a lot about her topic—which is part of the reason for writing in college. Although her position about the problems with standardized testing hadn't changed, she now appreciated the complexity of the issues much more than she did before writing her essay. "I have a better understanding of why there is a Regents Exam in New York State," she says. "I understand the need to measure everyone against a single standard." Nevertheless, her view about a test-prep approach to teaching high schoolers to write was strengthened as a result of this assignment. "I feel even stronger now that this approach is bad for students. My position is more informed as a result of the project."

Elizabeth also learned some important lessons about writing. "I learned that writing can be seen as something like a learning process, not necessarily just an assignment to be completed." These insights will help Elizabeth develop into an even more effective college writer.

Working with Ideas and Information 5

BY THE TIME they enter college, most students have developed the ability to write grammatically correct sentences, use proper punctuation, form verb tenses appropriately, spell correctly, and so on. Of course, *all* students, even the most successful writers, make mistakes and sometimes have trouble remembering certain rules of formal writing (such as when to use a semi-colon rather than a comma). But for the vast majority of students, learning to write effectively in college is not about learning these "basics." For most students, the main challenge is learning to write effectively in an appropriate academic style and conveying complex ideas and information clearly in the kind of authoritative voice that college instructors expect—in other words, learning to write like a scholar. And that means learning some strategies and skills that are essential for effective academic writing.

This chapter will help you learn essential stylistic strategies and develop key skills necessary to write the kind of prose expected in academic settings. These strategies and skills, which will enable you to convey complex ideas clearly without oversimplifying the subject matter, correspond to the Ten Core Concepts described in Chapter 2. For example, in most academic writing, supporting claims or assertions (Core Concept #5) requires *summarizing* the ideas or arguments of others, *quoting* from other texts, and *citing* appropriate sources. If you can't do these tasks well, your writing is likely to be less effective, no matter how compelling your point or how sound your ideas. Summarizing accurately and strategically, quoting appropriately, and citing sources properly not only enable you to convey your ideas clearly to your audience but also contribute to a strong, authoritative voice and help establish your credibility as a writer.

These skills and strategies are integral to the process of discovery and learning that academic writing should be (see Core Concept #1):

- developing an academic writing style
- writing effective paragraphs
- summarizing and paraphrasing
- synthesizing
- framing
- introducing
- making transitions

MarcelClemens/Shutterstock.com; Alexandr Mitiuc/iStockphoto.com

The more effectively you apply these skills, the more you are likely to learn from your writing—and the better your writing is likely to be.

Developing an Academic Writing Style

A few years ago, my son, who was a first-year college student at the time, complained to me about a comment a professor had written on his paper in a political science class. The assignment required students to use a certain theory to analyze a recent political event. My son was keenly interested in the topic, had read the assigned readings carefully, and understood the theory, but he had very little experience writing about such specialized topics. He tried his best to write prose that sounded like the scholarly articles he had been assigned to read. In other words, he tried to write like a scholar of political science. He worked hard on the paper and was confident that his analysis was sound. His professor agreed but nevertheless criticized the paper, calling it a parody of bad academic writing. In the professor's view, there was nothing wrong with the analysis my son had written; the problem was with *how* it had been written.

In trying to write like a scholar, my son was using unfamiliar language in a style he had not yet mastered. The professor's comment that the paper sounded like a parody of bad academic writing was unfortunate, but in a sense it was accurate. My son had not yet developed the skills a writer needs to write in an appropriate academic style about such a sophisticated topic. So it was inevitable that he would make some mistakes. After all, like just about every new college student, he was on unfamiliar terrain. Although he knew the material, he didn't have the tools to write about that material effectively in appropriate academic style.

Learning to Write Like a Scholar

My son was like a novice skier trying to descend an expert slope for the first time: the novice knows how to ski, but his skills are not developed enough to tackle the more challenging slopes. So, although he can descend an easy slope with smooth, controlled turns, on the expert slope his turns are sloppy, he loses control now and again, and he looks like a complete beginner. My son was venturing onto the expert slopes of a challenging kind of academic analytical writing without the experience and skill to negotiate that slope smoothly; as a result, his prose was full of sloppy turns and slightly out-of-control sentences.

This story underscores three important lessons for effective academic writing:

- *How* **you write affects** *what* **you write.** To complete most academic writing tasks successfully requires more than having something relevant to say (Core Concept #4); it also requires saying it well. In academic writing, that means adopting an appropriate style and presenting your ideas in a way that meets the expectations of an academic audience. Academic audiences expect writers to know how to summarize relevant information and other points of view, to quote properly from appropriate sources, to synthesize ideas clearly, to write coherent paragraphs about complicated subject matter, and to place their arguments or analyses in the context of the larger academic subject within which they are writing.

- **Good writing isn't necessarily always good writing.** Core Concept #2 ("Good writing fits the context") reminds us that what counts as good writing always depends upon the rhetorical situation. In college-level academic writing, students must learn to fit into the ongoing conversations about the subjects that are the focus of the academic disciplines they are studying. Sociologists examine how human societies function. Anthropologists explore culture. Biologists describe the living world. Scholars and researchers in every field engage in continuous conversations about specialized topics by reporting the results of their studies, proposing hypotheses, debating conclusions, and raising questions. This is the nature of academic discourse, and students must eventually learn to write in ways that enable them to become part of that discourse. Good academic writing is writing that fits into the relevant academic conversation.

- **Practice might make perfect, but it also means making mistakes.** My son was trying to write like a scholar without yet having mastered the skills of scholarly writing. So he made mistakes. His professor did not recognize that those mistakes were actually a sign of growth. My son was stretching just beyond his ability as a writer, and ultimately he learned from those mistakes, in the process gaining valuable experience and insight into academic writing. Like the novice skier trying to ski down the expert slope, my son was advancing his skills by challenging himself to go beyond his present level of ability. Through practice, he eventually acquired those skills and was able to write effective academic prose—but not without first making mistakes. Just like that skier, when you try to do something that is beyond your skill level, you'll stumble and fall, but by practicing you will eventually master the necessary skills and avoid those early mistakes. You'll make it down the expert slope smoothly. So expect some stumbling as you develop the specialized skills described in this chapter. If you struggle, it doesn't mean you're a "bad" writer; it just means you haven't yet developed the specialized skills needed to write effective academic prose.

Keep these lessons in mind as you work on your writing assignments. These lessons will help you keep your mistakes in perspective, understand and build on your strengths, and identify aspects of your writing that need improvement.

Principles of Academic Inquiry

The conventions of academic writing reflect the fact that writing is central to academic inquiry. Developing an effective academic writing style is partly a matter of learning to use language in a way that reflects the basic principles of academic inquiry.

- **Qualify your statements.** Academic writers must back up what they say (Core Concept #5). Often, that means avoiding unsupported generalizations and qualifying your statements. For example, in casual conversation or informal writing, it's acceptable to say something like this:

> Drivers just don't pay attention to speed limits.

In academic writing, which values accuracy and validity, such statements usually need to be qualified, depending on the rhetorical context:

Drivers *often* seem to ignore speed limits.

Many drivers ignore speed limits.

Studies show that *most* drivers *sometimes* exceed speed limits.

The italicized words in these examples make the statements more "true." If you can't support a statement with evidence, then qualify it so that it is valid.

■ **Be specific.** Academic audiences value specificity, and good writers avoid vagueness. Here's an example of a vague statement from a student essay:

In order for education to work, things need to change.

Such a statement seems reasonable enough, but it doesn't quite hold up under scrutiny. What does it mean to say that education must "work"? What "things" must change? And what kinds of "changes" are necessary? Often, vague terms like *things* are a sign that a statement itself might be vague. Even if this statement appears in a longer paragraph explaining those "things" and "changes," such a statement is weak by the common standards of academic writing. We might revise it as follows:

If schools are to solve the problems that prevent students from obtaining a sound education, several reforms should be implemented.

Notice that in this statement the writer avoids vague terms and tries to be more specific about what it means for schools to "work." Specificity isn't always possible or even desirable, but often vagueness can weaken your writing. (By the way, you'll notice that the revised sentence employs the passive voice, which many teachers discourage. See "Active vs. Passive Voice" on page 120.)

These examples illustrate that strong academic writing is partly a result of careful word choice, which should reflect your effort to make valid, accurate, and clear statements.

■ **Give credit.** Giving credit in academic writing is not just a matter of citing sources properly (which is discussed in Chapters 9–11); it is also a matter of using appropriate language to signal to readers that you are using source material or referring to someone else's ideas. For example, here's a student referring to a source in a paper about education reform:

The article states that money spent on schools can do little to improve educational outcomes.

Technically, there is nothing wrong with this sentence, but it is an awkward way of introducing information or referring to material taken from a source. For one thing, it isn't the article but the author who makes a statement. That might seem to be a minor point, but minor revisions can make this sentence stronger by bringing it into line with the conventions of academic writing:

The author claims that money spent on schools can do little to improve educational outcomes.

According to this author, money spent on schools can do little to improve educational outcomes.

These versions make it clear that the assertion being made is attributed to the author, not to the writer of this sentence.

In general, unless the assertion is yours, credit the author or source for the assertion. Because academic writing is essentially a matter of participating in ongoing conversations, crediting a source for a statement not only indicates to a reader who deserves credit for the statement but also helps place your own writing in the context of the larger academic conversation in which you are participating. It shows that you are part of that conversation.

■ **Use specialized terminology judiciously.** A common complaint about academic writing is that it is full of jargon. The complaint assumes that jargon is bad; however, when used properly, jargon—or specialized terminology—is not only useful but essential. All academic fields have specialized terminology that refers to important ideas and concepts within those fields. In education, for example, *pedagogy* refers to a teacher's instructional approach and the beliefs about teaching, learning, and knowing that inform that approach. It would be difficult to convey that concept efficiently and clearly without that term. Equivalent terms using common language, such as *instructional approach* or *teaching technique*, don't quite capture the complexity of the concept. In such a case, *pedagogy* is an efficient term that conveys important ideas to readers and reflects the writer's familiarity with the field. The challenge for student writers is to become familiar enough with such terminology so that it becomes a tool for effective writing.

In the following passage, for example, the writer discusses the increasing socio-economic inequality in higher education:

> At the same time that family income has become more predictive of children's academic achievement, so has educational attainment become more predictive of adults' earnings. The combination of these trends creates a feedback mechanism that may decrease intergenerational mobility. As children from higher socio-economic strata achieve greater academic success, and those who succeed academically are more likely to have higher incomes, higher education contributes to an even more unequal and economically polarized society.

This passage contains terms that are widely used in academic discussions about poverty, education, and education reform: for example, *academic achievement* and *intergenerational mobility*. These terms have specialized meaning in fields like sociology, education, political science, and public policy and therefore can be useful for writers in those fields. Not only do these terms convey important ideas efficiently to a reader, but they also signal that the writer is knowledgeable about the subject. At the same time, such terminology can make a passage dense and difficult to follow. Some careful revisions (which are highlighted) to reduce wordiness can make the passage clearer without eliminating necessary terms:

> At the same time that family income has become more predictive of children's academic achievement, so has educational attainment become more predictive of adults' earnings. The combination of these trends could decrease intergenerational mobility. As the children of the rich do better in school, and those who do better in school are more likely to become rich, we risk producing an even more unequal and economically polarized society. (Adapted from Edsall, Thomas. "The Reproduction of Privilege." *New York Times* 12 Mar. 2012. Web. 27 July 2012.)

In this revised version, some jargon (e.g., *higher socio-economic strata, greater academic success*) is replaced with more common language (*rich, do better in school*), but key terms (*academic achievement* and *intergenerational mobility*) are preserved. Replacing those key terms with common language would result in a lengthy passage that might not be clearer. For example, *intergenerational mobility* refers to the process by which children do better economically than their parents; in other words, children attain a higher socio-economic status than their parents. Explaining that idea in a sentence or two would unnecessarily lengthen the passage. If this passage were intended for a general audience, then it might be necessary to define the term or replace it entirely; for an academic audience, however, the term enables the writer to keep the passage shorter while at the same time making an important point.

The rule of thumb is to use language that communicates your ideas clearly to your intended audience:

- Use appropriate terminology to communicate specialized ideas, but make sure you understand the terminology.
- Replace confusing terms or unnecessary jargon with common words if you can do so without undermining your point or changing the meaning of the passage.

Following these guidelines will help you write prose that is both clear and sophisticated.

FOCUS   Active vs. Passive Voice

It is a common dictum to avoid the passive voice and use active voice in writing. The prevailing belief is that using the active voice strengthens your prose, whereas the passive voice weakens your writing by making it unnecessarily wordy and vague. Like most such "rules," this one is misleading. Remember Core Concept #2: "Good writing fits the context." Although it might be true that in many contexts the active voice makes for better writing, the passive voice is not only acceptable but also essential in academic writing. In some cases, the passive voice is actually preferable because it can change the focus of a statement to emphasize a point or idea. To illustrate, let's return to the example on page 118:

> If schools are to solve the problems that prevent students from obtaining a sound education, several reforms should be implemented.

The main point of this sentence is that school reform is needed. Notice that in the main clause (*several reforms should be implemented*), which is in the passive voice, the emphasis is on *reforms* (which is the subject of the clause). Revising the sentence to place the main clause in the active voice changes that emphasis. Here's how that sentence might look in the active voice:

> If schools are to solve the problems that prevent students from obtaining a sound education, they should implement several reforms.

Is this version clearer, more succinct, or more valid than the original sentence? Not necessarily. Notice that in the revised version the subject of the main clause is now *they* (presumably referring back to *schools*), which shifts the emphasis of the statement. But who exactly is "they"? School reform involves a lot of different people and institutions: teachers, administrators, school districts, government agencies, consultants, voters, politicians. Does "they" refer to all of these? Some of these? It isn't clear. In this regard, the passive voice enables the writer to keep the emphasis on the need for school reform—which is the main point of the sentence—not on *who* will accomplish the reform—which is an important and related topic but not the issue here. So the use of passive voice in this example does not weaken the writing but allows the writer to maintain the appropriate focus. If the writer's focus happened to be on a specific entity responsible for education reform, the active voice might be more appropriate. For example, let's assume that the writer was discussing reforms that only elected politicians could enact. In that case, the subject would be clear and the active voice more appropriate:

> If schools are to solve the problems that prevent students from obtaining a sound education, elected officials should undertake several reforms.

The passive voice should be used judiciously. Overuse or inappropriate use of the passive voice can weaken your writing. Usually, active voice results in more concise prose, but as this example illustrates, writers can use the passive voice as an important tool for emphasis and clarity.

EXERCISE 5A   PRACTICING ACADEMIC STYLE

Using the advice for academic writing style in this section, revise the following statements so that they are clearer and appropriately supported or qualified. For each item, imagine an appropriate rhetorical context and indicate how that context would shape your revisions. (For example, you might imagine the first statement in an argument supporting gun control for a criminal justice course.)

- We need better gun laws to make our communities safer. Otherwise, we'll just have more and more violence.

- Poverty-stricken Americans of low socio-economic status will be adversely affected by legislative actions that facilitate the attainment of citizenship by undocumented residents.

- Smartphones are convenient, but they are making everyone dumber because people rely on them rather than on their own minds.

Writing Paragraphs

By the time they enter college, most students have had many hours of instruction in writing correct sentences and paragraphs. Yet new college students often struggle to write effective paragraphs that convey complex ideas clearly and coherently. Part of the problem is that the subject matter in college writing is often new and challenging, and students have to learn how to write clearly about unfamiliar ideas, concepts, and information. But students can also improve their writing by learning how to create more effective paragraphs, no matter what subject they are writing about.

Effective paragraphs in academic writing have three key characteristics. They are:

- **Well-developed.** A paragraph should cover its topic sufficiently. Often, that means elaborating on key points, ideas, or facts and including examples. Under-developed paragraphs tend to be superficial and suggest that the writer has not explored the topic in sufficient depth.

- **Coherent.** Coherence refers to the extent to which the paragraph retains a focus on a main idea or point. In a coherent paragraph, all the sentences relate clearly to one another and communicate ideas or information relevant to the main point. Usually, but not always, a strong paragraph also has a clear topic sentence that states the main point and establishes the focus of the paragraph.

- **Cohesive.** Cohesion means that the statements, ideas, and information in a paragraph are explicitly linked together. To a great extent, cohesion is a function of the use of specific words and phrases that indicate to a reader that statements are connected: *similarly, by contrast, also, therefore, on the other hand, moreover, in addition,* and so on. Writers also achieve cohesion by repeating key words or phrases.

Writing Well-Developed Paragraphs

The key to writing a well-developed paragraph is making sure the topic of the paragraph is sufficiently explained or examined and the main point adequately supported. When necessary, elaborating on a point and illustrating it with examples also contribute to paragraph development. Here's an example of an under-developed paragraph from an essay about the relationship between poverty and educational achievement:

> The culture of poverty is defined by Paul Gorski as "the idea that poor people share more or less monolithic and predictable beliefs, values and behavior" (32). This is not true. Later studies show that a culture of poverty does not exist. This belief was constructed from data collected in the early 1960s showing that certain behaviors, such as increased violence and failure to foresee or plan for the future, were common among poor people. The original study portrayed stereotypes of poor students, not a culture of poverty.

In this paragraph the student tries to explain the idea of "the culture of poverty," relying on a source for information about the origins of that idea and how it has been interpreted. The author of that source, Paul Gorski, argues that the idea of a culture of poverty is actually a misunderstanding of a particular study of poverty; he cites subsequent studies that invalidate the whole idea of a culture of poverty. In this paragraph, the student attempts to communicate Gorski's position. However, although the student defines the term *culture of poverty*, the problems associated with that idea are not sufficiently explained. The student states simply that the idea "is not true" and that studies show it "does not exist," but the lack of explanation makes it difficult for readers to understand the problems with the original study and how the data were interpreted. In short, the paragraph does not communicate this complicated information well.

In situations like this one, in which the writer is trying to convey complex ideas and information in a single paragraph, the solution is to elaborate on key ideas. In this case, the student must provide more information about the origins of the idea of the culture of poverty, how it was misinterpreted, and how it was invalidated:

> The culture of poverty, according to Paul Gorski, is "the idea that poor people share more or less monolithic and predictable beliefs, values and behavior" (32). The idea emerged from a 1961 book by Oscar Lewis that reported on ethnographic studies of several small poor Mexican communities. Lewis's data indicated that those communities shared fifty attributes, such as frequent violence and a failure to plan for the future. From this small sample, he concluded that all poor communities share these attributes, which reflect a culture of poverty. The idea that "people in poverty share a persistent and observable 'culture'" (32–33) became popular among scholars trying to understand poverty. However, numerous later studies revealed great differences among poor communities and called the very idea of a culture of poverty into question. According to Gorski, these subsequent studies make it clear that "there is no such thing as a culture of poverty" (33). Gorski concludes that "the culture of poverty concept is constructed from a collection of smaller stereotypes which, however false, seem to have crept into mainstream thinking as unquestioned fact" (33).

In this developed version, the writer elaborates on specific points, such as how Lewis arrived at the idea of a culture of poverty and how the idea was subsequently challenged. The writer also uses quotations from the source text to provide additional information about this topic, which makes it much easier for a reader to grasp the main idea and supporting points.

Longer is not always better, of course, but when you are writing about complex ideas in academic contexts, under-developed paragraphs can result in superficial and sometimes confusing prose.

Achieving Coherence

In effective academic writing, paragraphs are not only sufficiently developed but also clearly focused and organized. In a coherent paragraph:

- The writer is in control of the subject matter and takes the reader deliberately from beginning to end.
- All the sentences contain relevant information.
- The discussion follows a clear and logical progression.

Often there is a topic sentence, but even without one, the main point of the paragraph is clear.

Students sometimes lose control of a paragraph when they are writing about complicated, abstract, or unfamiliar ideas and aren't sure what information to include and how to organize that information. In the following example, a student tries to explain what he believes is a basic principle of social life: competition. However, he struggles to make the main point of the paragraph clear and to present his ideas about competition in an orderly way:

> Our society is based on competition. It is natural for all of us to compete. Probably cheating is caused by our desire to succeed in competition. The first place we experience competition is at home when we cry to be held by our parents. We compete with their busy schedules to get their attention. Our next major competition is school, where we are all compared with other students. Until this time we only know that the time we spend with our parents is limited but if we exert ourselves we get what we want. Being compared with other students is when we first realize that we compete for others' time and compliments. As children we only know that we need get someone's attention to achieve what we need. We find that most competition is based upon being recognized.

Although this paragraph has a general focus, the main idea seems to shift. The opening sentence suggests that the paragraph is about the central role competition plays in human society, but the final sentence suggests a somewhat narrower point: that competition arises from the need to be recognized. In addition, the third sentence is irrelevant to the main point about competition, and the paragraph isn't well organized.

To address these problems, the first task is to identify the main point of the paragraph. Stating that point in a topic sentence can help, but the topic sentence does not have to be at the beginning of the paragraph. Let's assume that the writer wants to make the point that competition arises from the human need to be recognized. That can serve as a topic sentence. We want to keep the focus of the paragraph on that main point. We also want to order the sentences so that the reader can follow the discussion easily from one supporting point to the next. Here's a revised version:

> Our society is based on competition, and it is natural for all of us to compete. But why? Competition, it seems, arises from a basic human need to be recognized. We first experience competition very early in our lives when we cry to be held by our parents, actually competing with their busy schedules for their attention. For the first years of our lives, we learn that the time we spend with our parents is precious but limited, so we exert ourselves to get the attention we need. Our next major competition occurs in school, where we are compared with other students. We are still seeking the time and attention of others, but now we realize that we must compete with other students to be recognized. Every stage of our lives is characterized by different versions of this competition to fulfill our basic need for attention and recognition.

In this version, much of the original language is retained, but the focus on the main idea has been sharpened by adding a clear topic sentence (*Competition, it seems, arises from a basic human need to be recognized.*), eliminating unnecessary material (the sentence about cheating), rewriting some sentences so that they relate more clearly to the topic sentence, and reorganizing the paragraph. The paragraph is now more coherent, which makes its main point more evident to the reader.

Coherence can be difficult to achieve, but following these three steps can help make your paragraphs more coherent and effective:

1. State the main point of the paragraph in a sentence (topic sentence). ⟹ 2. Make sure every sentence in the paragraph relates to the main point. ⟹ 3. Order the sentences to make it easy for a reader to follow the discussion of the main point.

Achieving Cohesion

Cohesion refers to the extent to which statements, ideas, and information in a paragraph are related and explicitly connected to one another. In concrete terms, cohesion is a measure of how well the individual sentences in a paragraph are linked together so that the reader can see the relationship between the ideas or information in one sentence and those in another sentence. If a writer does not make those relationships clear, the paragraph becomes harder for a reader to follow. Even a coherent paragraph (that is, one in which all the sentences relate clearly to the main topic of the paragraph) can lack cohesion. Fortunately, cohesion can usually be achieved in two main ways:

- by the strategic use of certain "linking" words and phrases (e.g., *also, similarly, by contrast, in addition, then, therefore,* etc.)
- by the repetition of key words and phrases

Here's a paragraph that is coherent but not cohesive. Like the example in the section on developing a paragraph (page 122), this example also addresses the idea of "the culture of poverty" and draws on the same source. In this case, the paragraph retains its focus on the main topic, which is Paul Gorski's explanation of the concept of the culture of poverty, but the paragraphs lacks cohesion that would help a reader follow the writer's discussion more easily:

In "The Myth of the 'Culture of Poverty'" (2008), Paul Gorski examines the concept of the "culture of poverty" and how it relates to education. Numerous case studies and academic articles as well as first-hand experience are discussed. Research shows that the culture of poverty doesn't exist. Many teachers have a preconceived notion that a culture of poverty is responsible for creating unmotivated students and uninvolved parents. He goes into great detail about the bias of educators, which leads them to promote a "culture of classism" that results in an unequal education for those living in poverty. Gorski suggests several ways that teachers can better address the needs of poverty-stricken students and avoid the problems associated with bias in education.

Compare this paragraph with the following one, which has been revised to make it more cohesive. The key revisions are highlighted. Yellow highlighting indicates the repetition of key words or phrases; blue highlighting indicates a linking word or phrase.

> In "The Myth of the "Culture of Poverty" (2008), Paul Gorski examines the concept of the "culture of poverty" and how it relates to education. Gorski draws upon numerous case studies and academic articles as well as the first-hand experience of a classroom teacher to explain the origins and interpretations of this concept. In addition, he cites research to show that the culture of poverty doesn't exist. Gorski points out that many teachers have a preconceived notion that this "culture of poverty" is responsible for creating unmotivated students and uninvolved parents (2). He carefully examines this bias, which, he argues, leads educators to promote a "culture of classism" that results in an unequal education for those living in poverty (3). Gorski also suggests several ways that teachers can better address the needs of poverty stricken students and avoid this "culture of classism" and its damaging effects on poor children.

Notice how simple linking words (e.g., *also, this*) and careful repetition of key phrases (e.g., *"culture of poverty"*) create connections among the sentences and enable the reader to follow the discussion more easily. Students sometimes mistakenly believe that repeating words and phrases is a mark of poor writing, but, as this example illustrates, strategic repetition actually makes the passage more cohesive and therefore strengthens the writing.

EXERCISE 5B   WRITING EFFECTIVE PARAGRAPHS

Using the advice in this section, revise the following paragraph to make it more coherent and cohesive. Also, revise the sentences so that they reflect a more effective academic prose style:

> Religion is a man-made device that has allowed people to find a meaning in life. Whether it is monotheism or polytheism, or whether it is mixes of various beliefs regarding a creator, idols, or an overall power, people revert to some form of belief for solace. Spiritualism, which is not the same as religious faith, is on the rise. Studies routinely show that Americans are much more religious than most other nations. As religions grow, cultural aspects come into play, and it is the spiritual and physical actions that tend to dictate societal and personal beliefs. Some people want to hold onto traditional values. Many traditional values and actions have faded in religions, especially in mainstream, secular society. Judaism, among other religions, has become secularized, except for some sects. The same is true of many Christian denominations.

Summarizing and Paraphrasing

Summarizing and paraphrasing are among the most important skills in academic writing. It is a rare writing task that does not include some summary or paraphrase:

- In an argument about capital punishment, the writer summarizes the main positions for and against capital punishment before defending a position on the issue.

- A chemistry lab report about campus air quality includes summaries of previous analyses of air quality.

- An analysis of housing density in a neighborhood near campus for a sociology class includes a paraphrase of a seminal study about the relationship between housing density and key socio-economic and demographic factors.

- In a literary analysis essay for an English literature course, a student summarizes the plots of several plays by Shakespeare and paraphrases a critic's evaluation of them.

These examples underscore not only how common but also how useful summary and paraphrase can be in academic writing. They also indicate that, although students often need to summarize other texts, they might also need to summarize an argument, perspective, or theory that arises from multiple sources.

Usually, *summary* is distinguished from *paraphrase* (see "Summarizing vs. Paraphrasing"); in practice, however, the distinction is not always clear—or useful. For our purposes, distinguishing between summary and paraphrase is less important than understanding how to represent information and ideas from a source text accurately and how to credit the source appropriately. Accordingly, the advice in this section generally applies to both summarizing and paraphrasing.

5

FOCUS   Summarizing vs. Paraphrasing

Students are often confused by the difference between a summary and a paraphrase. That's understandable, because summary and paraphrase are very similar and textbooks as well as online resources often contribute to the confusion.

Paraphrase. The Merriam-Webster Dictionary defines *paraphrase* as "a restatement of a text, passage, or work giving the meaning in another form." A paraphrase expresses the ideas or information from a source text in your own words. Usually, a writer paraphrases when the information and/or meaning of a source text is important but the original wording of that text is not. Sometimes writers paraphrase when the source text is specialized and difficult to understand. (When it is important to convey the original wording to readers, the writer should *quote* from the source text. See "Quoting from Sources" on page 233 in Chapter 9.)

(Continued)

Summary. *Summary*, by contrast, is a condensed version of a source text that conveys only the main ideas or information from that text in the writer's own words. Writers summarize when they need to convey

- a key idea from a source text

- a point of view expressed in a source text

- the results of an analysis reported in a source text

- an argument made in a source text

The main difference between a summary and a paraphrase is that a summary boils a source down into a brief passage (a sentence, a few sentences, or a paragraph), whereas a paraphrase restates the source text. Both use the writer's own words, but the purpose of each is slightly different. In a summary, the writer conveys the main point or idea of a source text; in a paraphrase, the writer restates the source text to convey the information or ideas of that source text.

Although summarizing seems to be a straightforward task, students encounter **two main problems when summarizing:**

- inaccurately representing the main point, idea, or information from the source text

- using too much of the original language from the source

For example, here's a passage from an article in which a law professor offers an analysis of the so-called "war on poverty" initiated by President Lyndon Johnson in the 1960s:

> The commitment and symbolism of the "war on poverty"—and the energy and enthusiasm of those who fought it—were vital. For a brief period, the idea of conducting a war on poverty captured the nation's imagination. The phrase is surely one of the most evocative in our history. Yet the war's specific components were a tiny fraction even of the Great Society programs enacted between 1964 and 1968 during the administration of Lyndon Johnson, let alone those enacted during the New Deal and those added since, many during the presidency of Richard Nixon. And, even considering all these, we never fought an allout war on poverty.

> Source: Edelman, Peter. "The War on Poverty and Subsequent Federal Programs: What Worked, What Didn't Work, and Why? Lessons for Future Programs." *Clearinghouse Review Journal of Poverty Law and Policy* (May–June 2006): 8. Web.

The following summary misses the main point of the source text:

> According to Edelman, the war on poverty captured the nation's imagination.

The source text does state that the war on poverty captured the nation's imagination, but the author goes on to argue that the United States "never fought an allout war on poverty." The main point of the passage is that, despite the popularity of the idea of a war on poverty, the federal efforts intended to alleviate poverty were a small part of total government social programs. This summary, although accurate to an extent, misrepresents the point of the source passage. Here's a summary that better represents the point of the source text:

> Edelman argues that although the idea of a "war on poverty" captured the country's imagination, programs focused on addressing poverty never amounted to more than a small part of President Lyndon Johnson's Great Society programs and the social programs of other administrations both before and after Johnson's.

Notice that this summary represents the source passage *as a whole* rather than focusing on one part of it.

It's possible that a brief summary like this would be insufficient, depending upon the nature of the writing assignment and rhetorical situation. For example, you might be writing an argument in response to the source text, in which case you would probably need to include a more complete representation of that source. In such a case, you would probably need to paraphrase the source passage. Here's a paraphrase that illustrates the very common problem of using too much of the original language of the source text (the passages that are taken from the source text are highlighted in yellow):

> The commitment and symbolism of the "war on poverty" were important. For a short time, the idea of a war on poverty captured the nation's imagination. But the specific components of the war were a tiny fraction of government programs enacted during the administration of Lyndon Johnson, not to mention those enacted before then and those added since. Even considering all these programs, an allout war on poverty was never really fought.

In this example, not only are too many words and phrases taken verbatim from the source text, but much of the sentence structure is also reproduced in the paraphrase. A more acceptable paraphrase transforms the source passage into the writer's own words while preserving the original meaning of the source text:

> According to Edelman, the idea of a "war on poverty" was important for its symbolism as well as for the national commitment it reflected. But although this idea resonated with Americans for a time, the programs intended specifically to fight poverty were never more than a small part of total government social programs, whether those programs were part of Lyndon Johnson's Great Society, the earlier New Deal, or initiatives undertaken by Richard Nixon and subsequent presidents. As a result, Edelman states, a total war on poverty was never really fought.

This paraphrase borrows only essential phrases from the source text (such as "war on poverty") and restructures the passage so that the diction and syntax are the writer's own.

When summarizing or paraphrasing, follow these guidelines:

- **Accurately represent the main idea or point of the source text.** This is not simply a matter of including important information or ideas in your summary or paraphrase but also making sure that you convey the original author's intent or meaning.

- **Use your own language.** In many cases, using your own language means finding appropriate synonyms for words in the source text, but it also means writing your own sentences rather than using the sentence structure of the source text.

- **Place quotation marks around important words or phrases from the source text.** If you reproduce key words or phrases from the source text, place them in quotation marks to indicate that the language is taken from the source text. In the example above, the phrase *war on poverty* is placed in quotation marks not only because it is taken from the source text verbatim but also because it has become a phrase associated with a specific set of programs and period in history. (See "Quoting from Sources" on page 233 in Chapter 9 for advice about how to quote appropriately from a source text.)

- **Cite the source.** Whether you are summarizing, paraphrasing, or quoting directly from a source text, you must cite that source properly to indicate to your readers that you are taking ideas or information from another text. (See Chapters 10 and 11 for information about citing sources.)

EXERCISE 5C   PRACTICING SUMMARY AND PARAPHRASE

1. Write a summary and a paraphrase of the following passage:

Individualism-collectivism is perhaps the broadest and most widely used dimension of cultural variability for cultural comparison (Gudykunst and Ting-Toomey, 1988). Hofstede (1980) describes individualism-collectivism as the relationship between the individual and the collectivity that prevails in a given society. In individualistic cultures, individuals tend to prefer individualistic relationships to others and to subordinate ingroup goals to their personal goals. In collectivistic cultures, on the other hand, individuals are more likely to have interdependent relationships to their ingroups and to subordinate their personal goals to their ingroup goals. Individualistic cultures are associated with emphases on independence, achievement, freedom, high levels of competition, and pleasure. Collectivistic cultures are associated with emphases on interdependence, harmony, family security, social hierarchies, cooperation, and low levels of competition.

Source: Han, Sang-Pil, and Sharon Shavitt. "Persuasion and Culture: Advertising Appeals in Individualistic and Collectivistic Societies." *Journal of Experimental Social Psychology* 30 (1994): 327–28. Print.

2. Revise the summary below so that it more accurately reflects the original passage:

Original passage: Prior to the official acceptance of the low-fat-is-good-health dogma, clinical investigators, predominantly British, had proposed another hypothesis for the cause of heart disease, diabetes, colorectal and breast cancer, tooth decay, and a half-dozen or so other chronic diseases, including obesity. The hypothesis was based on decades of eyewitness testimony from missionary and colonial physicians and two consistent observations: that these "diseases of civilization" were rare to nonexistent among isolated populations that lived traditional lifestyles and ate traditional diets, and that these diseases appeared in these populations only after they were exposed to Western foods—in particular, sugar, flour, white rice, and maybe beer. These are known technically as *refined* carbohydrates, which are those carbohydrate-containing foods—usually sugars and starches—that have been machine-processed to make them more easily digestible.

Source: Taubes, Gary. *Good Calories, Bad Calories*. New York: Knopf, 2007. Print.

Summary: Another hypothesis was proposed based on decades of eyewitness testimony from physicians and the observations that these "diseases of civilization" didn't occur in isolated populations until they were exposed to Western diets of refined carbohydrates. Refined carbohydrates include sugar, flour, white rice, and maybe beer.

Synthesizing

In much academic writing, writers must do more than consult sources for relevant information. They must also bring together information or ideas from a variety of sources and synthesize the material into a coherent discussion that is relevant to the task at hand. Not only is synthesizing material from several sources an essential task in most academic writing, but it also lends depth to the writing. Consider this passage from *The Young and the Digital*, an analysis of the role of media in the lives of young people today:

In years past, social scientists expressed serious apprehension about the media content, especially violent and sexual imagery, that's exposed to young children and teenagers. And though violent and sexual themes in media continues to be a serious topic of debate, a growing amount of attention is shifting to the proliferation of screens in homes and in young people's lives. There is rising anxiety about the sheer amount of time children and teens spend with media and technology. According to a 2006 study conducted by the Kaiser Family Foundation, kids spend between six and eight-and-a-half hours a day with media. Today, playtime for many young children

Sean Gallup/Getty Images

usually involves time with a screen. As they observe their parents' connection to mobile phones, BlackBerrys, laptops, and other electronic gadgets, many young children mimic those behaviors. We often hear, and for good reason, that young people are leading the migration to digital. But in many homes across America, parents are unwittingly teaching their kids to be digital. In the midst of the marketing and selling of the digital lifestyle, the American Academy of Pediatrics recommends that children's daily screen time be limited to one to two hours.

Source: Watkins, S. Craig. *The Young and the Digital*. Boston: Beacon, 2009. Print.

In this passage, author S. Craig Watkins draws on several sources to make his main point about the increasing amount of time young people spend using digital media. Notice that Watkins cites two specific sources (a study by the Kaiser Family Foundation and a recommendation from the American Academy of Pediatrics), but the first few sentences of the paragraph provide an overview of an important development (the shift in attention from questionable media content to the amount of time children spend with media) that Watkins likely gleaned from several additional sources. In other words, Watkins is synthesizing ideas and information not only from the two sources he cites but also from other sources that he consulted while researching his topic. As this example suggests, synthesis can be extremely useful when a writer is working with complex subject matter and many different sources.

Effective writers follow three basic guidelines when synthesizing ideas and information.

- Keep larger goals in mind
- Identify a main point
- Use only source material that you need

Keep Larger Goals in Mind

When working with several different sources, especially in a longer project on a complicated topic, it can be easy to lose track of your reasons for consulting the specific sources you found. As you review sources and identify relevant information or ideas, remind yourself of the main goal of your project and identify how the section you are working on fits into that main goal. For example, the passage above from Watkins' book *The Young and the Digital* is taken from a chapter titled "The Very Well Connected: Friending, Bonding, and Community in the Digital Age," in which Watkins examines the increasingly central role digital media play in the social lives of young people. The passage above focuses on the increasing amount of time young people devote to digital media, a point that supports Watkins' analysis that digital media have become one of the most significant factors in how young people manage their social lives. Notice that in synthesizing material from his sources to make his point about the time young people devote to digital media, Watkins also connects that point to his larger point about the social impact of digital media.

Identify a Main Point

Source material is often varied and complicated, and when synthesizing this material, you must identify what is relevant to the task at hand. In effect, you are managing information from different sources that might seem unrelated and connecting them to make a point. That task is easier if you keep focused on a main point. Here's an example in which a writer synthesizes information from several very different sources to make a point about the longstanding debates about vegetarianism:

> Debates about the efficacy of vegetarianism follow us from cradle to wheelchair. In 1998 child-care expert Dr. Benjamin Spock, who became a vegetarian late in life, stoked a stir by recommending that children over the age of 2 be raised as vegans, rejecting even milk and eggs. The American Dietetic Association says it is possible to raise kids as vegans but cautions that special care must be taken with nursing infants (who don't develop properly without the nutrients in mother's milk or fortified formula). Other researchers warn that infants breast-fed by vegans have lower levels of vitamin B12 and DHA (an omega-3 fatty acid), important to vision and growth.

Source: Corliss, Richard. "Should We All Be Vegetarians?" *Time* 2002: 48+. Print.

In this passage, the author draws on at least three separate sets of sources: (1) material about the 1988 controversy surrounding Dr. Benjamin Spock's recommendations about feeding young children a vegetarian diet; (2) the American Dietary Association's recommendations; and (3) nutritional studies of infants who were breast-fed by vegans. Although these difference sources all relate to the topic of the impact of vegetarianism on children, they each have a different focus. The author brings them together to make a single main point, which is stated in the first sentence of the paragraph. The information from each source is clearly related to that main point. As a result, the author makes it easy for a reader to make sense of the information from these different sources.

Use Only the Source Material You Need

When working with multiple sources, you might find a great deal of relevant material that is interesting and seemingly important, but don't overwhelm your reader by trying to synthesize information from too many sources at once. In the examples in this section, the authors select information from their sources carefully and use only what they need to make their points. It is likely that in each case the author had much more information than he used. Part of your task when working with sources is to evaluate the information you have gathered and select the material that helps you achieve your rhetorical goals. Synthesis can be a powerful tool in academic writing, but if you try to squeeze too much information from too many different sources into a passage, it is likely that your prose will be less clear and your discussion more difficult for your readers to follow.

EXERCISE 5D   PRACTICING SYNTHESIZING

Write a brief paragraph in which you synthesize the following information about the job market for college graduates:

A Bachelor's degree is one of the best weapons a job seeker can wield in the fight for employment and earnings. And staying on campus to earn a graduate degree provides safe shelter from the immediate economic storm, and will pay off with greater employability and earnings once the graduate enters the labor market. Unemployment for students with new Bachelor's degrees is an unacceptable 8.9 percent, but it's a catastrophic 22.9 percent for job seekers with a recent high school diploma—and an almost unthinkable 31.5 percent for recent high school dropouts.

Source: Anthony, Carnevale, et al. *Hard Times: College Majors, Unemployment, and Earnings*. Publication. Georgetown University Center on Education and the Work Force, 2013. Web. 21 May 2013.

More than half of all recent graduates are unemployed or in jobs that do not require a degree, and the amount of student-loan debt carried by households has more than quintupled since 1999. These graduates were told that a diploma was all they needed to succeed, but it won't even get them out of the spare bedroom at Mom and Dad's. For many, the most tangible result of their four years is the loan payments, which now average hundreds of dollars a month on loan balances in the tens of thousands.

Source: McArdle, Megan. "Is College a Lousy Investment?" *The Daily Beast*. Newsweek/Daily Beast, 9 Sept. 2012. Web. 17 June 2013.

[In 2011] about 1.5 million, or 53.6 percent, of bachelor's degree-holders under the age of 25 last year were jobless or underemployed, the highest share in at least 11 years. In 2000, the share was at a low of 41 percent, before the dot-com bust erased job gains for college graduates in the telecommunications and IT fields.

Source: Associated Press. "Half of Recent College Grads Underemployed or Jobless, Analysis Says." *Cleveland.com*. Cleveland Live LLC, 23 Apr. 2012. Web. 17 June 2013.

Underemployment also tends to be temporary for college graduates. Even after the recession hit, Pew found that annually, about 27 percent of BA's stuck in high-school level jobs transitioned to college-level employment... Unemployment for college graduates is higher than normal. Underemployment is more prevalent, though it's less severe than college critics portray, and perhaps no worse than during the Reagan days.

Source: Weissmann, Jordan. "How Bad Is the Job Market for College Grads? Your Definitive Guide." *The Atlantic*. The Atlantic Monthly Group, 4 Apr. 2013. Web. 17 June 2013.

Framing

You might have heard an instructor comment about "framing" an argument, analysis, or discussion:

Be sure to frame your argument clearly.

Frame your analysis of the new health care law in terms of the ongoing debates about the role of government in citizens' lives.

Try to frame your discussion in a way that makes it relevant for your readers.

In these statements, "framing" means placing your project in a context that gives it relevance or significance for your audience. It is a technique for putting into practice Core Concept #2: "Good writing fits the context." All writing must fit into a specific rhetorical situation that includes an intended audience and a context for communicating with that audience. It is part of a writer's task to show his or her audience why the topic at hand is important and meaningful and how the writer will approach it. "Framing" is a term used to describe a technique for doing that.

For example, in the following passage, the authors, three biologists, frame their argument about "eusociality" in terms of an ongoing debate in their field:

> For most of the past half century, much of sociobiological theory has focused on the phenomenon called eusociality, where adult members are divided into reproductive and (partially) non-reproductive castes and the latter care for the young. How can genetically prescribed selfless behaviour arise by natural selection, which is seemingly its antithesis? This problem has vexed biologists since Darwin, who in *The Origin of Species* declared the paradox—in particular displayed by ants—to be the most important challenge to his theory. The solution offered by the master naturalist was to regard the sterile worker caste as a "well-flavoured vegetable," and the queen as the plant that produced it. Thus, he said, the whole colony is the unit of selection.
>
> Modern students of collateral altruism have followed Darwin in continuing to focus on ants, honeybees and other eusocial insects, because the colonies of most of their species are divided unambiguously into different castes. Moreover, eusociality is not a marginal phenomenon in the living world. The biomass of ants alone composes more than half that of all insects and exceeds that of all terrestrial nonhuman vertebrates combined. Humans, which can be loosely characterized as eusocial, are dominant among the land vertebrates. The "superorganisms" emerging from eusociality are often bizarre in their constitution, and represent a distinct level of biological organization.

Source: Nowak, Martin A., Corina E. Tarnita, and Edward O. Wilson. "The Evolution of Eusociality." *Nature* 466.26 (2010): 1057. Print.

In this passage, the authors place their specific argument in the context of a problem that evolutionary biologists have long confronted in their efforts to test Darwin's theories. In this way, the authors show how their argument is relevant to biologists by connecting it to a recognized problem in the field.

Here's another example, this one from a scholarly article reporting on a study of college students' use of digital media. In this passage, the author cites evidence of the increasingly important role that social media play in the lives of young Americans:

> According to the Pew Internet and American Life Project, as of August 2011, 83% of 18–29 year-olds used a social network site (Madden, 2012). Their interactions on these sites were also purposeful, as Pew reports that this age group is that most concerned with online identity management: 71% of them have changed the privacy settings on the sites they use (Lenhart, Purcell, Smith, & Zickuhr, 2010). Living a "literate life in the information age" (Selfe & Hawisher, 2004) increasingly means learning to navigate these spaces, managing one's identity and online data, and considering complex issues of privacy and representation. Using ethnographic case study data, this article examines how one undergraduate student integrated his use of social network sites into his everyday literacy practices to represent his identity. I approached this case study with three research questions: 1) How does this writer integrate social network sites into his everyday literacy practices? 2) How does this writer use those literacy practices to represent his identity for multiple audience groups on social network sites? 3) How does this writer negotiate site interfaces to represent his identity and communicate with others?

Source: Buck, Amber. "Examining Digital Literacy Practices on Social Network Sites." *Research in the Teaching of English* 47.1 (2012): 10. Print.

Here the author frames her own case study of a college student in terms of larger social and technological developments in contemporary society. She cites other research to establish the importance of social media and place her study in the context of these important developments.

Both these examples illustrate how authors use framing not only to introduce readers to the subject matter but also to identify why their arguments or analyses are relevant. By framing their discussions, these authors explicitly connect their arguments or analyses to larger debates or conversations that matter to their readers and show how their own arguments or analyses fit into those conversations.

Framing typically happens in the introduction to a piece, but a writer might see a need to frame a segment of a piece of writing, especially in a longer piece that might contain several sections. For instance, in an analysis of the economic impact of a proposed tax on gasoline, the writer might include a section presenting a specific kind of cost-benefit analysis using a new economic model. In such a case, the writer might frame that section in the context of, say, an ongoing debate about whether certain kinds of taxes hurt the average consumer or benefit the economy as a whole.

When framing an argument, analysis, or discussion, use these questions to guide you:

- What makes your argument, analysis, or discussion relevant to your intended audience? Why would your audience be interested in this topic?

- To which larger debates, conversations, or arguments is your topic related? How might you connect your topic to those larger debates, conversations, or arguments?

- What makes your topic important or relevant now? How can you show your readers that your topic is important and timely?

These questions can make it easier for you to frame your discussion in a way that makes it relevant for your readers and enables them to place it in a larger context.

1. Imagine an argument you might make about a current issue that interests you. Using the bulleted list of questions on page 137, describe briefly how you would frame this argument. In your answer, identify your intended audience and a purpose for your argument.

2. Using your answer for Question #1, reframe your argument for a different audience.

3. In a brief paragraph, describe how the authors of the following passage frame their research in this introduction to their series of studies about "Millennials" (that is, people born between 1981 and 2000):

Generations, like people, have personalities. Their collective identities typically begin to reveal themselves when their oldest members move into their teens and twenties and begin to act upon their values, attitudes and worldviews. America's newest generation, the Millennials, is in the middle of this coming-of-age phase of its life cycle. Its oldest members are approaching age 30; its youngest are approaching adolescence. Who are they? How are they different from—and similar to—their parents? How is their moment in history shaping them? And how might they, in turn, reshape America in the decades ahead? The Pew Research Center will try to answer these questions through a yearlong series of original reports that explore the behaviors, values and opinions of today's teens and twenty-somethings.

Source: Keeter, Scott, and Paul Taylor. "The Millennials." *Pew Research Center*. Pew Research Center, 10 Dec. 2009. Web. 17 June 2013.

Introductions

An introduction is a kind of roadmap to your paper: it tells your readers where you plan to go and why. In most forms of academic writing, the introduction not only presents the topic of the paper but also conveys a sense of why the topic is relevant and what the writer will say about it.

Below are four examples, each illustrating a common approach to introductions. The first three examples are from student essays: one from a paper written for an economics course, the second from a course on the history of modern China, and the third from an introductory psychology course. The fourth example is from an article by Deborah Tannen, a professor of linguistics at Georgetown University. Notice that, regardless of the approach, each introduction clearly establishes the focus of the paper and conveys a sense of the writer's main idea. Notice, too, how each introduction establishes the tone and style of the paper.

Getting Right to the Point

One of the most common mistakes students make when introducing an essay is saying too much. Often, the most effective introductions are those that get right to the point and move the reader quickly into the main body of the paper. Here's an example:

The Legalization of Prostitution

Prostitution is the "contractual barter of sex favors, usually sexual intercourse, for monetary considerations without any emotional attachment between the partners" (Grauerhold & Koralewski, 1991). Whenever this topic is mentioned, people usually shy away from it, because they are thinking of the actions involved in this profession. The purpose of this paper, however, is not to talk about these services, but to discuss the social, economic and legal issues behind prostitution.

Source: "Comments on an Economic Analysis Paper." *WAC Student Resources*. Coe Writing Center, 2001. Web. 17 June 2013.

This brief introduction quickly establishes the focus and main purpose of the paper. It also places the topic in the context of general perceptions of prostitution and clarifies that the writer will be examining that topic from a different angle. This is a good example of a writer efficiently introducing a topic. As this writer demonstrates, sometimes the best approach is the one that uses the fewest words.

Focusing on Context

This next example, from a history paper about the impact of Mao Zedong on modern China, illustrates how an academic writer can use techniques from narrative writing to introduce a topic and at the same time establish a context for the topic. This introduction begins with a brief description of the birthplace of Mao Zedong as a way to dramatize the main point of the paper that Mao "remains the central, dominant figure in Chinese political culture today." The second paragraph provides background information so that the reader can better appreciate Mao's significance to modern China, while the third paragraph establishes the focus of the paper, which examines Mao's enduring legacy in contemporary China.

Mao More Than Ever

Shaoshan is a small village found in a valley of the Hunan province, where, a little over a century ago, Mao Zedong was born. The first thing heard in Shaoshan is the music, and the music is inescapable. Suspended from posts towering over Mao's childhood home are loudspeakers from which the same tune is emitted over and over, a hit of the Cultural Revolution titled "We Love You, Mao."

The Chinese people were faced with an incredibly difficult situation in 1976 following the death of Mao Zedong. What was China to do now that the man whom millions accepted as the leader of their country's rebirth to greatness has passed away? China was in mourning within moments of the announcement. Although Mao rarely had been seen in public during the five years preceding his death, he was nevertheless the only leader that China had known since the Communist armies swept triumphantly into Peking and proclaimed the People's Republic twenty-seven years earlier. He was not only the originator of China's socialist revolution but its guide, its teacher, and its prophet.

Common sense foretold of the impossibility of erasing Communism and replacing Chairman Mao. He departed the world with his succession and China's future uncertain. With his death, historians and reporters around the world offered predictions of what was to become of China. They saw an instant end to Maoist theory. Through careful examination of Chinese life both under and after Mao, it is clear that the critics of 1976 were naïve in their prophecies and that Mao Zedong still remains the central, dominant figure in Chinese political culture today.

Source: "Comments on a Research Paper." *WAC Student Resources.* Coe Writing Center, 2001. Web. 17 June 2013.

In this example, the writer establishes the context by "telling the story" of Mao's enduring influence on China. This approach is common in the humanities (history, literature, and so on).

Using a Reference Point

Another common approach to introductions in academic writing is to use an established idea, point of view, development, text, or study as a reference point for the topic of the paper. In this example from a paper written for a psychology course, the writers begin by referring to a study of the anxiety people experience while waiting in hospital waiting rooms:

Sitting Comfort: The Impact of Different Chairs on Anxiety

Kutash and Northrop (2007) studied the comfort of family members in the ICU waiting room. They found that no matter the situation, waiting rooms are stressful for the patients and their families, and it is the nursing staff's job to comfort both. From this emotional distress many family members judged the waiting room furniture as "uncomfortable" and only talked about it in a negative context. From this study we have learned that there is a direct relationship between a person's emotional state and how that person perceives the physical state he or she is in, such as sitting in a chair. Is this relationship true in reverse as well? Can the way a person perceives his or her present physical state (such as sitting in a chair) affect his or her emotional state? This is the question that the present study sought to answer.

hxdbzxy/Shutterstock.com

Source: Baker, Jenna, Ashlynn Beacker, and Courtney Young. "Sitting Comfort: The Impact of Different Chairs on Anxiety." *Schemata* (2011): n. pag. Web. 15 June 2012.

Here the writers cite a previously published study that raises a question that is relevant to readers interested in psychology ("Can the way a person perceives his or her present physical state (such as sitting in a chair) affect his or her emotional state?"). The study serves as the reference point for the paper, and the question the writers pose clearly establishes the focus of the paper. One advantage of this approach is that the question sets up the expectation that the writer will answer the question. In this way, the writer gives the audience a clear sense of what will follow.

Telling an Anecdote

Using an anecdote to introduce a topic, which is common in many different kinds of writing, can be effective in academic writing as well. In this example, linguist Deborah Tannen shares an anecdote to illustrate the problem she will address in her article. Notice how she uses the anecdote to establish the focus of her paper and encourage the reader to continue reading:

Sex, Lies and Conversation

I was addressing a small gathering in a suburban Virginia living room—a women's group that had invited men to join them. Throughout the evening, one man had been particularly talkative, frequently offering ideas and anecdotes, while his wife sat silently beside him on the couch. Toward the end of the evening, I commented that women frequently complain that their husbands don't talk to them. This man quickly concurred. He gestured toward his wife and said, "She's the talker in our family." The room burst into laughter; the man looked puzzled and hurt. "It's true," he explained. "When I come home from work I have nothing to say. If she didn't keep the conversation going, we'd spend the whole evening in silence."

This episode crystallizes the irony that although American men tend to talk more than women in public situations, they often talk less at home. And this pattern is wreaking havoc with marriage.

Source: Tannen, Deborah. "Sex, Lies and Conversation: Why Is It So Hard for Men and Women to Talk to Each Other?" *Washington Post* 24 June 1990: C3. Print.

Using an anecdote can be very effective, but students sometimes devote too much time to the anecdote, which can make it more difficult for readers to see where the paper might be going. If you use this approach, keep the anecdote brief and follow it up with a few sentences indicating why you're sharing the anecdote and what it means—as Tannen does in her second paragraph.

Transitions

Earlier in this chapter we noted that, in effective academic writing, paragraphs must be coherent and cohesive (see page 122). The same is true for an essay or other kind of document as a whole. Your sentences can be clear and your paragraphs coherent and cohesive, but if you don't connect them to one another, your essay is likely to be more difficult for your readers to follow. The main tool for keeping your essays coherent and cohesive is the transition, which is why writing effective transitions is an essential skill in academic writing. Fortunately, it is a skill that is easy to develop.

What exactly is a *transition*? It is a device to get your reader from one paragraph—or section of your document—to the next. Transitions amount to signposts that keep your readers oriented and enable them to know where they are in your text. If you have written an effective introduction that tells your readers what to expect in your text, transitions signal when they have reached each main section.

It is important to remember that you don't need a transition between every paragraph in a document. Often, the connection between paragraphs is clear because the subject matter of one paragraph explicitly relates to the subject of the next. However, transitions are usually necessary

■ when there is an important shift in the focus of discussion from one paragraph to the next

■ when moving from one main section of a document to another

The section on "Achieving Cohesion" in paragraphs (page 125) describes two strategies for writing cohesive paragraphs that also can be used to write effective transitions between paragraphs to create more cohesive essays:

■ using linking words or phrases (e.g., *first, second, in addition, then, therefore, that*)

■ repeating key words and phrases

In addition, a third important strategy is to set up your transitions by letting a reader know what to expect in a section or in your entire document. For example, your introduction might explain that your essay will address four key questions. When making the transitions between the four main sections of your essay, you can refer back to those questions to remind your reader what will follow.

The following passage from a student literacy narrative illustrates these common strategies for transitions between paragraphs. In this slightly humorous narrative about the student's experience in a college writing class, the writer explains the first few weeks of the class. Notice how the transitions help keep the narrative coherent and enable the reader to follow the story more easily. (Key transition strategies are highlighted in yellow.)

5

1 Prior to college I had never had a true intensive course. My high school English classes consisted mostly of reading assigned literature, with the occasional plot summary, known as a book report, thrown in for variety. Never had a teacher of mine critiqued papers with anything more in mind than content, unless it was to point out some terrible structural flaw. That changed when I enrolled in college and found myself in a required course called Introduction to Academic Writing.

The introductory paragraph establishes the focus of the narrative. The final sentence in particular conveys a sense of what will follow.

2 Introduction to Academic Writing was designed in part to eliminate from the writing of incoming students any weaknesses or idiosyncrasies that they might have brought with them from high school. Run-on sentences, incoherent paragraphs, and incorrect footnoting were given particular emphasis. To address these issues, the professor assigned a great deal of work. Weekly journal assignments and multiple formal essays kept us very busy indeed. And then there were the informal in-class essays.

> This paragraph begins with a repeated phrase (*Introduction to Academic Writing*) that clearly links it to the last sentence of the preceding paragraph. Also, the final sentence of this paragraph sets up the transition to the next paragraph.

3 The first such essay took place on the second day of classes so that our professor could evaluate each student's strengths and weaknesses. Before accepting our work, however, she had us exchange papers with one another to see how well we could spot technical flaws. She then proceeded to walk around the room, interrupting our small-group discussions, and asked each of us what we thought of what we had read. It was not a comfortable situation, though the small size of the groups limited our embarrassment somewhat.

> The writer uses linking words (*the first such essay*) to make the transition to this paragraph. The same strategy is used for the transition to the following two paragraphs (*This unique brand; Eventually*).

4 This unique brand of academic humiliation was a palpable threat in class, which consisted mostly of students with little confidence in their writing abilities. Most of them seemed to be enrolled in majors other than English, and they viewed this remedial writing course as a painful, albeit necessary, endeavor. Our professor sympathized, I believe, and for the most part restricted her instruction to small groups and one-on-one sessions. But the in-class writing exercises were a daily hardship for the first few weeks of the semester, and I think most of us dreaded them.

5 Eventually, we were deemed ready for the first formal essay, which was a kind of expository writing in which we were to select an academic subject of interest to us and report on that subject to the rest of the class. Most of the students seemed wary of the assignment, because it was the first one in which we were given a choice of topic. All the in-class essays were on assigned topics. So the first source of anxiety was the uncertainty about which topics would be acceptable.

Although this example is narrative writing, which is less common than other forms of academic writing, its strategies for effective transitions are the same strategies used in analytical and argumentative writing. For example, here's a passage from a psychology research report published in a professional journal. The style of this passage reflects the formal writing typical of the social sciences, yet the transition strategies the authors use are the same as those in the passage from the student narrative essay above.

1 The Action-to-Action (ATA) model of Norman and Shallice (1986) has three subcomponents: *action schemas, contention scheduling,* and a *supervisory attentional system* (SAS).

> This paragraph establishes the expectation that the authors will discuss these three key concepts in turn, thus setting up the transitions in the following paragraphs.

2 Action schemas are specialized routines for performing individual tasks that involve well-learned perceptual-motor and cognitive skills. Each action schema has a current degree of activation that may be increased by either specific perceptual "trigger" stimuli or outputs from other related schemas. When its activation exceeds a preset threshold, an action schema may direct a person's behavior immediately and stereotypically toward performing some task. Moreover, on occasion, multiple schemas may be activated simultaneously by different trigger stimuli, creating error-prone conflicts if they entail mutually exclusive responses (e.g., typing on a keyboard and answering a telephone concurrently).

3 To help resolve such conflicts, the ATA model uses contention scheduling. It functions rapidly, automatically, and unconsciously through a network of lateral inhibitory connections among action schemas whose response outputs would interfere with each other (cf. Rumelhart & Norman, 1982). Through this network, an action schema (e.g., one for keyboard typing) that has relatively high current activation may suppress the activation of other potentially conflicting schemas (e.g., one for telephone answering). Contention scheduling allows task priorities and environmental cues to be assessed on a decentralized basis without explicit top-down executive control (Shallice, 1988). However, this may not always suffice to handle conflicts when new tasks, unusual task combinations, or complex behaviors are involved.

> In the first sentence of paragraph 3 the authors use two sets of repeated words or phrases along with a linking word (*such*). The first repeated word (*conflicts*) links this paragraph to the preceding one. The second repeated phrase (*contention scheduling*) links this paragraph to the first paragraph and reminds the reader that the discussion has now moved to the second of the three main concepts mentioned in that paragraph

4. Consequently, the ATA model also has an SAS. The SAS guides behavior slowly, flexibly, and consciously in a top-down manner. It helps organize complex actions and perform novel tasks by selectively activating or inhibiting particular action schemas, superseding the cruder bottom-up influences of contention scheduling and better accommodating a person's overall capacities and goals. For example, one might expect the SAS to play a crucial role during switches between unfamiliar incompatible tasks that are not ordinarily performed together.

> Like the previous paragraph, this one demonstrates two transition strategies: linking words (*Consequently* and *also*) and a key repeated term (*SAS*).

Source: Rubinstein, Joshua S., David E. Meyer, and Jeffrey E. Evans. "Executive Control of Cognitive Processes in Task Switching." *Journal of Experimental Psychology: Human Perception and Performance* 27.4 (2001): 764. Print.

The best time to strengthen the transitions in a piece of writing is during revision (Core Concept #8). Step #8 in Chapter 3 includes advice on revising to improve your transitions. At that point in the process of revision, review your entire draft, focusing only on transitions. As you do so, keep the following **guidelines for effective transitions** in mind:

- **Set up your transitions.** An effective introduction will convey a sense of the main parts of your text. Your transitions from one main part to the next should refer back to the key terms you use in your introduction. In addition, you can make transitions more effective by letting the reader know what will follow in each main section. In effect, write a brief introduction to each main section—as the authors did in the example above.

- **Use linking words or phrases.** As the examples in this section demonstrate, there are many common words and phrases that writers use to signal a transition from one point or topic to the next or from one main section of a document to the next. Here's a brief list of some of the most common linking words and phrases:

  next

  then

  also

  in addition

  similarly

  on the other hand

  therefore

  consequently

  first, second, third, …

finally

at the same time

sometimes

- **Repeat key words or phrases.** The examples included in this section illustrate how writers repeat key words or phrases to link one paragraph to the next and to signal to readers that they are making a transition from one point to another. Select these words and phrases carefully so that you can keep your writing cohesive without being repetitive. Repetition in itself is not a weakness in writing, but unnecessarily repeated words or phrases can make your prose tedious and distracting for readers.

WRITING PROJECTS | PRACTICING TRANSITIONS

Add transitions to the following passage to make it more cohesive and easier for a reader to follow:

Writing developed as a visual means of communication, and a long, continuing history of close incorporation of visual elements in many different text forms has been maintained. Illustrated manuscripts, calligraphy, and tapestries are but a few of the art forms in which distinctions between word and form are blurred to the point of meaninglessness. Olson (1992) reminds us, "The calligraphic (meaning 'words written by hand') form incorporates all the elements of a painting—line, shape, texture, unity, balance, rhythm, proportion—all within its own unique form of composition" (131).

The distance between the visual and the verbal forms of information practiced in verbal-based classrooms is highly artificial. Shuman and Wolfe (1990) draw what they see as "two pertinent conclusions": (1) Early composition that was used as a means of preserving and transmitting ideas and information through the ages took the forms of singing and drawings. (2) Early alphabetic writing was an art form that may have had less to do with composing the content of what was to be communicated than with the art form itself. "Obviously, connections between language and the arts have roots deep in antiquity" (2).

Olson explores connections between writing and art. She notes that the "Greeks chose to represent each spoken sound with a symbol (or letter). Just as speech developed out of the imitation of sound, writing developed out of the imitation of forms of real objects or beings. At the beginning of all writing stands the picture" (130).

Currently educators are interested in interdisciplinary approaches at all levels, primary through postsecondary. It is a particularly opportune moment to attempt instructional approaches that bring together art and writing.

Source: Pamela B. Childers, Eric H. Hobson, and Joan A. Mullin, Eds. "ARTiculating: Teaching Writing in a Visual World." *WAC Clearinghouse Landmark Publications in Writing Studies* (1998): 3–4. Print.

Designing Documents 6

RECENTLY, a friend of mine who works as a regional planner was asked to review a proposal. The proposal had been submitted to her organization by a consulting company that manages commercial and residential projects, such as strip malls, parks, and housing developments. The consulting company was seeking to be hired to create a development plan for the rural county where my friend works. It was a big proposal for a big project, and my friend had to evaluate it to help the county decide whether to hire the company to develop its regional plan. So she carefully studied the proposal, assessing the company's ideas for regional development as well as its ability to complete a good plan on time. The document was nearly 100 pages, with detailed analyses of issues like water flow, population density, and infrastructure (roads, bridges, and so on). My friend liked many aspects of the proposal, but her biggest complaint was that the document itself looked unprofessional. Although its analysis was sophisticated, with many graphs and tables, its design, she said, looked amateurish. More important, she found it difficult to locate important information in the document. The proposal, she said, just didn't look professional, which influenced her evaluation of it.

This anecdote underscores the importance of design in many documents—not only in professional settings such as my friend's workplace, but in many other contexts as well:

- A campus group that trains volunteer mentors for first-year students creates a flier to announce a meeting for new volunteers.

- A community organization that runs a food pantry develops a brochure to advertise its services to local residents.

- A college rugby club compiles an annual report, complete with photos and charts, for the campus athletic department.

And of course many college instructors expect students to include graphs, tables, and other visual elements in print reports and to make presentations using tools such as Prezi. In each case, a well-designed document is more likely to achieve its rhetorical purpose.

Because widely available technologies make it easy to create professional-looking documents, readers often expect more than well-written content. They want the content to be presented with appropriate graphics, attractive color schemes, and pleasing layouts. Such features are much more than ornamentation. The design of a document is a rhetorical tool that helps writers communicate ideas and information effectively to their audiences and convince readers that a document is worth reading. Effective document design also lends credibility to the writer. Today, knowing how to design a document well is an increasingly important part of being an effective writer.

This chapter will help you develop the skills you need to design documents that will achieve your rhetorical goals.

Understanding Document Design as a Rhetorical Tool

Imagine that you want to raise awareness among students on your campus about alcohol abuse. Here's a public service poster from a university health center that does just that:

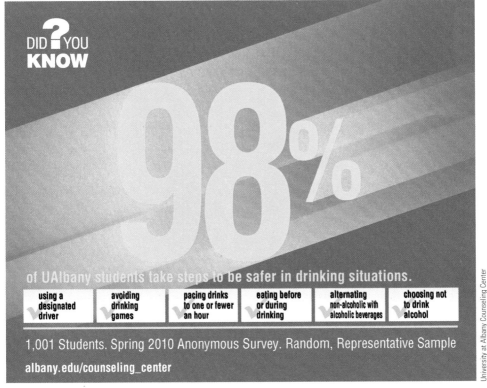

Source: Freidenberg, Brian M. *Did You Know?* Digital image. *Counseling Center.* University at Albany, State University of New York, n.d. Web. 17 June 2013.

What do you notice about this document? The authors certainly intend to catch your eye with the large yellow "98%" in the center of the page that contrasts with the darker background and the smaller text below it. Using color, layout, and font size strategically, they communicate a great deal of information with relatively few words. For example, they describe six different steps students can take to drink alcohol safely (using a designated driver, avoiding drinking games, and so on), and they identify the source of the information (a survey of students at that university). The layout of this information in a horizontal line of checked items at the bottom of the page sets it apart, making it more likely that you will read that information. And notice that the question in the upper left-hand corner of the document invites you into a kind of dialogue, a provocative way to entice students to read the entire document.

The authors of this poster have designed their document, first, to attract the attention of their intended audience (students at their university), and second, to communicate specific information efficiently to that audience. A more conventional document might be less effective in achieving these rhetorical goals, especially given how much information busy college students encounter in a typical day. For example, compare the poster to an email with the same information that might be sent to students as a public service announcement:

> Do you know that 98% of UAlbany students take steps to be safer in drinking situations? A random, anonymous survey of 1,001 students conducted during spring 2010 found that students take the following steps: using a designated driver, avoiding drinking games, pacing drinks to one or fewer an hour, eating before or during drinking, alternating non-alcoholic with alcoholic beverages, and choosing not to drink alcohol.

Which document is more likely to reach students? Which is more likely to grab students' attention? Which is more likely to be memorable to students?

Document design is a powerful way to make sure you reach an audience and convey ideas and information effectively. In designing your own documents, keep these points in mind:

- **Consider your audience.** The first step in designing a document is to identify the expectations of your intended audience and the rhetorical goals for your document. Who is your audience for this document? What kind of document are they likely to expect? What design features will appeal to them? A flier announcing a campus farmer's market probably won't appeal to residents of a local retirement community if it has the flashy colors and provocative features of the public service poster on page 150, which is intended for a much younger audience with very different tastes.

- **Consider your message.** Be clear about the ideas, information, or point you want to convey to your audience. What features will best help you convey your message? How might you use those features to emphasize key ideas and help readers find important information? For example, the large font and bright color of the figure "98%" in the poster on page 150 help emphasize the key point of the poster, which is that the vast majority of students on that campus try to use alcohol safely.

- **Avoid ornamentation.** Just as you should try to eliminate unnecessary information from a piece of writing, you should avoid design features that do little more than decorate your document. The images, graphics, font styles, colors, and layout you use should help you accomplish your rhetorical goals by communicating or emphasizing important ideas or information. If a design element doesn't help you accomplish your rhetorical goals, consider eliminating or changing it.

- **Make a good impression.** First impressions can influence how an audience responds to your document. If the design is effective, your audience is more likely to take your message seriously, and you are more likely to achieve your rhetorical goals. If your design is weak, you risk undermining your credibility, as happened to the authors of the poorly designed proposal in the anecdote at the beginning of this chapter.

EXERCISE 6A   EXAMINING THE DESIGN OF DOCUMENTS

1. Visit the websites of two or three restaurants in your town or neighborhood, and review their menus. Compare the way the menus present information. How are the menus organized? How easy is it to find information about specific items that you might want to order? Which menu looks most professional? Now identify specific features that make each menu appealing or not: the colors, the layout of the pages, the use of images or graphics, and so on. Consider how these elements help you find the menu items you are looking for. What conclusions about document design might you draw from this exercise?

2. Compare the design of two or more textbooks that you are currently using for your classes (or textbooks you have used in the past). Select a representative page from each textbook and compare them. What do you notice about each page? Which pages do you find most appealing? Which are easiest to read? On the basis of this compari-son, draw your own conclusions about which textbook has the most effective design.

Principles of Document Design

The public service poster on page 150 demonstrates four basic principles of document design:

- **Contrast:** a pronounced difference in color, size, or other design elements that can be used for emphasis or to help readers navigate a document
- **Repetition:** strategic repeating of text, color, patterns, or other features to emphasize infor-mation or ideas and show connections between content or sections of a document
- **Alignment:** the layout of elements of a page or document in relation to each other and to the page borders
- **Proximity:** the positioning of information or features next to one another to show connec-tions or emphasis

These four principles can guide your decisions about how to design a document to meet the needs of your rhetorical situation.

Contrast

Notice how the white text stands out against this black background.

This light-colored text is more difficult to see against the yellow background.

These two examples illustrate the value of contrast—in this case, contrasting colors—to communicate or emphasize ideas and information. Contrast that is sufficiently strong, as in the top example, helps convey information more easily. Poor contrast can obscure information and make it difficult for readers to navigate a document.

Writers use contrast for three main reasons:

- **To emphasize ideas or information.** Notice, for example, the color, size, and font style of the phrase "to emphasize ideas or information" make it stand apart from the rest of this paragraph and give it greater emphasis. Contrasting images—say, of a crying baby and a smiling child—might be used to communicate an idea or point—for example, about the nature of childhood.

- **To organize a document.** Contrast is a common way to help readers navigate a document. For example, headings or subtitles that appear in sizes or colors that are different from the main text indicate to readers where different sections of a document begin and end. Icons can be used to indicate special information.

- **To establish a focus.** Contrast can be used to convey a sense of the focus or main idea of a document. In the poster on page 150, for example, the large contrasting type size for the figure "98%" helps focus the reader's attention on the point that most students use alcohol safely.

Contrast is commonly created with color and different font sizes or styles. For example, **this 18-point font** is immediately noticeable in a paragraph full of 12-point font. Similarly, you can use **a different font style like this** to set a title, subheading, or key sentence apart from surrounding text.

FOCUS   Understanding Typography

Typography refers to letters and symbols in a document. It includes features such as *italics*, underlining, and **boldface** as well as the size and style of the font. You can use typography to make documents more readable, appealing, and easy to navigate. You can also use it to emphasize important ideas or information. Understanding a few basic concepts can help you use typography effectively in your documents.

(Continued)

Serif and sans serif. Fonts appear in two basic types: *serif*, which has small horizontal lines attached to the main lines of a letter, and *sans serif*, which does not.

serif   sans serif

Although the uses of these styles can vary, serif fonts are considered more traditional and are generally used in formal writing (such as academic assignments), whereas sans serif fonts tend to be considered more contemporary. Serif fonts are generally considered easier to read and are therefore the best choice for long passages of text (as in a traditional academic paper).

Font styles. Writers can choose from hundreds of font styles, including common styles such as Courier, Arial, and Garamond, as well as unusual styles, such as *Lucida Calligraphy* and Old English Text. Although it is tempting to use uncommon font styles, the rule of thumb is to select fonts that make your document readable. For most academic assignments, a traditional font such as Times Roman, is preferable. Also keep in mind that different font styles take up different amounts of space.

Font size. Fonts sizes are measured in points. The standard font size for most extended text is 12-point. Sometimes, larger font sizes, such as this 14-point font or this 18-point font, are used for titles and headings or in tables and charts. However, varying the font size too often can be distracting to readers, so select font sizes strategically and be consistent in sizing the fonts you use. For example, use the same font size for all extended text and another font size for all subtitles.

Repetition

The careful repetition of specific features of a text—such as words, color, graphics, and font sizes or styles—can help make a document more readable and coherent. For example, the repetition of certain design features on the first page of each chapter of this textbook (such as color, the placement and style of images, the font size, and the layout of the page) enables you to identify the beginning of a chapter quickly and easily. In this same way, you already use repetition to help readers navigate your conventional print documents. For example, numbers in the same location on each page and subheadings separated from the main text are common features of essays or reports to help readers follow a document.

This use of repetition is so common that we might not even notice it, yet it can be used to communicate or emphasize important information very efficiently. For instance, the familiar repetition of the shape and color scheme of road signs tells motorists unequivocally that the signs contain relevant information, such as whether a traffic light or a pedestrian crossing lies ahead.

FIGURE 6.1 Standard Road Signs

In the same way, a writer might use the repetition of a color or font style to indicate that certain information is important. Notice the repetition of the color blue on the web page about maintaining health in college in Figure 6.2. Blue is used to signal main ideas: the page title ("College Health: How to Stay Healthy) and the questions that represent key points ("What can I do to stay healthy?" "What should I know about nutrition and eating well?"). Blue is also used to lend a sense of cohesion to the page; notice, for example, that the bullets are blue.

FIGURE 6.2 College Health Web Page

College Health:
How to Stay Healthy

- Knowing About My Health
- First Aid Supplies
- Health Services
- How to Stay Healthy
- Common Health Problems
- Mental Health
- Homesickness

- Eating Disorders
- Alcohol and Drugs
- Sexual Health
- Sexual Assault/Rape
- Abusive Relationships
- Survival Tips
- Resources

What can I do to stay healthy?

Eat nutritious food, exercise, and get plenty of rest.

What should I know about nutrition and eating well?

Eating well will keep your body strong, and help your immune system fight off germs that cause colds and other common illnesses.

Learn to:

- Eat a variety of healthy foods. Try to eat 5-7 servings of fruits and vegetables every day.
- Choose foods that are baked, steamed, or grilled, rather than fried.
- Choose fresh foods such as steamed vegetables, fresh fruits, and grilled chicken instead of fast food or processed food.
- Limit the amount of salt that you use. Check out food labels to see if the food you choose is low in sodium.
- Cut down on junk food (candy, chips, soft drinks, etc.).
- Snack on healthy foods such as popcorn, string cheese, fruits, and vegetables.
- Drink 8-10 glasses of water or non-caffeinated fluids every day.
- Remember dairy products. Dairy products such as milk, yogurt, and cheese are high in calcium, which keeps your bones healthy. Eat or drink 3 servings a day of low-fat or fat-free dairy products.
- Take a daily multivitamin (with iron and 0.4 mg folic acid) and 600 units of vitamin D each day.
- If you're a vegetarian, get all the nutrients that you need .

What do I need to know about exercise?

Another important way to stay healthy, reduce stress, and manage your weight is to exercise. Try to include aerobic exercise, muscle strengthening, and stretching exercises into your daily routine. It is recommended that you exercise approximately 60 minutes each day.

- Aerobic exercises include biking, running, fast walking, swimming, dancing, soccer, step aerobics, etc. You can tell that you are doing aerobic exercise because your heart will speed up and you will start breathing faster. However, you should still be able to talk when you are doing aerobic exercise.
- Strengthening exercises (such as sit-ups, push-ups, leg lifts, or weight training) will build up your muscles and keep your bones healthy.
- Stretching exercises (such as yoga) will make you more flexible, so you will be less likely to strain a muscle.
- You can also get exercise by doing simple things, such as walking or riding a bike (with a helmet, of course), instead of driving or taking the bus.

Center for Young Women's Health

Source: College Health: How to Stay Healthy. *Center for Young Women's Health.* 1 Feb. 2013. Web. 24 June 2013

Alignment

Alignment is the primary means by which writers make documents easy to read and create a sense of unity on a page or screen. When you set margins for a report or essay and keep all the paragraphs justified to the left-hand margin, you are using alignment to make your document easier to follow.

Readers depend on conventions for alignment—such as justifying paragraphs to the left or centering titles—which standardize some elements of document design to avoid confusion.

Because of these conventions, most readers find it annoying to read text that is aligned to the right-hand margin. And notice how the insertion of columns in the middle of this paragraph makes it harder to follow.

Writers can use alignment to present information efficiently and in visually appealing ways. Notice how the columns at the top of the web page in Figure 6.2 make it easy for a reader to find the right link to other pages on that website. Notice, too, that the bullet points are all aligned in the same way: indented from the left margin. Such an alignment helps set off the main questions and makes it easier for readers to follow the text.

In some kinds of documents, including brochures, newsletters, and web pages, alignment is an essential tool for designing a page or screen that is both visually appealing and easy for a reader to navigate. When aligning elements on a page, consider how the placement of elements will draw a reader's eye and enable the reader to move comfortably from one element to the next.

Proximity

Proximity creates cohesion and shows relationships among elements on a page or screen. Using this principle can help you create documents that are less cluttered and more efficiently organized, especially when you are combining text with visual elements.

Proximity can have a big impact on the appearance and effectiveness of a page. Let's imagine that you are part of a student organization that oversees all club sports on your campus, and you are creating a one-page flier to inform students about the different club sports available to them. You might simply list all the sports:

Join a Club Sport!

Softball	Swimming
Ski Team	Badminton
Bowling	Men's Baseball
Field Hockey	Equestrian
Fencing	Women's Ultimate Frisbee
Wrestling	Men's Ultimate Frisbee
Men's Soccer	Women's Soccer
Snowboarding	Ice Hockey
Men's Volleyball	Men's Lacrosse
Mixed Martial Arts	Women's Volleyball
Women's Rugby	Tae Kwon Do

This unorganized list is visually aligned but tedious to read. To make it easier for students to make sense of the information, you can organize the sports by categories and place similar sports together:

Join a Club Sport!

Co-Ed Sports
- Badminton
- Bowling
- Equestrian
- Fencing
- Swimming
- Tae Kwon Do
- Ultimate Frisbee

Winter Sports
- Hockey
- Ski Team
- Snowboarding

Men's Team Sports
- Baseball
- Lacrosse
- Mixed Martial Arts
- Soccer
- Wrestling

Women's Team Sports
- Field Hockey
- Rugby
- Softball
- Soccer
- Volleyball

Simply by placing similar items together and adding space between the groups, you have organized the page in a way that makes it easier for a reader to find relevant information.

In more sophisticated documents that include images and graphics as well as text, the proximity of elements can significantly improve appearance and readability. For example, notice how many different elements catch your eye on this main web page from Yahoo.com. To make it easier for viewers to find information on a screen with so many elements, similar items are grouped together:

Key links are listed vertically here.

News stories appear together in the center of the page.

Current updated information is placed together in the right-hand column.

Source: *Yahoo!* Yahoo!, n.d. Web. 1 May 2013.

Strategic use of proximity can make such a complex page even more readable. Here's the main page for the social media site Flickr:

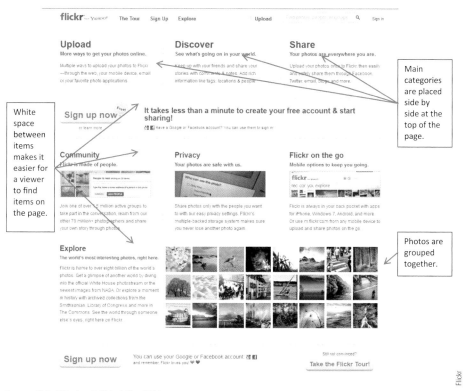

Source: *Flickr*. Yahoo!, n.d. Web. 1 May 2013.

Careful grouping of similar items and the use of white space make this page appear clean and coherent, even though it contains a great deal of information. Notice, too, that repetition, contrast, and alignment make the page visually appealing and well organized: The main titles appear in similar font style and size (repetition) but in larger fonts than other text on the page (contrast), which makes them more noticeable; in addition, all the main items are aligned vertically and horizontally, creating a balanced, cohesive, and unified page.

The most effectively designed documents, even relatively simple print texts, use all four design principles together. **When deciding on the design of a document, follow three basic steps:**

1. **Consider your rhetorical situation.** Who is your intended audience? What are your goals in addressing that audience with this document? What expectations might this audience have when it comes to the design of a document?

2. **Be clear about your message.** What is the central point you want to make with this document? What primary information do you hope to communicate?

3. **Apply the four principles of basic design.** How can you use contrast, repetition, alignment, and proximity to communicate your message effectively to your intended audience? How can you use these principles to make your document appealing and efficient?

Use the four basic principles of document design to evaluate this flier from a public television station. The document is intended to help parents identify potential reading problems in their children. Assess how effectively the document uses design elements to convey its message to its intended audience.

Place your school name
or logo here

Helpful information about learning brought to you by Reading Rockets, Colorín Colorado, and LD OnLine

Recognizing Reading Problems

Learning to read is a challenge for many kids, but most can become good readers if they get the right help. Parents have an important job in recognizing when a child is struggling and knowing how to find help.

What to look for:
- Difficulty rhyming
- Difficulty hearing individual sounds
- Difficulty following directions
- Difficulty re-telling a story
- Struggles to sound out most words
- Avoids reading aloud

What to do:
- **Step 1: Meet with your child's teacher**
  Gather examples of your child's work that reflect your concerns. Ask the teacher for his/her observations and discuss what can be done at school and at home. Stay in touch with the teacher to monitor your child's progress.
- **Step 2: Meet with the principal and/or reading specialist**
  If your child's performance does not improve, meet with other professionals in the building to see if there are classes, services, or other interventions available.
- **Step 3: Get a referral for special education**
  If you have tried all interventions, request an evaluation. Talk to the principal to schedule this.
- **Step 4: Get an evaluation**
  A professional team—which may include a school psychologist, a speech-language pathologist, or a reading specialist—gives your child a series of tests and determines whether s/he is eligible to receive special education services.
- **Step 5: Determine eligibility**
  - If your child is found eligible for services, you and the school develop your child's Individualized Education Program (IEP), a plan that sets goals based on your child's specific learning needs and offers special services like small group instruction or assistive technology.
  - If your child is not eligible, stay involved and keep talking to the teacher about your child's progress. You can also turn to private tutoring for extra support.

Check out the *Assessment* section for more information on identifying reading problems:
www.ReadingRockets.org/article/c68

Visit our sister sites, ColorinColorado.org and LDOnLine.org, for more information about learning.

Reading Rockets, Colorín Colorado, and LD OnLine are services of public television station WETA, Washington, D.C. Reading Rockets is funded by the U.S. Department of Education, Office of Special Education Programs. Colorín Colorado, a web service to help English language learners become better readers, receives major funding from the American Federation of Teachers. Additional funding is provided by the National Institute for Literacy and the U.S. Department of Education, Office of Special Education Programs. LD OnLine is the world's leading website on learning disabilities and ADHD, with major funding from Lindamood-Bell Learning Processes.

Reading Rockets

Source: *Recognizing Reading Problems*, Reading Rockets. WETA. 2012. Web. 12 April 2013.

Working with Visual Elements

Many documents include photographs, charts, graphics, and other visual elements. Increasingly, college instructors expect students to incorporate such elements into conventional papers. However, visual elements should never be used simply as ornamentation; rather, they should be used in a way that communicates information, conveys important ideas, and enhances the effectiveness of the document.

This section provides advice on using two common kinds of visual elements:

- tables, graphs, and charts
- images

Working with Tables, Graphs, and Charts

Many college assignments require students to work with quantitative information. For example, an analysis of the economic impact of college loan debt for an economics course will likely include various kinds of statistical data. Often, such data are most effectively presented in a table, bar graph, line graph, or pie chart. Contemporary word processing programs make it easy to create such elements in a variety of formats. However, the key to using such elements effectively is knowing what you want your readers to understand from the information you are presenting. Consider:

- **What is the nature of the information?** Numerical data can be easy to convert into a chart or table. Other kinds of information, such as directions for a procedure or a list of specific responses to a survey question, might not work as well in a graphical format. A chart or table should make the information easier for a reader to understand. Avoid using a graphical format if it makes the information more complicated or confusing.

- **What is the purpose of the information?** You present information for various reasons: to explain a concept, event, or development; to support a claim or assertion; to strengthen an argument; to illustrate a key idea or principle. The purpose can shape your decision about how best to present the information. For example, if you want to emphasize a specific set of statistics to support a central claim in an argument, using a graph or pie chart to present the data can make them more persuasive.

- **Tables, charts, and graphs have four basic elements:**
  - a title
  - a vertical axis, called the y axis
  - a horizontal axis, called the x axis
  - the main body of data

6

Numerical data such as survey results are commonly reported in the form of tables or graphs, but deciding how best to present that information depends on how you are using it in your report. Let's imagine you are writing a report on the benefits of a college education and want to report the results of a survey of students who graduated in the past three years from three different departments on your campus. The survey was intended to learn about average starting salaries of graduates from your school. If you are simply reporting the survey results to help your readers understand the average salaries of recent graduates, you might use a simple **table**. In this example, the *y* axis is used for the three different departments and the *x* axis for the three recent years; the main body of data is the starting salaries. The table would look like this:

Title ⟶ **Average Starting Salaries in Three Departments by Year of Graduation**

x axis: graduation years

Department	2009	2010	2011
A	30,653	32,898	49,519
B	42,289	44,904	52,698
C	46,172	61,538	66,357

y axis: departments

main data: salaries

This table helps readers easily find the average salary for a specific department in a specific graduation year. Consider how much more tedious it is for readers to read an explanation of this information, which might look like this:

> The average starting salary for students who graduated from Department A in 2009 was $30,653; in 2010 it was $32,898, and in 2011 it was $49,519. For students who graduated from Department B in 2009, the average starting salary was $42,289; in 2010 it was $44,904, and in 2011 it was $52,698. Students who graduated from Department C in 2009 earned an average starting salary of $46,172; for 2010 graduates the average starting salary was $61,538, and in 2011 it was $66,357.

Although presenting numerical information visually isn't always the most effective approach, in a case like this one, it is much more efficient than a verbal explanation.

A simple table might be too limited for presenting more complicated bodies of data, especially if you want to compare information. Let's say that for the same report on the benefits of college, you wanted to emphasize differences in the potential earnings of students entering specific professions. A **bar graph** is an effective means for comparing information. This graph presents salary ranges in a way that makes it easy for a reader to compare the top, median, and bottom salaries in three different professions:

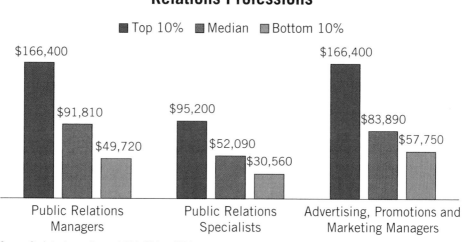

Salary Range for Advertising and Public Relations Professions

■ Top 10%   ■ Median   ■ Bottom 10%

Public Relations Managers: $166,400 / $91,810 / $49,720
Public Relations Specialists: $95,200 / $52,090 / $30,560
Advertising, Promotions and Marketing Managers: $166,400 / $83,890 / $57,750

Source: *Gradschools.com*. N.p., n.d. Web. 15 June 2013.

Here the *y* axis is used for salary ranges and the *x* axis for the type of position; the data are the salaries.

If you wanted to show a trend or trajectory reflected in statistical information over time, **a line graph** might be a better option. For example, let's say you included in your report data to show trends in the starting salaries of male and female college graduates over the past two decades. This line graph makes it very easy for readers to see those trends and compare the salaries of men and women who earned college degrees:

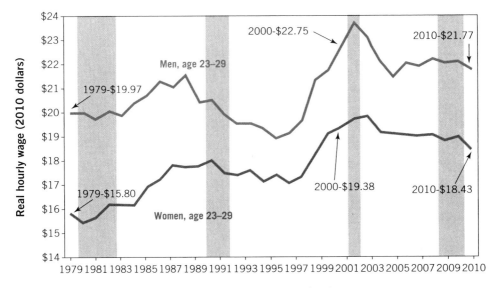

New college graduates losing ground on wages
Entry-level wages of male and female college graduates, 1979–2010

Source: EPI's analysis of the Current Population Survey, Outgoing Rotations Group.

Source: *New College Graduates Losing Ground on Wages.* Digital image. *Trends in Starting Salaries for College Grads.* Sociological Images, 4 Sept. 2011. Web. 17 June 2013.

In this example, the *y* axis shows hourly wages and the *x* axis shows the years from 1979 to 2010.

Tables, graphs, and charts can present information efficiently, but they also can be misleading. For example, let's say you want to show the percentage of four items in the budget of a student organization you work for: item A (11%), item B (42%), item C (5%), and item D (42%). In addition, you want to highlight item C, which is the smallest expenditure. Your pie chart might look like this:

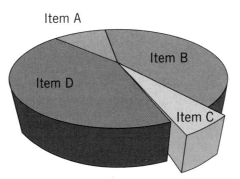

Source: "Misleading Graph." *Wikipedia.* Wikipedia Foundation. N.d. Web. 15 June 2013.

This three-dimensional chart, which makes it seem that you are looking at it from the side and slightly above it, is visually striking. Notice, however, that item C, which is only 5% of the budget, appears bigger than item A, which is 11% of the budget. Now here's the same information presented in a simpler, two-dimensional pie chart:

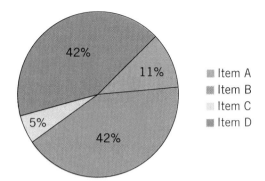

Source: "Misleading Graph." *Wikipedia*. Wikipedia Foundation. N.d. Web. 15 June 2013.

In this case, the simpler chart presents the information more accurately. Keep in mind that small changes in the design of a table, chart, or graph can dramatically affect the appearance of the information, sometimes making small differences appear much larger and thus conveying a misleading idea about that information. Although such strategies might seem effective in supporting a claim or point of view, they might also be ethically questionable. You should always use graphical elements in a way that presents information not only accurately but also ethically.

Working with Images

For many documents, effective design includes the use of images, but simply incorporating images into a document isn't necessarily enough to improve its design. Using images effectively is a matter of making sure the images are appropriate for your document and help address your rhetorical situation.

When using images, follow the same basic principles that apply to document design in general (see page 152):

■ **Consider your audience.** The images you select should be relevant to your subject matter and appropriate for your rhetorical situation. For example, a photograph of a car on a brochure about campus transportation services is probably a poor choice if the majority of students live on campus, do not drive cars to campus, and use the campus bus service. Moreover, consider whether the images you select might seem confusing or offensive to your audience. A photograph that might convey relevant information dramatically could also weaken your document if the image is considered inappropriate for some reason by your readers.

■ **Consider your message.** Images in your document should reinforce important ideas or information. Ideally, images should convey information rather than just supplement written text. For example, a photograph of a specific location should enable the audience to gain an understanding of that location without a lengthy verbal description to accompany the image.

- **Avoid ornamentation.** Sometimes, images are used to enhance the appearance of a document, but too many images used simply as decoration can become distracting for readers and therefore undermine the document's effectiveness.

- **Make a good impression.** Any images used in a document should contribute to the overall impression a document makes on the intended audience. A poorly selected image could weaken an otherwise effective document.

In addition to these basic principles, **consider how the content and perspective of an image fit your rhetorical situation**. For example, compare these two versions of the same photograph:

artcphotos/Shutterstock

artcphotos/Shutterstock

What is the difference between them? How does the potential impact of each differ? As this example demonstrates, simply "cropping" an image—that is, selecting a section of it and eliminating the rest—can dramatically change its impact and message. In this example, the version on the left might be appropriate for a report in a zoology class that includes descriptions of various kinds of raptors; the photograph could be used to show the size and color of a specific species of raptor. The cropped version on the right might be used to emphasize the extraordinary eyesight of raptors or to dramatize the fierce nature of a particular species. Your rhetorical purpose should dictate how you use an image and how you might alter it.

The **perspective** of an image can have a powerful effect on the message it communicates. Let's imagine you are writing an analysis of the social and economic impact of severe weather, such as a hurricane. The photograph on the next page dramatically conveys the devastating effects of the storm on property as well as the lives on local residents.

FEMA/Alamy

Notice that the perspective from which the photograph was taken (above and at a distance from the subjects) highlights the sense of vulnerability of the people in the photo, who appear small in comparison to the damaged homes surrounding them. This photo would be less effective in conveying these ideas if it were taken from ground (or water) level or from closer to the subjects. This photograph dramatically highlights the extent of storm-caused devastation and its impact on residents in a way that would be challenging to explain in words alone. At the same time, such an image can provoke strong emotions in readers and therefore can be used to influence readers—for example, to convince readers of the need to prepare for future storms or to contribute to a fund to help storm victims.

Like any other design elements, images should be placed strategically so that they convey their messages without undermining the overall appearance of a document. Images that are too large, for example, might distract a reader from other important information on a page. Images that are too small might not communicate important information clearly.

1. Imagine you are writing an analysis of the impact of smartphone technology on college students for a general audience. For each of the following items, decide whether to present the information in a chart, table, graph, or written description; explain your reasons for your decision in each case:

   - The most common uses of smartphone among college students are surfing the Internet, texting, and playing games; 85% of students report using their smart phones for playing games much more often than for any other purpose.

   - In 2010, 42% of college students reported owning a smartphone. In 2013, 73% of college students reported owning a smartphone. In 2010, 27% of Americans owned smartphones. In 2013, 65% of Americans owned smartphones.

   - Since 2008, sales of smartphones have increased by an average of 15% annually.

   - In 2009, college students spent an average of $65 per month for their cell phone service. In 2012, college students spent an average of $80 per month for smartphone service.

2. Using some of the information in Question #1, create a table, graph, and chart. (You can easily create these elements using a word processing program such as Microsoft Word.) Use the same information for each graphic. Compare the table, chart, and graph. What are the differences in the way they present the same information? What advantages and disadvantages do you see to each kind of graphic?

3. Using the example from Question #1, search online to find one or two images that you might use in your analysis of smartphones. Explain how you would use each image in your analysis. Justify your selection of images in terms of how they would help you accomplish specific rhetorical goals.

Designing Documents: Three Sample Projects

This section presents three common kinds of projects that illustrate how the same basic design features can make different kinds of documents effective in meeting the needs of a rhetorical situation.

Print Documents

For most college assignments, you are likely to be asked to submit a conventional paper, whether in hard copy or in a digital form (such as a Microsoft Word file), but even conventional papers can be more effective when writers apply the principles of design. Whenever you submit a conventional paper for an assignment, be sure to follow the appropriate conventions for formatting, which include such elements as font size, the uses of underlining and boldface, and the format for citing sources. (See Chapters 10 and 11 for information about proper format for papers in MLA and APA style.) You can also use the design principles in this chapter to enhance even the most traditional kind of paper by making sure that your font sizes and styles are consistent, you use features such as underlining strategically, and you avoid ornamentation.

Sometimes, however, your rhetorical situation might call for a print document that is not a conventional paper—for example, a flier, brochure, or memo. In such cases, applying the principles of document design can enhance the document's effectiveness, even when the document is relatively simple. Here, for example, is a one-page flier with information for college students about getting proper sleep. The flier was developed by a college health and counseling center and made available in print as well as in PDF format on the center's website. It illustrates how even a basic print document can more effectively meet the needs of a rhetorical situation when design principles are carefully applied.

1. Consider the rhetorical context. ⇒ **2. Be clear about your message.** ⇒ **3. Apply the principles of design.**

- The health and counseling center helps students deal with lifestyle and health issues common to college life. One such problem is insomnia. The center's goal is to inform students on its campus about the importance of proper sleep without overwhelming busy students with information.

- The main point is to show that students can use several easy strategies to avoid insomnia and get proper rest. Also, knowing the common causes of poor sleep can help students avoid sleep problems.

- The one-page flier incorporates no images and only two small graphics, but it uses the principles of contrast, alignment, and repetition to convey a great deal of information efficiently and to reinforce the main point about getting proper sleep.

Contrast: Titles and headings are larger and in different font styles than the main text, making them easier to see and more helpful to readers looking for information.

Layout: Contact information is placed prominently in the upper-right-hand corner to make it easy for students to find.

health.geneseo.edu

Division of Student and Campus Life
State University of New York at Geneseo
1 College Circle, Geneseo, New York 14454
Phone: (585) 245-5716; Fax: (585) 245-5071

GETTING A GOOD NIGHT'S SLEEP

Insomnia Triggers to Avoid

Diet. caffeine; alcohol; nicotine; prescription and non-prescription medication, including sleeping pills
Lifestyle. irregular bedtimes; exercising just before bedtime/lack of exercise; daytime naps

Bedroom Environment. noise; light
Psychological Factors. academic and other stress; family problems; other interpersonal issues

Alignment: Document is aligned vertically. Main text is justified on both the left and right margins to highlight the connections among the main points and give the page a coherent appearance.

Behavioral Strategies for Improving Sleep

Develop a Bedtime Routine. Stop doing anything stimulating (including studying!) about a half hour *before* you are ready to go to bed. Develop a wind-down ritual that includes doing something relaxing—such as reading for pleasure, listening to soft music, watching a mindless TV show, performing gentle stretches—followed by set pre-bed activities (e.g., washing up, brushing your teeth). As much as possible, you should try to go to bed at about the same time every night. Finally, try to get up at approximately the same time every day as well; don't oversleep to make up for lost sleep.

Plan the Right Time to Go To Bed. Go to bed *at the time when you usually fall asleep*—i.e., if you usually fall asleep at 2 a.m., go to bed *then*, not at 12 a.m. Once your body adjusts to this, you can gradually try pushing this time back earlier, first to 1:45 a.m., then to 1:30 a.m., etc.

Stop Intrusive Thoughts. Keep a pad and pencil handy by your bed. If you think of something you want to remember, jot it down. Then let the thought go; there will be no need to lie awake worrying about remembering it. You might also want to try this visualization technique: pretend that your mind is a chalk board. Every time a worrisome thought enters your head, visualize it as written on the chalk board and then immediately erase it. Keep erasing these thoughts as they pop up and refuse to think about them until later. Remember that sometimes it doesn't hurt to be like Scarlet O'Hara and say "I'll think about that tomorrow!"

Reduce Physical Stress. If you find that your are physically unable to relax, you might benefit from progressive muscle relaxation, a technique which involves alternately tensing and relaxing each major muscle in your body one-by-one. For example, starting with your upper body, flex your shoulders tightly towards your ears. Hold this position, making the muscles as tight as you can, for 10 seconds. Release and relax your shoulders, noticing the difference between the tense and relaxed positions and feeling the warmth associated with the relaxation of the muscle; relax and breathe for 15-20 seconds. Continue this process with the other muscles in your body, working from your shoulders, neck, and arms down to your midsection, buttocks, and legs.

Get Out of Bed! If you are lying in bed and are unable to sleep, the best thing you can do is to get *out of bed.* Most people fall asleep within 15 minutes of going to bed, so if you're not asleep after half an hour, get up and go elsewhere to engage in a quiet activity—reading, writing letters, etc. Do not eat, drink, or smoke, which could cause you to wake up for these things in the future. When you start to feel sleepy, return to bed. Repeat this routine as often as necessary, and follow these same steps if you wake up in the middle of the night and can't fall back asleep. If you awake in the early morning hours, get up to start your day. Try to avoid naps; instead, go to bed your usual time the following night.

Repetition: Main points all appear in italics and boldface and have the same sentence structure.

Other Resources

NOTE: Both of the books below can be borrowed from the Counseling Services Self-Help Lending Library, Lauderdale 205.

📖 *Getting a Good Night's Sleep*—This book by Moore-Ede and LeVert helps identify factors which affect sleep, find solutions to common sleep problems, develop more healthy sleep habits, and work towards stress reduction.

📖 *The Relaxation and Stress Reduction Workbook*—This book by Eshelman and McKay contains in-depth descriptions of various techniques for increasing relaxation and reducing stress, both of which improve sleep.

Contrast: Icons indicate that this information is different from the main text.

Proximity: Like items are grouped together, making it easier for readers to sort through the information.

Still having problems? Visit us on the web at go.geneseo.edu/HotTopics and select "College Students & Sleep."

because it's your health.

Rev. 2/12

Source: Division of Student and Campus Life. Getting a Good Night's Sleep. Geneseo, NY: State University of New York at Geneseo, 2008. Web. 15 May 2013. Available at http://www.geneseo.edu/health/sleep; see also http://www.geneseo.edu/health/sleep.

Prezi Presentation

College students today are routinely asked to make presentations as part of their assignments. Often, students turn to presentation software, especially PowerPoint, which enables a speaker to present information visually to an audience. Prezi is an online tool for making presentations that is similar to PowerPoint in that it enables a writer to convey information efficiently and in visually engaging ways on screens or "slides." (See "Using Prezi.") Like PowerPoint, Prezi also allows the writer to embed images, sound, and video in a presentation. However, there are **two important differences between Prezi and PowerPoint:**

- PowerPoint presentations usually supplement the presenter's spoken words. By contrast, Prezi presentations are generally intended to be viewed online rather than presented by the author. However, increasingly students use Prezi in place of PowerPoint to supplement their oral presentations.

- Unlike PowerPoint, which requires you to present information sequentially from one slide to the next, Prezi is a dynamic tool that enables you to arrange text and images on a single screen according to an organizing theme or metaphor; a viewer clicks arrows to move from one place on the screen to another to follow a story or access information. Each individual screen in a Prezi presentation is therefore a section of the whole presentation rather than a discrete slide, as in PowerPoint.

Despite these differences, the same principles for designing an effective PowerPoint presentation apply to Prezi. The best presentations

- are well organized
- have a coherent visual theme
- do not overwhelm the viewer with text
- take advantage of the visual capabilities of the presentation tool
- apply the principles of design

SIDEBAR   USING PREZI

Although there are differences between Prezi and PowerPoint, learning to use Prezi is no more difficult than learning to use PowerPoint. To use Prezi, you must create a Prezi account (visit prezi.com). The Prezi website includes a great deal of information and advice for using the tool and taking advantage of its multimedia capabilities.

Here's an example of a Prezi presentation that meets these criteria and uses design principles effectively. The author, Hayley Ashburner, created this presentation for an assignment in a writing class at the University of North Carolina at Wilmington. The assignment called for students to tell their own literacy histories and how their experiences fit into larger cultural and historical contexts. Hayley's narrative focused on her journey from her birthplace in South Africa to a new home in Australia and the impact of that journey on her literacy and use of technology.

1. Consider the rhetorical context. ⇒ **2. Be clear about your message.** ⇒ **3. Apply the principles of design.**

- Hayley's presentation was intended for students in her writing class, but because it would be available online at prezi.com, it might also be viewed by a much broader audience. Her primary purpose was to tell her literacy history in a way that was consistent with the expectations of her course, but she also wanted her story to resonate with viewers outside her class who might simply be interested in her unique story.

- Hayley's main idea was that her experiences growing up in two different cultures shaped her as a person and as a reader and writer. She wanted to explore how her experiences affected her sense of herself and her uses of literacy and technology in her life.

- Hayley developed her presentation so a viewer could follow her journey as a person who grew up in two different cultures. She relied on the principles of proximity and alignment to make her presentation engaging and to organize her journey into a coherent story.

Here's the main screen of Hayley's presentation, titled "African Dreams":

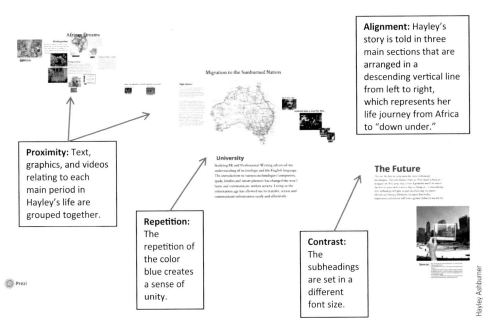

Alignment: Hayley's story is told in three main sections that are arranged in a descending vertical line from left to right, which represents her life journey from Africa to "down under."

Proximity: Text, graphics, and videos relating to each main period in Hayley's life are grouped together.

Repetition: The repetition of the color blue creates a sense of unity.

Contrast: The subheadings are set in a different font size.

Hayley Ashburner

A viewer navigates the presentation by clicking arrows that appear at the bottom of the screen. Here's what a viewer sees after the first three clicks:

1. The first click emphasizes the title, "African Dreams":

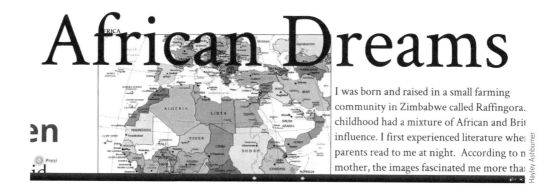

I was born and raised in a small farming community in Zimbabwe called Raffingora. childhood had a mixture of African and Brit influence. I first experienced literature whe parents read to me at night. According to n mother, the images fascinated me more tha

2. The next click zooms in on a map to show Hayley's birthplace:

3. The next click highlights text describing Hayley's early years:

I was born and raised in a small farming community in Zimbabwe called Raffingora. My childhood had a mixture of African and British influence. I first experienced literature when my parents read to me at night. According to my mother, the images fascinated me more than the words. My brothers and I were exposed to a variety of music by my parents and encouraged to perform in community plays.

Hayley Ashburner

Throughout her presentation, which included 35 separate screens, Hayley combined carefully written text with images and video clips to keep her audience engaged and to make her story coherent. Her selection of these elements also reflected her effort to communicate her main point about the influence of culture on her. The text in the following screen, for example, explains how various media helped her become familiar with Australian culture:

Television, phones, radio and computers helped my family adjust to life in Australia. The internet offered a cost effective way to communicate with friends and family back in Zimbabwe. Whilst, local television and radio exposed us to Australian culture, lifestyle and events. Listening to the radio, watching television and communicating with new peers changed the way I spoke. "Ya" became "yeah", "Chum" became "Mate" and "That's tight" became "hell good!" It also advanced my taste in music.

Hayley Ashburner

The next few clicks take the viewer through two embedded videos that illustrate her evolving taste in music:

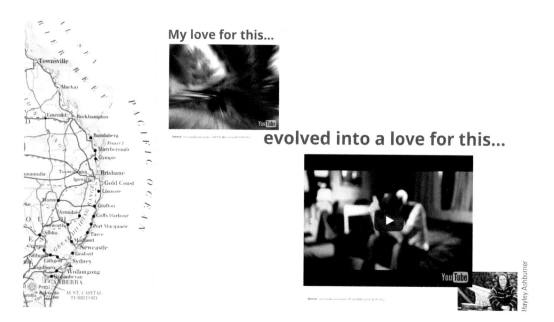

My love for this...

evolved into a love for this...

Hayley Ashburner

Clicking the video on the left starts a video clip with music that Hayley listened to in South Africa; clicking the right-hand video starts music that she listened to in Australia. Using sound and video in this way, she conveys to the viewer a deeper sense of her experience. The proximity of these videos and the contrast between them highlight the change in her musical tastes over time and communicate a sense of her development as a person.

(You can view Hayley's complete presentation at http://prezi.com/c1q2bitx009e/literacy-narrative/).

Designing a Website

Websites are an invaluable means by which organizations and individuals establish a presence and communicate information to various audiences. Web authoring software (e.g., Dreamweaver) can make it easy to create a sophisticated website, but the use of basic design principles is what makes a website rhetorically effective. The most effective websites are:

- **Clean and uncluttered.** Too much text and too many images can make a website messy and difficult for visitors to find information. A website should not overwhelm visitors. Use relevant graphics that bconvey important ideas or information, and keep text limited and easy to read.

- **Easy to navigate.** Websites are tools that should be easy for visitors to use. The design should enable visitors to find information easily and quickly. Even extensive websites with many separate pages can be designed so that visitors don't get lost or confused as they seek specific information.

- **Coherent.** Appealing websites have a consistent appearance that unifies the various pages and gives the entire site a feeling of coherence. Color schemes, font styles, and graphics tend to be consistent from one page to another, which can give the site a sense of focus and make it easier for visitors to find what they are looking for.

Following these guidelines and applying the principles of design can give a website a professional appearance and enhance its ability to address its intended audience. This website was developed for the Capital District Writing Project, a non-profit organization that promotes effective writing instruction in schools and provides services to teachers, students, and communities to help improve writing. Shown here is the main page of the site. Notice how clean and uncluttered the page appears. It also has a coherent visual theme, with two main colors and consistent font styles and sizes, that is applied to all individual pages on the site. Significantly, the page is designed so that various audiences—teachers, school administrators, and parents—can get a sense of the organization's purpose and find the specific information they need.

1. Consider the rhetorical context.	2. Be clear about your message.	3. Apply the principles of design.
• The organization serves teachers, students, and schools in its region. Its website is intended to convey a sense of its mission to those audiences and to provide relevant information about its services. It must compete with many other organizations that are involved in education.	• The central point of the main page of the website is that the organization is an important resource for teachers and administrators interested in improving writing, teaching, and learning in their school districts.	• The main page of the website uses contrast, alignment, and proximity to convey its message and highlight important information contained on the website. It presents a clear and professional image through its strategic use of image, layout, and color.

Capital District Writing Project

Notice that the main elements on this page are easier to find because of the strategic use of white space between them. Also, the single image of a teacher writing reflects the organization's purpose without distracting a visitor. The navigation bar includes links for specific audiences.

Finding Source Material

RECENT STUDIES INDICATE that research-based writing, which has always been a mainstay of academic writing, is becoming ever more common in the assignments students encounter in their college courses. So being able to work effectively with sources is essential for successful college writing. This chapter will guide you in learning how to locate relevant information from a variety of sources.

Understanding Research

To understand research-based writing, we have to go back to the beginning, Core Concept #1: "Writing is a process of discovery and learning" (see Chapter 2). When you write, you are engaged in a powerful form of inquiry. You are writing to learn, to explore an idea, to examine an issue or problem, to understand an experience, to solve a problem, to participate in conversations about subjects that matter to you. You are *not* writing for the purpose of using source material. Consulting sources is part of the process of inquiry that writing should be; it is not the *reason* for writing.

Let me illustrate with a story about my own writing. While I was still in college, I made a road trip with a friend that took me through the Badlands of South Dakota, a remote, sparsely populated, and starkly beautiful region of pastel-colored hills, mesas, and prairies etched with countless canyons and dry creek beds. As we drove along a desolate stretch of Interstate 90, we passed one of those large green exit signs. Under that sign someone had attached another sign: a weathered plank with hand-painted red letters that read, "Doctor wanted." The sign surprised us and made us wonder: Were the residents of that isolated area really so desperate for medical care that they resorted to posting hand-painted signs on the Interstate? Was their situation common in rural areas? Was medical care scarce for Americans who lived in such areas? I had never really thought about what it might be like to live in a remote area where things that I took for granted—like medical care—might not be available.

When I returned from my trip, I contacted a cousin who is a family doctor and told him about the sign. He explained that providing doctors for remote rural areas was a longstanding challenge in the United States that was complicated by rising health care costs and the growing use of expensive medical technology. I was intrigued and wanted to know more. I contacted a magazine editor, who expressed interest in an article on the topic. At that point, I had a topic, an interesting and relevant experience, some basic information, and a lot of additional questions. I also had a goal: to inform the readers of the magazine about a little-known problem in American health care. I was ready to learn more. I could now begin my research.

As my story suggests, research should begin with a question or problem that you want to address—one that matters not only to you but also to a potential audience. Once you have a topic and a sense of your rhetorical situation, you can begin gathering information to help you understand your topic and answer your questions. Finding sources is then a purposeful activity: the sources help you achieve your rhetorical goals.

So the most important thing to remember about working with sources is that it isn't about the sources. In other words, your focus should be, first, on the purpose of your project and how it fits your rhetorical situation. So start there:

- What are you writing about and *why*?
- What are you trying to accomplish with a particular writing project?
- What do you need to know in order to accomplish your rhetorical goals?

By the time you're ready to begin consulting sources, you should already have begun exploring your subject and have a sense of your intended audience and the purpose of your project. Your rhetorical goals should guide your research—not the other way around.

A common mistake many students make in research-based writing is moving too quickly to the process of finding sources. After receiving an assignment, the first thing they do is go online to search for information about a possible topic before they have begun to develop some idea of what they will say about that topic. As a result, what they find online (or elsewhere), rather than their rhetorical purpose, guides their project. In such cases, the resulting project is often a compilation of source material rather than a genuine inquiry into the subject.

To avoid that mistake, follow the steps in Chapter 3 and don't focus on looking for source material until you have begun exploring your topic and have a good sense of your rhetorical situation. It's certainly OK to peruse source material to get ideas about a topic, but if your research is purposeful rather than haphazard, finding sources will be part of the process of inquiry that writing should be.

Doing research today is a kind of good news/bad news proposition. The good news is that students have ready access to an astonishing amount and variety of material online so that they can quickly find information on almost any conceivable topic. The bad news is that having access to so much information can be overwhelming and make it difficult to distinguish useful information from erroneous or dubious information. Following a few simple guidelines will enable you to take advantage of the wealth of material available to you and avoid the common pitfalls of finding useful and reliable sources.

The key to finding appropriate sources is threefold:

- determining what you need
- understanding available sources
- developing a search strategy

The remainder of this chapter is devoted to examining these three aspects of finding relevant source material.

Determining What You Need

To make your research efficient and successful, it's best to identify the kinds of information you need. Otherwise, your searches are likely to be haphazard and overly time-consuming. Follow these basic steps:

1. Consider the purpose of your project and your intended audience.

2. Generate questions you will probably need to address.

3. Identify possible sources of information to address those questions.

To illustrate, let's look at three writing assignments that call for research:

- a literacy narrative requiring you to analyze your own experiences as a young reader and writer in terms of available research on literacy development

- an argument in favor of abolishing the electoral college in U.S. presidential elections

- a history of your neighborhood focusing on the period since the end of World War II

1. Consider Your Purpose and Audience

Literacy narrative	• To gain insight into your own literacy experiences • To understand literacy development in general • To share this learning with students in your writing class
Argument against electoral college	• To illuminate problems with the current election system • To propose an increasingly popular solution to an important problem • To encourage other voting citizens to consider this solution
History of your neighborhood	• To understand important developments in your neighborhood's past • To understand how the past affects the present • To share these insights with other students of history and neighborhood residents

7

2. Generate Questions You Might Need to Address

Literacy narrative	• What important childhood experiences shaped you as reader and writer? • What role did literacy play in your life as an adolescent? • What influence did your family have in your writing and reading habits? • What does research indicate are the key factors that affect literacy ability?
Argument against electoral college	• How exactly does the electoral college work? Why was it developed? • What are the main criticisms of the electoral college? • What problems have occurred in past elections? • What solutions have others proposed? What concerns do critics have about these solutions?
History of your neighborhood	• What key economic, political, and social developments occurred in your neighborhood since WWII? What changes have taken place in that time? • How do these developments relate to broader developments in your region or the nation? • What problems does the neighborhood face today? How are those problems related to past developments?

3. Identify Possible Sources to Answer Your Questions

Literacy narrative	• Family members; former teachers • Relevant artifacts from your childhood (school papers, books, letters) • Scholarly articles and books about literacy development • Published studies of childhood literacy
Argument against electoral college	• Reference works on political science and elections • Articles in political journals, newspapers, newsmagazines • Blog posts, public affairs websites • Materials from political watchdog groups
History of your neighborhood	• Archived newspaper articles • Documents from local historical society or state museum • Op-ed essays in local newspapers, websites, blogs • Interviews with local leaders

These examples illustrate **several important points about finding sources:**

- **The kind of information you need and the possible sources for that information depend on the nature of your project and rhetorical situation.** For example, the literacy narrative assignment requires finding specialized information about literacy development that is most likely available only in academic publications. Moreover, because of the specialized nature of the assignment and the fact that it is intended for an academic audience, the instructor will probably expect students to consult scholarly sources. By contrast, the argument about the electoral college is intended for a more general, less specialized audience. It addresses a topic that has been discussed in a variety of contexts, including academic journals as well as the popular press and digital media. Given that rhetorical situation and the more general appeal of the topic, some relevant sources will probably be less specialized than those for the literacy narrative assignment.

- **Identifying what you don't know will help you find the right sources for what you need to know.** By starting the research process with questions that you need to answer, you will quickly identify what you don't know about your topic, which will help you identify what you *need to know*. For example, for the argument against the electoral college, you might already have a sense of the problems with the current election system, but you might have little knowledge of the history of that system or what experts and others have said about it. Similarly, for the neighborhood history, you might know a lot about the present economic and political situation in your neighborhood but little about how it came to be that way. Posing questions about your topic helps you identify such gaps in your knowledge and points you to possible sources of information to fill those gaps.

- **Some projects call for original research.** Two of these three examples point to the possibility of students doing their own *primary research* (see "Primary vs. Secondary Research"). For the neighborhood history project, for example, students might interview politicians and other local leaders as well as examine archived documents in a local historical society or museum. For the literacy narrative assignment, students might interview family members and former teachers and use documents such as old school papers. These original sources will be supplemented by *secondary sources*, such as academic journals, newspapers, books, or websites.

- **Research begets research.** The more you learn about your topic, the more questions you are likely to have. That's as it should be. For example, in researching the history of your neighborhood, you might discover that the closing of a local factory after World War II left many residents out of work, which led to an exodus of young people to other towns and states. Learning about that development might lead to questions about the basis for the local economy, which in turn might lead you to look at sources (e.g., economic data) that you had not previously considered. Similarly, in reading a journal article about childhood literacy for your literacy narrative, you might encounter a reference to a study about the relationship between literacy development and social class. That study in turn might prompt you to re-examine your own literacy development in terms of your socio-economic background. As you proceed with your research, you will learn more about your topic, which will probably mean that you will begin to understand better what you need to know to complete your project.

7

Scholars usually distinguish between two kinds of research.

Primary research is first-hand investigation. It involves conducting experiments, collecting various kinds of data (such as through surveys, interviews, or observation), or examining original documents (such as manuscripts, public records, or letters) or artifacts in libraries or museums. If you interview someone, design and distribute a survey, conduct a laboratory experiment, or analyze data that have not been previously published, you are conducting primary research. Most college students do not engage in primary research, although some college assignments require such research.

Secondary research is based on the work of others. It involves investigating what other people have already published on a given subject—in other words, finding information about a topic online, in books, in magazine or journal articles, and in similar sources. Most of the research college students do is secondary research. The advice in this chapter generally assumes that you are doing secondary research.

Understanding Sources

The examples in the previous section suggest the wide variety of available sources for research-based writing. The main challenge is finding the right sources containing the material you need to meet the rhetorical goals for your project. Understanding the different kinds of available sources will help you do so.

In this section, we will examine **two main categories of sources**:

- print materials
- online resources

The distinction between print and online resources has become increasingly blurred as many traditional print sources become available online or disappear altogether. Most print newspapers and magazines now have websites where online versions of print articles are available. Similarly, scholarly journals usually make articles available in both print and online form. For our purposes, *print materials* will refer to anything that appears in conventional print form (e.g., books, newspaper articles, magazines), whether or not it appears in an online version; materials that appear only online, such as blogs and websites, will be considered *online resources*. Despite some similarities between traditional print and online materials, there are important differences between these two categories of source materials, and understanding those differences will enable you to make the best use of available resources.

Print Materials

Despite the growing importance of online resources, print materials remain essential for much academic research. The main kinds of print materials that students are likely to consult for college assignments are the following:

- books (scholarly or trade)
- scholarly journals
- magazines and newspapers

Books. In today's instant-access digital age, books can seem archaic. It can be easy to find up-to-the-minute information on media websites, quickly get facts about a topic by using a search engine like Google, or instantly access information about a subject on a reference website like Wikipedia. Getting information from a book, on the other hand, requires you to go to the library (or bookstore) and physically page through the book to find what you need (unless you are using an e-reader like a Kindle, which enables you to search the contents of the book digitally). Nevertheless, printed books tend to be stable sources of information compared to many online resources, which can change without notice or even disappear, making it difficult for readers to access or verify the information. The involved process of producing a book requires writers and editors to consider the relevance of the content over a longer term than is necessary for much online material. Unlike websites, which can be revised and updated constantly, books are likely to remain in print for years before being revised or updated. In general, that means that if you cite information contained in a book, readers who want to track it down will be able to do so.

In addition, books, notably scholarly books, often contain the best of what is known about a subject. That's partly because scholarly publishers generally do not publish with an eye toward what is trendy or popular; rather, they look for material that reflects state-of-the-art understanding in a particular field. As a result, scholarly books often reflect the knowledge that an academic field has generated over many years. This does not mean that books are always accurate or unbiased (see "Detecting Bias" in Chapter 8); sometimes a new development in a field will significantly change or even invalidate previous thinking about an important subject in that field, and like trade books, scholarly books can reflect a particular perspective or school of thought. But by and large, scholarly books and many trade books are credible, stable sources of information.

Scholarly journals. If you search your college library's periodical holdings, you will discover that there are thousands of scholarly journals devoted to every academic subject and their many sub-specialties. For example, in 2012 the library of the State University of New York at Albany listed 429 scholarly journals in the field of general biology and an additional 597 journals in subspecialties such as genetics and microbiology. Taken together, these journals (most of which appear online as well as in print form) reflect the most up-to-date knowledge in biology and its subfields. Every academic field, no matter how small or specialized, has its own scholarly journals. In addition, some prestigious journals publish articles from many related fields. The journal *Science*, for example, publishes articles from all fields of science.

As a general rule, scholarly journals are considered reputable, dependable, and accurate sources of information, ideas, and knowledge. Most scholarly journals are *peer-reviewed*, which means that each published article has been evaluated by several experts on the specific subject matter of the article. By contrast, articles in trade and popular magazines are usually reviewed by an editor (or sometimes by an editorial team); they are generally not evaluated by an outside panel of experts. Consequently, articles that appear in scholarly journals are generally considered to meet rigorous standards of scholarship in their respective fields. If your research leads you to material in a scholarly journal, you can usually be confident that it is credible.

The challenge facing most student writers, however, is that scholarly articles are written by experts for other experts in their respective fields. These articles can often be difficult for a novice (as almost all students are) to understand, and students can find it hard to assess whether the material in such articles fits the needs of their project. If you find yourself in such a situation (and you probably will at some point), use the following strategies to help you decide whether the material in a scholarly article is useful to you:

- **Read the abstract.** Most scholarly articles include an *abstract*, which is a summary of the article. Reading the abstract will generally give you a good idea about whether the article contains the kind of information you need.

- **Ask a librarian.** Librarians are trained to understand the characteristics and nuances of the many different kinds of source materials available in their libraries. If you're not sure about whether a specific scholarly article is relevant for your project, ask a librarian.

- **Search the internet.** Often a scholarly article is part of a larger body of work by the author(s) and others in a specific field. If you find an article that seems relevant but are not sure whether it contains material you need, do a quick Internet search using the subject or title of the article and/or the authors' names. Such a search might yield links to websites, such as the authors' university web pages, that are less technical and contain information that can help you decide whether the scholarly article is useful for your project.

Magazines and newspapers. For many topics, especially topics related to current events, magazines and newspapers provide rich sources of information. But there are many different kinds of magazines and newspapers, and their quality and dependability can vary widely. Here are the main categories:

- **Trade magazines.** Trade magazines and journals are specialized periodicals devoted to specific occupations or professions. Many are considered important sources for information and opinions relevant to those occupations or professions. *Automotive Design and Production,* for example, publishes articles about the latest technology and news related to the automobile industry. Other well-known trade journals include *Adweek, American Bar Association Journal, Business & Finance,* and *Publishers Weekly.* Although most trade publications do not peer-review the articles they publish, they nevertheless can provide reliable information and important perspectives on subjects related to their professions.

- **Popular magazines.** This category includes numerous publications on every conceivable topic, but the main feature that distinguishes popular publications from trade or public affairs journals is that they are intended for a general, non-specialist audience. *Sports Illustrated*, for example, a popular magazine, might publish an article about the top track and field athletes competing in the Olympic Games, whereas *Track & Field News*, a trade publication, might include technical articles about the latest training techniques used by world-class sprinters to prepare for the Olympics. Popular magazines tend to value the latest news and often cater to specific segments of the general population (for example, *Seventeen Magazine* targets teenage girls) in an effort to attract advertising revenue. Although they vary widely in quality and dependability, they can be an important source of information, depending upon the nature of your project. However, some college instructors consider many popular magazines less credible sources than either trade or scholarly publications, so check with your instructor to determine whether to use such magazines as sources for your project.

- **Public affairs journals.** A number of periodicals focus on politics, history, and culture and publish carefully researched articles, often by well-known scholars and other experts. Many public affairs journals have developed reputations as respected sources of the most knowledgeable perspectives on important political, economic, and social issues. Some of these journals have been publishing for many decades. Among the most well-known public affairs journals are *The Atlantic, National Review, The Nation*, and *Foreign Affairs*.

- **Newspapers and newsmagazines.** Daily and weekly newspapers and weekly or monthly newsmagazines are general sources for the most up-to-date information. Among the advantages of these publications for researchers is that they tend to be accessible, are intended for a wide audience, and publish material on a wide variety of topics. Like popular magazines, newspapers and newsmagazines can vary significantly in quality, focus, and dependability. In general, well-established newspapers, such as *The New York Times, The Washington Post*, and the *Los Angeles Times*, and newsmagazines, such as *Time*, tend to have rigorous editorial review and often employ fact-checkers to verify information they publish. However, like all sources, these publications are subject to bias, no matter how objective and thorough they might claim to be (see "Detecting Bias" in Chapter 8). They might be dependable and well respected, but they also represent various points of view. Don't assume that because something is published in a reputable newspaper or newsmagazine, it is free from bias.

Depending on the nature of your project, any of these kinds of publications can provide useful material, but it is important to be aware of the differences among them so that you can better judge the appropriateness of a specific source.

Online Resources

Because the Internet contains an almost inconceivable amount of material, it can be a boon for researchers. At the same time, the great variety of resources available online can create challenges for students looking for credible, accurate information.

As noted earlier, many print resources are now available online. If your search leads you to a journal or newspaper article, check to see whether it is available online. For example, major newspapers like *The New York Times* archive their articles, so that you can usually gain access to them through the newspapers' websites or an online database offered through your college library.

There are **three main kinds of online sources of information.**

- **Websites.** Businesses, government agencies, media outlets, individuals, and organizations of all kinds maintain websites that can be excellent sources of information for researchers. For example, if you looking for information about standardized testing in K–12 schools, you can search the website of the U.S. Department of Education; you can visit the websites of state education departments, school districts, and related government agencies; and you can consult the websites of the many not-for-profit organizations and advocacy groups devoted to education issues, many of which provide a wide variety of information on education-related issues. Similarly, for-profit organizations that provide education services maintain websites that can also be useful sources for information. In addition, the websites of media organizations devoted to education issues can be excellent resources. It's safe to say that with careful searching you can almost always find relevant websites that provide useful and reliable information, no matter what subject you are researching.

- **Reference materials.** The Internet has become the digital equivalent of the traditional reference section of a library, providing such resources as encyclopedias, statistical abstracts, dictionaries, maps, almanacs, and related reference materials. If you need statistical information about employment rates in the United States, for example, you can search the *Statistical Abstract of the United States* as well as databases maintained online by the U.S. Department of Labor and the U.S. Census Bureau, among other such resources. Venerable reference resources such as *Encyclopedia Britannica* are now available online along with more recently developed resources such as *Wikipedia*. Many organizations, agencies, and institutions (such as universities) also maintain specialized reference materials online.

- **Social media.** Increasingly, social media have become important sites for debate, discussion, and the exchange of information. Many blogs have become as important and respected as the most reputable journals as sources of ideas, opinions, and information, and even sites like Tumblr and Facebook can be useful sources for some kinds of information. Often, such sites contain the most up-to-date perspectives and information because they are constantly revised to reflect current developments.

The nature of your project and your rhetorical situation will dictate which sources are the most relevant. For many academic writing tasks, some sources will be considered inappropriate. If you're not sure whether a specific source is appropriate for your project, check with your instructor or a reference librarian.

Locating the Right Sources

Given the wealth and variety of available resources, how do you find the information you need? There are **three primary tools for finding the right source materials** for your project:

- library catalogs
- databases
- online search engines

Library Catalogs

A library lists all the materials it holds in its online catalog, which is usually easily accessible from the library's home page. In addition to listing books held by the library, the library website typically enables you to access other resources maintained by the library, including its reference collections; periodicals (scholarly journals as well as newspapers and magazines); audio, video, and digital media holdings; government documents; and special collections (such as local historical materials or manuscripts from a well-known author). If you are searching for books on your subject, the library online catalog is the best place to start. But the library website is also a good place to start your search for other materials as well. Get to know what is available on your college library's website. It will serve you well in your research.

Databases

Databases are listings of published materials that enable you to locate articles in scholarly journals, trade journals, or popular newspapers and magazines. Some databases provide only citations or abstracts of articles in the periodicals they list; some also provide direct access to the full texts of the materials they list. The most popular databases are general and interdisciplinary because they index a wide variety of materials from all subject areas. However, many databases are specialized and index only periodicals relevant to their subject. For example, MedLine indexes periodicals and related materials on medicine, nursing, dentistry, veterinary medicine, the health care system, and pre-clinical sciences.

Chances are that you will need to search several different databases for many of your college writing projects, so it makes sense to become familiar with the databases available through your college library. Among the most widely used databases are the following:

- **Academic Search Complete** is a multidisciplinary scholarly database that includes thousands of full-text periodicals in the social sciences, humanities, science, and technology.
- **Article First** is a general database that indexes the content page of journals in science, technology, medicine, social science, business, the humanities, and popular culture.
- **EBSCOhost** is one of the most widely used general databases. It includes citations and abstracts from thousands of journals in many different disciplines and provides access to full-text articles from many journals.

- **FirstSearch Online Reference** is a general reference portal that provides access to a wide variety of databases in many different subject areas.

- **Google Scholar** is an increasingly popular multidisciplinary scholarly database that lists citations for articles, papers, books, and related scholarly documents in all major academic disciplines.

- **JSTOR** is a scholarly database that provides access to full-text articles from many different journals in a variety of academic disciplines.

- **LexisNexis Academic** is an extensive database providing citations and full-text articles from newspapers, magazines, and many different periodicals in law, business, biography, medicine, and reference.

- **MasterFILE Premier** is a general database that includes access to full-text articles from periodicals in general reference, business, health, education, culture, and science.

- **Scopus** is a general database that indexes abstracts and provides access to the contents of thousands of international journal titles as well as conference proceedings, book series, and scientific web pages and patents, with a focus on science, technology, and medicine.

Keep in mind that although some databases (such as Google Scholar) are freely available on the Internet, others are available only through a subscription or license. If your library has a subscription to these databases, you can usually access them by signing in through your library's website.

Search Engines

Search engines are websites that search the Internet for available materials. Typically, search engines return a list of links to websites and other web-based resources. Google is the most popular search engine, but there are many other search engines, including specialized search engines that focus on specific subject areas, such as automobiles, business, computers, or education. Among the most commonly used general search engines are Yahoo!, Bing, Ask.com, and Answers.com.

Like databases, search engines enable you to find relevant materials very quickly; however, unlike databases, search engines typically do not screen the results of searches, which means that you often have to work harder to sort through and evaluate the references returned by a search engine. If you find a citation in a specialized database, it is likely to be related to the specific subject area and from a source that has been evaluated by the editors of the database. By contrast, search engines return links to *any* site or resource related to the search term, no matter the source of that site.

Although these three kinds of resources overlap, in general you can use them as follows:

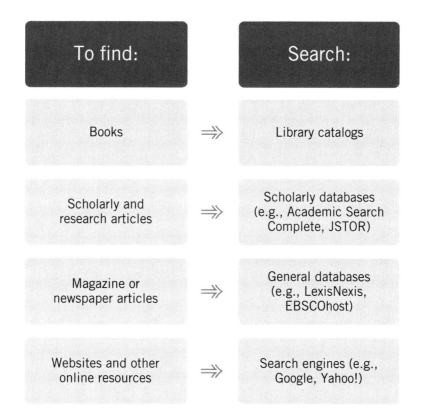

To find:		Search:
Books	⟹	Library catalogs
Scholarly and research articles	⟹	Scholarly databases (e.g., Academic Search Complete, JSTOR)
Magazine or newspaper articles	⟹	General databases (e.g., LexisNexis, EBSCOhost)
Websites and other online resources	⟹	Search engines (e.g., Google, Yahoo!)

Of course, you can use an Internet search engine such as Google to find references to books, scholarly articles, and newspaper and magazine articles, but if you limit your search tools to Internet search engines, you might miss important resources, especially if your topic is specialized and your assignment is academic in nature. It is best to use the three basic kinds of online resources in combination to be able to identify the most useful sources for your project.

Developing a Search Strategy

Understanding the many different sources available to you and knowing which search tools to use still isn't quite enough for successful research. For example, your library catalog lists thousands of book titles, but how do you even know whether searching for a book makes sense for your project? Similarly, a search engine such as Google can point you to thousands of links related to a certain topic, but what will you look for among those many links? How do you know which ones to pursue? You will more likely find what you need if you develop a general search strategy that focuses on the kinds of information you need for your project and takes advantage of all potential sources to find that information rather than limiting your search to one set of resources, such as online materials or scholarly journals.

To illustrate, let's return to one of the examples from the section titled "Determining What You Need" (page 181): an argument in favor of abolishing the electoral college in U.S. presidential elections. We identified the purpose of the project as follows:

- to illuminate problems with the current election system

- to propose an increasingly popular solution to an important problem

- to encourage other voting citizens to consider this solution

Let's imagine that you are writing this essay with several overlapping audiences in mind: classmates in your writing course, other college students, and voting citizens. So your audience is both general and academic. You have become interested in the topic because you have heard many young people of voting age express apathy about the presidential election, partly because the popular vote does not necessarily elect the president. You have also read several op-ed essays about this issue, some of which have called for abolishing the electoral college.

After reading about the electoral college online, you have decided you support the idea of replacing it with a system in which the national popular vote elects the president. However, you need to learn more about how the electoral college works, and you need to examine the various arguments for and against that system.

Here's the list of questions you have identified as a starting point for your research:

- How exactly does the electoral college work? Why was it developed?

- What are the main criticisms of the electoral college?

- What problems have occurred in past elections?

- What solutions have others proposed? What concerns do critics have about these solutions?

And here are some potential sources you have identified for addressing these questions:

- reference works on political science and elections

- articles in political journals, newspapers, and newsmagazines

- blog posts, public affairs websites

- materials from political watchdog groups

How should you proceed? When you have a general idea about what you might want to say about your topic (in this case, that the electoral college should be replaced with a national popular vote for U.S. presidential elections) but limited knowledge of the subject, a good search strategy is to start broadly and narrow your search as you learn more about your topic and refine your main point (Core Concept #4). That means beginning with general searches of the major categories of resources—library catalogs, databases, and Internet search engines—and then searching for more specific materials as you identify questions or subtopics that you need to explore, using the appropriate search tools at each stage. In our example, the process might look like this:

1. General search for materials on electoral college:
- Library catalog for books
- Search engine (e.g., Google)
- General database (e.g., LexisNexis, EBSCOhost)

2. Narrower search for critiques and studies of electoral college:
- Specialized databases (e.g., Worldwide Political Science Abstracts, Google Scholar)

3. Targeted search for alternatives to the electoral college:
- Advanced search of relevant database (e.g., LexisNexis, Google Scholar) and search engine

1. Do a General Search for Materials on the Electoral College

Recall your questions about your topic:

- How exactly does the electoral college work? Why was it developed?
- What are the main criticisms of the electoral college?
- What problems have occurred in past elections?
- What solutions have others proposed? What concerns do critics have about these solutions?

These should guide your general searches. You need basic information about the electoral college, its history, and the criticisms of the system. You also need information about proposed solutions. Search the three main kinds of resources for relevant materials:

Library catalogs. Libraries have different kinds of search mechanisms, but most allow users to do **keyword searches** of their catalogs for subjects or titles of books and related materials in their collections. In this case, you could use *electoral college* as a subject keyword. In 2012, a search using these keywords yielded 47 books in the library of the State University of New York at Albany. Here's what the first page of the results screen looked like:

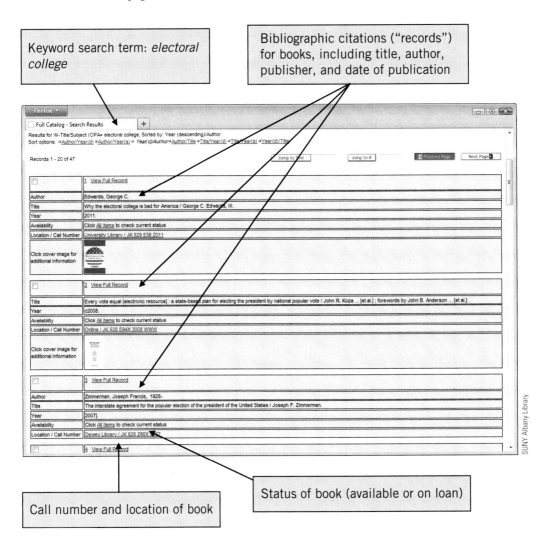

Keyword search term: *electoral college*

Bibliographic citations ("records") for books, including title, author, publisher, and date of publication

Status of book (available or on loan)

Call number and location of book

This screen shows the first three of 47 total "records," which provide bibliographic information about each book as well as its call number so that you can locate it in the library. You can also click a link to check on the status of each book (whether it is out on loan, when it is due, and so forth). Although the search screen will differ from one library to the next, each screen will have these key components, including complete bibliographic information about the book (author, publisher, date of publication) and the status of the book (whether it is available for loan, where it is located in the library).

Review the search results to see which books seem most likely to contain the information you need about the electoral college. Some of the books found in this sample search will likely provide general information about the electoral college:

> *After the People Vote: A Guide to the Electoral College* (2004), edited by John C. Fortier

> *Electoral College and Presidential Elections* (2001), edited by Alexandra Kura

Some specifically address the controversy about the electoral college and proposals to reform it:

> *Every Vote Equal: A State-Based Plan for Electing the President by National Popular Vote* (2008), by John R. Koza et al.

> *Enlightened Democracy: The Case for the Electoral College* (2004), by Tara Ross

> *Why the Electoral College Is Bad for America* (2004), by George C. Edwards

Some might be too specialized for your purposes:

> *Electoral Votes Based on the 1990 Census* (1991), by David C. Huckabee

Based on the information in the search results, select the books that seem most useful and visit the library to review them. (You might also do an online search to find additional information about each book before visiting the library. For example, a Google search of the book's title and author will often yield descriptions of the book, reviews, and related information that can help you determine whether the book is worth borrowing from the library.)

General databases. Search one or more general databases using the same or similar keywords. A good place to start is *LexisNexis Academic*, which indexes many different newspapers and magazines as well as other kinds of materials; it also indexes more specialized journals.

Like many databases, *LexisNexis Academic* has an "easy" search screen and an "advanced" search screen. Begin with an "easy" search of the news using your keywords *electoral college*. Notice that this database allows you to select categories of sources (newspapers, magazines, blogs).

In some cases, it might make sense to narrow your search to one such category; in this example, however, a broader search is appropriate:

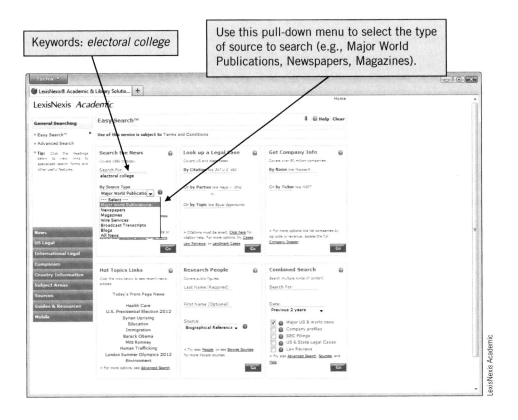

This search of "Major World Publications" returned 995 entries. Here's the first screen:

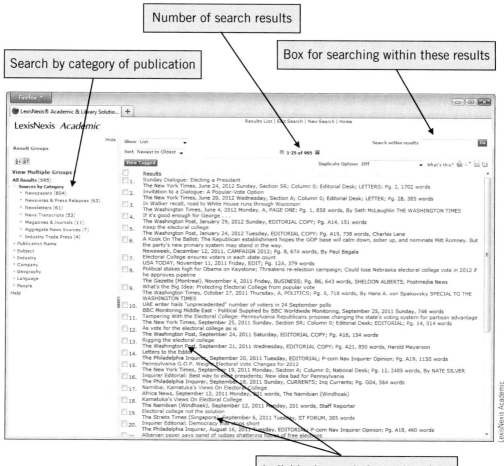

Number of search results

Box for searching within these results

Search by category of publication

Individual records for each article. Click to retrieve the article.

Databases have very different search screens, and it might take some time to become familiar with the ones you are using. However, all major databases allow you to specify the parameters of your search (e.g., by publication type, date, author, title, keywords, and so on) so that you can search broadly or be more strategic. Moreover, they all provide the same basic information about the sources that are returned in a search, which in this example are called "records." Usually, that information includes the author, title, publication, and date of the entry. Sometimes the entry will include an abstract or summary of the source. You can use this information to review the entries and decide which ones to examine more closely.

Obviously, the 995 records returned in this sample would be too many to review, but you can **narrow your search** in several ways:

- **Search within the results.** Use more specific terms to search within the results of searches that yield too many entries. For example, you can use the keywords *presidential election* to exclude any articles about other elections. Using those keywords reduced the search results in this example to 776 records.

- **Search specific publications.** Because you are interested in the American electoral college, you might search only American newspapers. You can limit your search further by searching only major newspapers (e.g., *The Washington Post, The New York Times*). You can do the same for magazines and other types of publications.

- **Specify dates.** If you want to find materials related to a specific time period, you can specify the dates of the materials you want. For example, if you want articles about the 2000 presidential election, you might search for materials published from 1998 through 2001.

Notice that you can also search by subject. Expanding the subject list reveals a number of subtopics. The numbers in parentheses after each subtopic indicate how many of the 995 records relate to that subtopic. For example, among the 995 entries in the original search in this example, 343 are related to the subtopic "U.S. Presidential Elections":

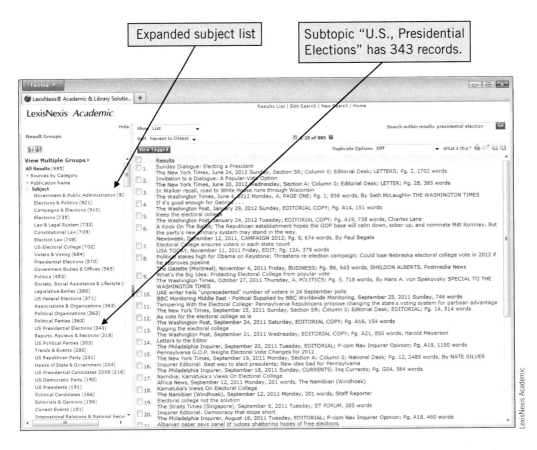

You can use the subject categories to narrow your search further. For example, you could click on the subject "U.S. Presidential Elections" and search within that category, which contains 343 sources. In this way, you can find sources that are more likely to be relevant to your specific topic.

As you gain experience in research, you will become more efficient in finding the materials you need. In the meantime, **when searching databases, follow these guidelines:**

- **Experiment with keywords.** Sometimes it takes several different combinations of search terms before you begin to see the search results you want. In our example, the search term *electoral college* returned good results, but depending upon what you are looking for, you might have to try various other search terms: *elections, popular election, presidential elections, election controversies,* and so on.

- **Use several search strategies.** Sometimes a basic keyword search gets you right to the materials you need. More often you will have to try different search strategies to narrow your search to manageable numbers and to find the most relevant materials. If various keyword searches don't yield what you need, try subject searches. Try various searches within your search results. Don't rely on a single approach.

- **Use different databases.** Different databases have different search options and will return different results. Although most databases allow for refined or advanced searching, each database has its own interface with its own peculiarities. So the same keywords are likely to yield different results in different databases. In this sample search, for example, using the same keywords (*electoral college*) with the *EBSCO* database will turn up some of the same sources but also different sources. You might also find some databases easier to use than others. Be aware that it can take some time to become familiar with the characteristics of each database, so if you have trouble finding what you need in a specific database, ask a librarian or your instructor for guidance.

Internet search engines. Having searched your library catalog and one or more databases, you can expand your search to include online materials using a general search engine such as Google or Yahoo!. Remember that search engines will return many more entries than a library catalog or database, so you might have to adjust your search terms to keep the search results manageable. In our sample search, you might begin with a general search term, such as *electoral college*, but be aware that such general searches will usually yield an enormous number of results. A search of Google using this term in 2012 yielded more than 10 million items, for instance. That kind of result isn't surprising when you remember that Google is searching the entire Internet for anything (websites, documents, and so on) that contains those two words. So try different strategies for

7

narrowing your search. For instance, placing those terms in quotation marks (see "An Important Tip for Searching Databases and Search Engines") reduced the results by half:

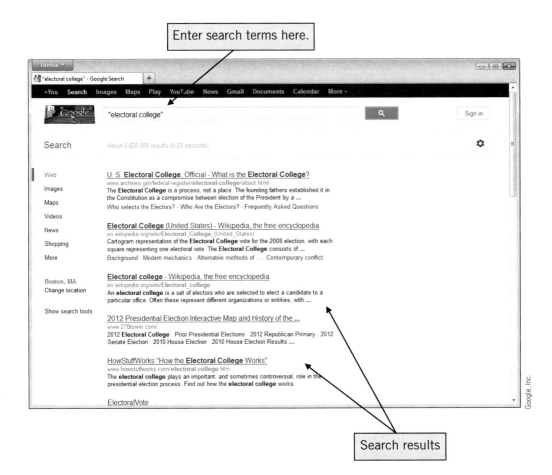

Five million is still an unmanageable number, but you can review the first few pages of search results to determine whether any of the links might be useful. In this example, the very first item is a link to the website of the U.S. Electoral College itself, which probably has relevant information for your purposes.

After reviewing the first several pages of search results, narrow your search using different search terms: e.g., *electoral college presidential election, electoral college controversy, history of electoral college.* Each of these terms will yield different results. Review each set of results for materials that seem promising. Continue to narrow your search so that the results are not only relevant but manageable.

As you proceed with these three kinds of general searches, you will gather relevant information and begin to gain a better understanding of your subject, which can help you search more strategically for additional materials.

You can search databases and search engines more efficiently by using quotation marks strategically. Placing search terms in quotation marks tells the search engine to look for exactly those words in exactly that order. For example, if you search for *online privacy,* your search will turn up sites with both those words as well as sites that have either one word or the other; however, placing that term in quotation marks (*"online privacy"*) will yield only sites containing the phrase *online privacy,* which is more likely to point to relevant sources. Experiment with different combinations of search terms, with and without quotation marks, to find the most useful sources.

2. Narrow Your Search for Specific Critiques of the Electoral College

Your general search should yield enough information for you to begin to identify specific issues, questions, and subtopics that you need to explore further. The general searches in our example have yielded a lot of information about the electoral college, how it works, its history, criticisms of the system, and proposals to reform it. Although much of that information is general (e.g., books and websites explaining the electoral college), some is more specialized (e.g., analyses of specific elections in which the popular vote did not elect the president, scholarly critiques of the system). Given that your intended audience is both general and academic, you might now look more closely at what scholars and other experts have to say about the pros and cons of the electoral college.

- **Examine the references in the books you have found.** Most books contain bibliographies or works cited pages that can point you to additional sources. The references in those bibliographies often include citations of relevant scholarly articles. Make a list of citations that seem promising, and use your library catalog or a general database to track down the articles that seem most relevant.

- **Search specialized databases.** Your library website will list its available databases. Find one or more that relate specifically to your subject. In this example, you could search general scholarly databases, such as *JSTOR, Academic Search Complete,* or *Google Scholar,* as well as databases specific to political science or the social sciences, such as *Worldwide Political Science Abstracts, PAIS,* or *Social Sciences Abstracts.* Given the nature of your project (which is intended for a general academic audience rather than a more specialized audience of readers in political science), it makes sense to search a general scholarly database, such as *JSTOR.* If you were writing your argument for a political science course, it might make more sense to search the specialized databases specific to that field, such as *Worldwide Political Science.*

Boolean, or logical, operators are words that command a search engine to define a search in a specific way. The most common Boolean operators are *AND, OR*, and *NOT*. Understanding how they work can help you search the Internet and databases more efficiently:

- *AND* tells the search engine to find only sources that contain both words in your search. For example, if you entered *sports AND steroids*, your search would yield sources that deal with steroids in sports and would not necessarily return sources that deal with steroids or sports in general.

- *OR* broadens a search by telling the search engine to return sources for either term in your search. Entering *sports OR steroids*, for instance, would yield sources on either of those topics.

- *NOT* can narrow a search by telling the search engine to exclude sources containing a specific keyword. For example, entering *steroids NOT sports* would yield sources on steroids but not sources that deal with steroids in sports.

In addition, keep these tips in mind:

- You can use parentheses for complex searches: (*sports AND steroids*) NOT (*medicine OR law*); this entry would narrow the search to specific kinds of sources about sports and steroids that did not include medical or legal matters.

- With most search engines, you can use Boolean operators in combination with quotation marks to find a specific phrase. For example, "steroid use in sports" would return sources that included that exact phrase. (See "An Important Tip for Searching Databases and Search Engines.") Using this strategy allows you to narrow your search further: ("*steroid in sports*") AND ("*steroid controversies*"). Such a search would find sources that include both phrases in the parentheses.

- Generally, you should capitalize Boolean operators.

Let's imagine that after reviewing the materials you found in your general searches, you want to know what scholars say about the implications of the electoral college for modern elections. You can search *JSTOR* for relevant scholarly articles. Here's the opening screen:

Box for entering search terms

Link to advanced search screen

Firefox ▼

J JSTOR   +

JSTOR HOME   SEARCH ▼   BROWSE ▼   MyJSTOR ▼

Used by millions for research, teaching, and learning. With more than a thousand academic journals and over 1 million images, letters, and other primary sources, JSTOR is one of the world's most trusted sources for academic content.

SEARCH

electoral college   SEARCH

Advanced Search

BROWSE BY DISCIPLINE

African American Studies (19 titles)	Health Sciences (36 titles)
African Studies (55 titles)	History (334 titles)
American Indian Studies (8 titles)	History of Science & Technology (38 titles)
American Studies (125 titles)	Irish Studies (49 titles)
Anthropology (93 titles)	Jewish Studies (27 titles)
Aquatic Sciences (17 titles)	Language & Literature (294 titles)
Archaeology (94 titles)	Latin American Studies (54 titles)
Architecture & Architectural History (33 titles)	Law (96 titles)
Art & Art History (191 titles)	Library Science (17 titles)
Asian Studies (73 titles)	Linguistics (41 titles)
Astronomy (1 title)	Management & Organizational Behavior (31 titles)
Bibliography (22 titles)	Marketing & Advertising (14 titles)
Biological Sciences (240 titles)	Mathematics (71 titles)
Botany & Plant Sciences (57 titles)	Middle East Studies (55 titles)
British Studies (17 titles)	Music (86 titles)
Business (231 titles)	Paleontology (12 titles)

Links to lists of journals in specific disciplines

JSTOR

7

Notice that, like most scholarly databases, *JSTOR* allows you to browse journals by discipline. However, doing so is very time-consuming. Also, a general search using the search term *electoral college* is likely to yield too many results (in this case, such a search returned more than 23,000 articles in 2012), so an **advanced search** would make more sense. Here's the *JSTOR* advanced search screen:

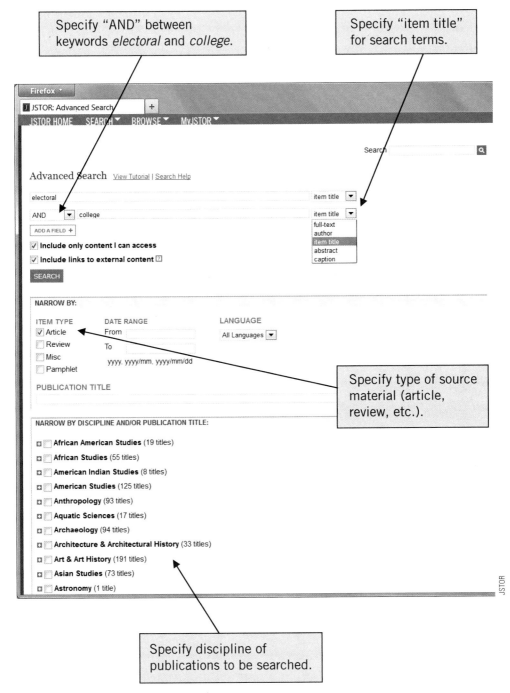

Specify "AND" between keywords *electoral* and *college*.

Specify "item title" for search terms.

Specify type of source material (article, review, etc.).

Specify discipline of publications to be searched.

Such an advanced search screen allows you to limit your searches in various ways to increase the likelihood that the results will be useful. For example, you can specify that the search terms appear in the article titles rather than the body of the articles, making it more likely that the focus of the article will be relevant to your needs. Also, you can use the *Boolean operator* "AND" to make sure that the titles of the articles have *both* search terms (see "Using Boolean Operators with Databases and Search Engines"). In addition, you can search only journals in certain disciplines and limit your search by dates and type of publication. Doing so can dramatically narrow your search and yield much more relevant results. For example, a search of *JSTOR* in 2012 using the search term *electoral college* only in the title of political science journal articles yielded 36 results:

Number of articles in search results

Search results. Click the link to access the article.

These results include several older articles as well as more recent ones. For example, the first three results shown in this image were published in 1960, 1950, and 1974, respectively. If you wanted to narrow your focus to more recent elections, you could modify your search to include only articles published since 1998. Such a search returned 11 articles in 2012. Here's part of the results:

Browse these results to find articles that are most relevant for your needs. In this example, several articles promise to examine the implications of the electoral college for modern elections, including #8: "In Play: A Commentary on Strategies in the 2004 U.S. Presidential Election," by Jennifer Merolla, Michael Munger, and Michael Tofias, published in 2005 in a journal called *Public Choice*. Click the link to access the article. The first page of the article appears:

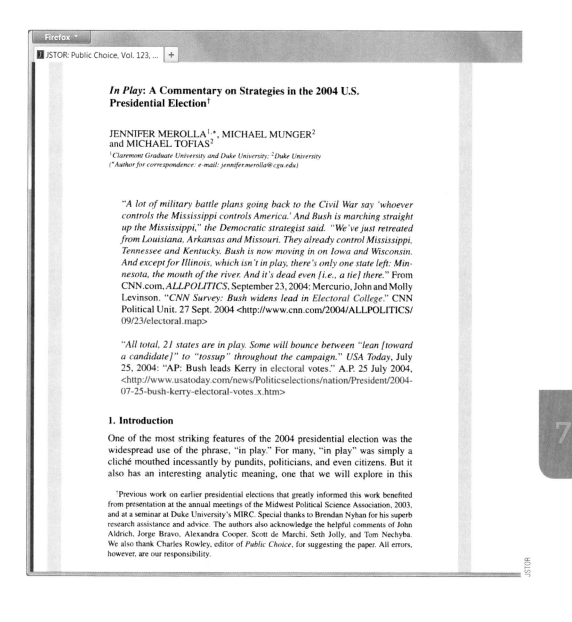

Firefox ▾

J JSTOR: Public Choice, Vol. 123, ... +

In Play: A Commentary on Strategies in the 2004 U.S. Presidential Election[†]

JENNIFER MEROLLA[1,*], MICHAEL MUNGER[2] and MICHAEL TOFIAS[2]
[1]*Claremont Graduate University and Duke University;* [2]*Duke University*
(*Author for correspondence: e-mail: jennifer.merolla@cgu.edu)

"*A lot of military battle plans going back to the Civil War say 'whoever controls the Mississippi controls America.' And Bush is marching straight up the Mississippi,"* the Democratic strategist said. *"We've just retreated from Louisiana, Arkansas and Missouri. They already control Mississippi, Tennessee and Kentucky. Bush is now moving in on Iowa and Wisconsin. And except for Illinois, which isn't in play, there's only one state left: Minnesota, the mouth of the river. And it's dead even [i.e., a tie] there."* From CNN.com, *ALLPOLITICS*, September 23, 2004: Mercurio, John and Molly Levinson. "*CNN Survey: Bush widens lead in Electoral College.*" CNN Political Unit. 27 Sept. 2004 <http://www.cnn.com/2004/ALLPOLITICS/09/23/electoral.map>

"*All total, 21 states are in play. Some will bounce between "lean [toward a candidate]" to "tossup" throughout the campaign."* USA Today, July 25, 2004: "AP: Bush leads Kerry in electoral votes." A.P. 25 July 2004, <http://www.usatoday.com/news/Politicselections/nation/President/2004-07-25-bush-kerry-electoral-votes.x.htm>

1. Introduction

One of the most striking features of the 2004 presidential election was the widespread use of the phrase, "in play." For many, "in play" was simply a cliché mouthed incessantly by pundits, politicians, and even citizens. But it also has an interesting analytic meaning, one that we will explore in this

[†]Previous work on earlier presidential elections that greatly informed this work benefited from presentation at the annual meetings of the Midwest Political Science Association, 2003, and at a seminar at Duke University's MIRC. Special thanks to Brendan Nyhan for his superb research assistance and advice. The authors also acknowledge the helpful comments of John Aldrich, Jorge Bravo, Alexandra Cooper, Scott de Marchi, Seth Jolly, and Tom Nechyba. We also thank Charles Rowley, editor of *Public Choice*, for suggesting the paper. All errors, however, are our responsibility.

JSTOR

7

A quick review of the opening passage reveals that the article focuses on strategies employed by the campaigns in the 2004 election, which is relevant for your project.

Like general databases, specialized databases can differ noticeably, and you might have to experiment with several different databases to become familiar enough with their search screens to conduct effective searches. But all databases will have features such as those in this example that allow you to target your search by entering specific parameters (type of publication, dates, subject terms, and so on). No matter which database or search engine you are using, you can apply these same basic strategies to make your searches successful. As always, consult your librarian for help, if necessary.

3. Do a Targeted Search for Alternatives to the Electoral College

As you narrow your search further, more specific questions might arise or you might identify subtopics that you hadn't previously considered. For example, in reviewing scholarly articles about the role of the electoral collect in recent U.S. presidential elections, you might come across references to legal challenges to the electoral college, a topic that seems relevant to your project but one that you had not previously encountered. At this point, if you decide you need more information about such a specialized topic, you can return to the databases that you have already searched (such as *JSTOR*) and do an additional search focused on legal challenges to the electoral college system; you can also search specialized databases, such as *Westlaw Campus*, which provides access to legal decisions. The goal at this stage is to identify any specific issues or questions you need to explore as well as gaps in the information you have already gathered.

Keep in mind that a search is not necessarily a linear process. The strategy described here assumes you will be continuously reviewing the materials you find. As you do, you might need to return to a general search for information on a new topic that seems important. For example, as you examine arguments in favor of using the popular vote to elect the president, you might discover that some experts have concerns about the wide variety of voting systems used by different states. If you decide that this concern is an important topic for your project, return to your library catalog or a general database or search engine to find some basic information about the regulations governing the way states allow citizens to vote.

Remember that writing is a process of discovery (see Core Concept #1 in Chapter 2), and research is part of that process. You are learning about your subject matter to achieve your rhetorical goals. (The advice for Core Concepts #2 and #5 in Chapter 2 can also help you conduct more effective searches for useful source materials.)

WIKIPEDIA
English
The Free Encyclopedia
4 240 000+ articles
Español
La enciclopedia libre
1 020 000+ artículos
Русский
Свободная энциклопедия
1 000 000+ статей
日本語
フリー百科事典
860 000+ 記事
Deutsch
Die freie Enzyklopädie
1 590 000+ Artikel
Français
L'encyclopédie libre
1 390 000+ articles
Polski
Wolna encyklopedia
970 000+ haseł
Italiano
L'enciclopedia libera
1 030 000+ voci
Português
A enciclopédia livre
780 000+ artigos
中文
自由的百科全書
690 000+ 條目

Evaluating Sources

8

FINDING INFORMATION for your project is one thing. Deciding whether a source is appropriate, credible, and reliable is another. Given the enormous variety of available sources, evaluating the materials you find can be challenging, but it is an integral part of research.

When evaluating sources, you need to address two main questions:

- Is the source trustworthy?
- Is the source useful for your purposes?

Answering the first question involves understanding the nature and purpose of the source itself. For example, a newspaper article about a political campaign and a campaign flier can both be useful sources, but they are very different kinds of documents with different purposes. The purpose of a newspaper is to provide readers information about important and relevant events—in this example, a political campaign. A political campaign flier, by contrast, is intended to present a candidate in the best possible light to persuade voters to support that candidate. Both documents can provide accurate information about the candidate, but the information they present must be considered in terms of their different purposes. The campaign flier, for instance, might emphasize the candidate's record of voting against tax increases, whereas the newspaper article might explain that the candidate's vote against a specific tax increase resulted in reduced funding for a special program for disabled military veterans. Both sources are technically "true," but each presents information from a particular perspective and for a specific purpose.

As a writer evaluating sources for a project, you have to sort through these complexities to determine how trustworthy a source might be and whether it suits your own rhetorical purposes. The advice in this chapter will help you do so.

Determining Whether a Source Is Trustworthy

Evaluating source material requires understanding the different kinds of sources that are available to you. (Chapter 7 describes the characteristics of various kinds of sources.) It helps to develop a sense of the main similarities and differences in the general categories of sources you are likely to consult:

Source ⇒	Example ⇒	Purpose ⇒	Authors ⇒	Audience
Scholarly books	Elizabeth L. Eisenstein. *The Printing Revolution in Early Modern Europe.*	To share ideas and research about relevant topics	Scholars	Other scholars and experts
Scholarly journal articles	Mishra, Ashok, et al. "Precautionary Wealth and Income Uncertainty: A Household-Level Analysis." *Journal of Applied Economics* 15.2 (2012)	To share ideas and research about relevant topics	Scholars	Other scholars and experts
Reference books	*Encyclopedia Britannica; Oxford Companion to the History of Modern Science*	To provide accurate information about general or specialized subjects	Experts	General
Trade books	Ben Goldacre. *Bad Pharma: How Drug Companies Mislead Doctors and Harm Patients.*	To provide information, share knowledge, advance an argument	Experts, professional writers	General
Newspaper and newsmagazine articles	Kluger, Jeffrey, and Alice Park. "Frontiers of Fertility." *Time* 30 May 2013.	To provide information on current issues; to report current events	Reporters, professional writers	General
Newspaper and magazine editorials and commentary	Strassel, Kimberly A. "Conservatives Became Targets in 2008." *Wall Street Journal* 23 May 2013.	To present a viewpoint; to advance an argument	Columnists, experts	General
Sponsored websites	The Blues Foundation, www.blues.org	To provide information about a topic or an organization	Varied	General; specialized

A glance at this graphic reveals that different kinds of sources can be very similar in some respects (e.g., their intended audiences) but very different in others (e.g., their primary purpose). Having a general sense of the characteristics of these categories of sources can help you evaluate information from specific sources and determine its usefulness for your project.

Source materials within any of these general categories can also vary in terms of three important considerations when it comes to trustworthiness: credibility, reliability, and bias.

Credibility

Credibility is the extent to which a source is respected and can be trusted. It refers to your sense of whether a source is reputable and dependable and the information found there generally reliable. The credibility of a source can arise from a reputation built over time. Well-established newspapers, magazines, and publishers are usually considered credible sources because of their record of publishing certain kinds of reliable, accurate information and their commitment to high standards of integrity. Scholarly publications, for example, are generally considered credible because they tend to be peer-reviewed and because of their commitment to holding their authors to high standards of quality and accuracy. The fact that an article published in a scholarly journal has likely been carefully evaluated and critiqued by established scholars can give readers confidence that the article meets high standards for accuracy and integrity.

Credibility can also be a function of a writer's general approach to the subject matter: his or her tone, the level of fairness with which subject matter is treated, how carefully he or she seems to have examined the subject, how accurate or believable his or her statements are, and so on. For example, if you notice a writer making easy generalizations or drawing dubious conclusions about a complicated subject, you might be skeptical of the writer's credibility when it comes to that subject. Consider this passage from a post on Alternet, a website devoted to politics and culture; the writer, an editor for Alternet, is reporting on a newspaper survey of recent Harvard graduates regarding their career choices after college:

> Wall Street's propensity to ravage the economy, launder money, and illegally foreclose on families with no harsher punishment than a slap on the wrist seems to have irked some of the nation's brightest. Either that or the shrinkage of jobs in the finance sector is turning them off. According to a survey by the student newspaper the *Harvard Crimson*, Harvard graduates are just saying "No" to Wall Street, with some of them looking instead to put their smarts to work making America a better place.
>
> The paper reports that about a third of new graduates plan to work in finance, with 15 percent working on Wall Street and 16 percent doing consulting. In 2007, before the recession, 47 percent of Harvard grads went onto work in finance and consulting, a number that fell to 39 percent in 2008, and 20 percent in 2012.
>
> As the Huffington Post noted, it looks like the financial crisis may have triggered a change in the aspirations of the nation's brightest, prompting millennials to prefer work in industries where they can contribute to social good, like health and tech, although

many of them, no doubt, want to score big in tech. At the same time, Wall Street is laying off more employees than it hires, so grads' reasons for career shifts may be more pragmatic than idealistic.

Source: Gwynne, Kristen. "Even Harvard Grads Don't Want to Work on Wall Street Anymore." *Alternet*, 29 May 2013. Web. 1 Jun. 2013.

As the editor of an established news website, the writer might be seen as a credible professional source for information about current political, economic, and cultural issues. At the same time, Alternet is well known for having a left-leaning political slant, which can affect the kind of information it publishes and how that information is presented. (See "Understanding Bias" later in this chapter.) That does not mean that the information in this passage is inaccurate, but it does mean that the information is likely to be presented in a way that reflects a certain political perspective on the issue at hand. Notice, for example, that the first sentence of the passage makes an unsupported assertion that financial firms on Wall Street have a "propensity to ravage the economy, launder money, and illegally foreclose on families." Such a claim is debatable, but it is presented here as fact. Moreover, the writer draws a conclusion from the newspaper survey that even she acknowledges might be mistaken. She suggests that the survey conducted by the student newspaper the *Harvard Crimson* indicates that the behavior of Wall Street firms has "irked some of the nation's brightest" college graduates. Although the survey results, which are reported in the second paragraph of the passage, indicate a decline in the percentage of Harvard graduates seeking employment in finance, the reasons for that decline are unclear. In the final sentence of the passage, the writer herself acknowledges that the decline might be a result of a decline in the number of job opportunities on Wall Street. The conclusion that Harvard graduates are "irked" by Wall Street is not supported by the evidence presented here.

This example illustrates that skepticism can be healthy when evaluating source material. In this case, the writer could be considered credible as a professional journalist, but the way she presents the information about the student survey and the rhetorical situation (that is, the fact that she is writing for a left-leaning website whose readers would very likely be critical of the financial firms on Wall Street) should make you look carefully and critically at the information she presents. Moreover, her conclusions and claims about the views of Harvard graduates regarding Wall Street are questionable. So when it comes to this particular issue—the financial industry—it might make sense to be skeptical about what the writer states, even if she can be considered a credible source, and to be judicious in deciding how you use any information from this source. You might, for example, use the figures from the student survey to show that college graduates' career decisions have changed in recent years, but you might avoid using the writer's conclusions about the reasons for that change.

In determining the credibility of a source, consider the following:

- **Author.** Who is the author? Do you know anything about his or her background? Is the author an expert on the subject at hand? Does he or she have an agenda with respect to this subject?

- **Publication.** What is the source of the publication? Is it a scholarly book or journal? A trade magazine? A sponsored website? What do you know about this source? What reputation does it have? Is it known to have a particular slant? Is it associated with a group that espouses a particular point of view on the subject?

- **Purpose.** What is the purpose of the source? To what extent might the purpose influence your sense of the trustworthiness of the information in the source? For example, is the author presenting a carefully researched analysis of a controversial topic—say, gun control—as in a scholarly journal article, or is the writer vigorously arguing against an opposing perspective on that topic for an audience of people who share the writer's views, as in an op-ed essay on a sponsored website? Both sources might be credible, but having a sense of the purpose of the source and the rhetorical situation can help you determine how skeptical to be about the information contained in the source.

- **Date.** How recent is the publication? Is it current when it comes to the subject at hand? For some kinds of information, the date of publication might not matter much, but for many topics, outdated information can be problematic.

Reliability

Reliability refers to your confidence in the accuracy of the information found in a source and the reputation of a source for consistently presenting trustworthy information. In general, credible sources gain a reputation for publishing accurate information over time. For example, major newspapers and magazines, such as the *Los Angeles Times* and *The New Yorker*, usually employ fact checkers to verify information in articles they are preparing to publish; respected publishing houses usually edit manuscripts carefully to be sure they are accurate; and scholarly publishers employ expert reviewers to evaluate manuscripts. These practices usually mean that material published by these sources tends to be consistently accurate and trustworthy, so they gain a reputation for reliability. By contrast, many popular news outlets emphasize breaking news and sometimes publish information quickly before it can be carefully verified. Often, such publications are not subject to the kind of rigorous editorial review that characterizes scholarly publications, which can result in inaccuracies and weaken your confidence in their reliability.

Because you are not likely to be an expert on many of the subjects you write about in college, you often won't have a sense of the reliability of a particular source, so you will have to make judgments on the basis of the nature of the source and its credibility. **Follow these guidelines:**

- **Choose credible sources.** In general, if you have a choice of sources, use those that you know or believe to be credible. Sources with reputations for credibility are more likely to supply reliable information. In general, scholarly publications, reference works (such as encyclopedias), well-established newspapers or magazines, and respected government agencies or non-governmental organizations (such as the Centers for Disease Control and Prevention or the American Heart Association) tend to be safe bets as sources for your research.

- **Consult multiple sources.** Using multiple sources on the same topic can help you avoid using unreliable information. If you have information that is consistent across several sources, including sources you consider to be credible, that information is more likely to be reliable as well.

Determining whether a source is trustworthy is usually not an either–or proposition. Even credible and reliable sources might have information that isn't accurate or is inappropriate for your purposes. Your decisions about the trustworthiness of a source, then, should be guided by your rhetorical situation as well as by your own growing understanding of your subject. As you gain experience in reviewing unfamiliar sources, you will begin to develop a sense of what to look for and what to avoid when determining whether information from a source can be trusted. Such decisions about source material must also be made with an understanding of the potential bias of a source, which is discussed in the following section.

Understanding Bias

Bias is a tendency to think or feel a certain way. It is the inclination of a source to favor one point of view over others that might be equally valid—the privileging of one perspective at the expense of others. Bias is sometimes thought of as prejudice, though bias is not necessarily a negative quality. One might have a bias in favor of cats rather than dogs as pets, for example. In this textbook, bias generally refers to a source's perspective or slant.

It is important to understand that all sources are biased in some way. We tend to think of some kinds of source material, such as encyclopedias and other kinds of reference works, as objective or neutral. But even a venerable reference such as the *Encyclopedia Britannica* can be said to have certain biases, despite its extensive efforts to present accurate information as objectively as possible. For example, the kind of information that is considered appropriate for inclusion in *Encyclopedia Britannica* reflects a set of beliefs about what kinds of knowledge or information are relevant and important for its purposes. Although such a reference work is intended to be comprehensive, it inevitably excludes some kinds of information and privileges others. For instance, extremely technical information about the rhythms of hip hop music might be excluded from an encyclopedia, even though more general information about that musical form might be included. The decisions the editors make about what to include in and what to exclude from the encyclopedia represent a bias, no matter how open-minded the editors might be.

Bias, then, is not necessarily a negative quality in a source, but it is essential to recognize bias in any source you consult so that you can evaluate the usefulness of information from that source. Some kinds of sources are transparent about their biases. Scholarly journals, for example, tend to make their editorial focus and purpose clear. Here is a statement of the editorial policy of a journal titled *Research in the Teaching of English,* published by a professional organization called the National Council of Teachers of English (NCTE):

> *Research in the Teaching of English* publishes scholarship that explores issues in the teaching and learning of literacy at all levels. It is the policy of NCTE in its journals and other publications to provide a forum for open discussion of ideas concerning the teaching of English and language arts.

Scholarly journals often provide such descriptions of the kinds of articles they seek to publish; they might also provide explanations of the processes by which manuscripts are reviewed. These editorial policy statements help make the biases of a journal explicit.

Many sources, even credible and reliable ones, are not so transparent about their biases. For example, although many readers consider newspapers to be trusted sources of information, many newspapers have well-established points of view. *The New York Times* is generally considered to have a liberal bias, whereas *The Washington Times* is usually thought to reflect a more conservative viewpoint. However, if you did not already have a sense of such biases, you might find it difficult to determine them. Here, for example, is the description that *The New York Times* provides of its editorial board:

> The editorial board is composed of 18 journalists with wide-ranging areas of expertise. Their primary responsibility is to write *The Times's* editorials, which represent the voice of the board, its editor and the publisher. The board is part of the *Times's* editorial department, which is operated separately from the *Times* newsroom, and includes the Letters to the Editor and Op-Ed sections.

Source: "The *New York Times* Editorial Board." *The New York Times*, 2013. Web. 3 June 2013.

Although this statement explains that the editorial department is separate from the newsroom at *The New York Times*, which might give readers confidence that the newspaper's reporting is not influenced by its editorial opinions, the statement does not describe a particular political slant or perspective. You would have to examine the newspaper more carefully—and probably over time—to gain a sense of its political bias. Similarly, consider the following statement from the "About" page on the website of *The Washington Times*:

> *The Washington Times* is a full-service, general interest daily newspaper in the nation's capital. Founded in 1982, *The Washington Times* is one of the most-often-quoted newspapers in the U.S. It has gained a reputation for hard-hitting investigative reporting and thorough coverage of politics and policy. Published by The Washington Times LLC, *The Washington Times* is "America's Newspaper."

Source: "About." *Washington Times*, 2013. Web. 3 June 2013.

Nowhere in this statement is there any indication that the newspaper tends to reflect a conservative point of view.

These examples underscore the important point that even the most credible and reliable sources will have biases that might not be obvious; however, a bias does not mean that a source is untrustworthy. Rather, bias influences the kind of information a source might contain and how that information is presented, even when the information is trustworthy. For example, like major newspapers, major public affairs magazines are usually considered to have either a liberal (e.g., *The Nation*) or conservative (e.g., *National Review*) bias. Those biases mean that each magazine is likely to focus on some issues as opposed to others and to examine issues from a particular perspective. For instance, *The Nation* might publish an argument in favor of a proposal to increase the national minimum wage, reflecting a liberal perspective on the government's role in economic matters. *National Review*, by contrast, might publish a critique of the same proposal, reflecting a conservative bias in favor of less government intervention in economic matters. Both articles might contain reliable and accurate information about the proposal, but the information is presented in a way that reflects the political bias of the publication.

Often, the bias of a source is much more subtle and difficult to detect. For example, advocacy groups often try to appear objective in their treatment of certain issues when in fact they have a strong bias on those issues. For example, an environmental advocacy group might oppose the development of a large wind farm in a wilderness area. Its website might seem to be a neutral source of information about various kinds of energy, including wind power, but its opposition to large wind farms means that its treatment of wind power is likely to focus on the disadvantages of wind power and the harmful impact of wind turbines on wilderness areas. In such a case, even though the information on the website might be accurate, that information might also be incomplete or presented in a way that paints a negative picture of wind power. (See "Detecting Bias.")

When evaluating a source for bias, consider these questions:

- Does this source reflect a particular perspective or point of view?

- Does this source represent a specific group, political party, business, organization, or institution?

- Does the source seem to have an agenda regarding the subject at hand?

- To what extent is the bias of this source evident? Are there blatantly slanted statements? Do you notice questionable information? To what extent does this bias seem to affect the trustworthiness of the information it presents?

FOCUS **Detecting Bias**

Many sources appear at first glance to be neutral or objective on a particular issue or subject but actually reflect a strong bias. The website shown on page 219, for example, contains information about education reform but is sponsored by an organization that advocates a particular perspective on school reform in favor of charter schools and related movements that are controversial. Notice that nothing on the web page conveys a sense of the organization's strong views about specific kinds of education reforms; instead, the language is neutral ("The leading voice for lasting, substantive and structural education reform in the U.S.") and seemingly nonpartisan ("Join us in our fight to make *all* schools better for *all* children."). The information on such a site can be useful, but it is important to understand that it is being presented from a particular point of view. In this case, you might find accurate information about charter schools, but you are unlikely to find studies whose results are not flattering to charter schools; therefore, although the information might be accurate, it might also be incomplete or present a misleading view of the impact of charter schools.

Before using information from a source, try to determine how the source's bias might affect the usefulness and reliability of the information. Identifying any bias in a source can help you determine whether to trust the information you find there and whether you might need to balance it with information from other sources.

Source: *The Center for Education Reform.*

All sources should be evaluated for trustworthiness, but different sources can present different challenges when you are trying to determine trustworthiness. **Use the following questions to guide you as you evaluate specific sources:**

Print Sources

- **Who published this article or book?** (scholarly press, trade publisher, respected newspaper or magazine, professional organization, non-profit organization, government agency, advocacy group, business)
- **Who is the author?** (Is the author's name provided? Is the author an expert on the subject?)
- **What is the purpose?** (to share information or knowledge, to advocate for a point of view)
- **Does the source have a reputation for reliability?** (Is the source known to have a bias or slant? Is the source generally considered credible?)
- **When was it published?** (Is the date of publication indicated? Is the book or article current or outdated?)

Websites

- **Who sponsors the site?** (a news organization, business, political organization, advocacy group, non-profit foundation, government agency)
- **What is the purpose of the site?** (to inform, to advertise or sell a product, to promote a point of view)
- **What are the contents of the site?** (Does it include relevant information? Does it have advertisements? Does it seem to contain accurate information? Are the sources of information indicated?)
- **Is the site current?** (Is the site regularly updated? Are the web pages dated? Is the information current?)

8

Determining Whether a Source Is Trustworthy **219**

Although the advice in this chapter applies to all kinds of sources, you can follow additional steps to help you determine the trustworthiness of online sources:

- **Read the "About" page.** Many websites have pages titled "About" or "About Us" that provide useful information about the authors, the purpose, and sometimes the history of the site. Sites sponsored by advocacy groups and non-profit organizations often include information about their boards of directors or administrators. Such information can help you evaluate the trustworthiness of a site and determine the extent to which it might be biased. For example, a site of an organization that seems to advocate green energy but whose board of directors includes mostly business leaders from large energy companies might have a bias in favor of large business interests. By contrast, the site of a clean energy advocacy group whose directors are members of well-known environmental organizations will be less likely to support business interests when it comes to energy issues.

- **Look for a date.** Most websites sponsored by legitimate organizations indicate the date when the website or individual web pages were updated. Many organizations, especially respected media organizations, update their websites daily. However, some websites are never adequately maintained. Such sites can be readily available on the Internet many years after they cease to be updated or revised. If you cannot find dates on a website or if the only dates you find are well in the past, be wary of the material on that site.

- **Check the links.** Many websites contain pages with various kinds of resources, including links to related websites sponsored by other organizations. Often, those links reflect a website's own biases and can help you determine whether the site is trustworthy or biased in a way that should concern you. If these links are not active, it indicates that the site is not well maintained—another reason to be skeptical about information you find there.

Evaluating Source Material for Your Rhetorical Purposes

Once you have determined that information from a source is trustworthy, you must still decide whether it is useful and appropriate for your project. It isn't enough to determine whether a source is credible and reliable or to identify its biases; you must also evaluate the information in terms of your own rhetorical situation and especially in light of the purpose of your project.

To illustrate, let's imagine two related but different kinds of writing assignments: an analysis of the debate about health care reform in the United States and an argument about the Affordable

Care Act (ACA), often called Obamacare, which was passed by the U.S. Congress and became law in 2010. The analysis is for an assignment in a writing course that requires students to examine public debates about a controversial issue; the audience includes other students in the course as well as the instructor. The argument is intended for the student newspaper on your campus. Both pieces require research.

Let's consider how these different rhetorical situations, with their different audiences and purposes, might shape your decisions about whether and how to use information from the following three sources: an article posted on the website of Fox News, a blog post from a website called California Healthline, and an article from Alternet:

Smoke? Overweight? New Regulations Could Raise Your Insurance Rates

by Jim Angle

Foxnews.com 31 May 2013

If you smoke or you're overweight, have high cholesterol or high blood pressure, you could be forced to pay a lot more for health insurance, according to new regulations just issued by the Obama administration.

"For smoking, for being overweight, for being obese and basically, for generally not meeting the health guidelines, the employer can charge 30 percent more—for smoking, 50 percent more," explains John Goodman, President of the National Center for Policy Analysis in Dallas.

Obamacare does prevent insurers from charging more for pre-existing conditions, or from charging as much as they currently do for older people who use more health care.

But when it comes to smoking and being overweight as well as other health problems, if employees don't participate in wellness programs, they could pay more.

Ed Haislmeier of the Heritage Foundation says "on the one hand they're trying to ban discrimination based on health status, but on the other hand they're trying to say that some discrimination based on health status is good discrimination."

Goodman adds that "it is definitely the nanny state trying to tell us what we're going to do, and unleashing the employers to be the agent of the government in telling us what we're going to do."

Smokers, of course, run up more health care bills than non-smokers. But that habit and some other unhealthy conditions are associated with lower incomes, so higher rates would hit those the administration was aiming to help.

(Continued)

8

"Allowing premium differentials based on these factors will push premiums higher primarily on people that will be struggling to pay the premiums in the first place," says Jim Capretta of the Ethics and Public Policy Center.

Many employers already offer wellness programs, but the new 123-page regulation tells them exactly how they must operate.

"This is just one more massive regulation on top of the thousands and thousands of pages that have already been issued that employers have to deal with," says Capretta. "I think the whole system is starting to choke on so many rules."

Ironically, on the day officials released the new regulations, a Rand Corporation study about wellness programs was released—and not with good news.

Goodman noted it was "a Rand Corporation study, which was paid for by the Obama administration, and called for in the affordable care act. And the Rand Corporation has studied wellness programs all over the country, and basically says they don't work."

In fact, the study found that those trying to lose weight in these programs lost an average of a pound a year. And although some employers offer gym memberships, those who take them are the ones using the gym already—not those who need it most.

Source: Angle, Jim. "Smoke? Overweight? New Regulations Could Raise Your Insurance Rates." *Foxnews.com*, 31 May 2013. Web 1 June 2013.

The Premium Conundrum: Do Smokers Get a Fair Break under Obamacare?

by Dan Diamond

California Healthline 23 Jan. 2013

The Affordable Care Act contains a number of provisions intended to incent "personal responsibility," or the notion that health care isn't just a right—it's an obligation. None of these measures is more prominent than the law's individual mandate, designed to ensure that every American obtains health coverage or pays a fine for choosing to go uninsured.

But one provision that's gotten much less attention—until recently—relates to smoking; specifically, the ACA allows payers to treat tobacco users very differently by opening the door to much higher premiums for this population.

That measure has some health policy analysts cheering, suggesting that higher premiums are necessary to raise revenue for the law and (hopefully) deter smokers' bad habits. But other observers have warned that the ACA takes a heavy-handed stick to smokers who may be unhappily addicted to tobacco, rather than enticing them with a carrot to quit.

Under proposed rules, the department of Health and Human Services would allow insurers to charge a smoker seeking health coverage in the individual market as much as 50% more in premiums than a non-smoker.

That difference in premiums may rapidly add up for smokers, given the expectation that Obamacare's new medical-loss ratios already will lead to major cost hikes in the individual market. "For many people, in the years after the law, premiums aren't just going to [go] up a little," Peter Suderman predicts at Reason. "They're going to rise a lot."

Meanwhile, Ann Marie Marciarille, a law professor at the University of Missouri-Kansas City, adds that insurers have "considerable flexibility" in how to set up a potential surcharge for tobacco use. For example, insurers could apply a high surcharge for tobacco use in older smokers—perhaps several hundred dollars per month—further hitting a population that tends to be poorer.

Is this cost-shifting fair? The average American tends to think so.

Nearly 60% of surveyed adults in a 2011 NPR-Thomson Reuters poll thought it was OK to charge smokers more for their health insurance than non-smokers. (That's nearly twice the number of adults who thought it would be OK to charge the obese more for their health insurance.)

And smoking does lead to health costs that tend to be borne by the broader population. Writing at the Incidental Economist in 2011, Don Taylor noted that "smoking imposes very large social costs"—essentially, about $1.50 per pack—with its increased risk of cancers and other chronic illness. CDC has found that smoking and its effects lead to more than 440,000 premature deaths in the United States per year, with more than $190 billion in annual health costs and productivity loss.

As a result, charging smokers more "makes some actuarial sense," Marciarille acknowledges. "Tobacco use has a long-term fuse for its most expensive health effects."

But Louise Norris of Colorado Health Insurance Insider takes issue with the ACA's treatment of tobacco users.

Noting that smokers represent only about 20% of Americans, Norris argues that "it's easy to point fingers and call for increased personal responsibility when we're singling out another group—one in which we are not included."

As a result, she adds, "it seems very logical to say that smokers should have to pay significantly higher premiums for their health insurance," whereas we're less inclined to treat the obese differently because so many of us are overweight.

(Continued)

This approach toward tobacco users also raises the risk that low-income smokers will find the cost of coverage too high and end up uninsured, Norris warns. She notes that tax credits for health coverage will be calculated prior to however insurers choose to set their banding rules, "which means that smokers would be responsible for [an] additional premium on their own."

Alternate Approach: Focus on Cessation

Nearly 70% of smokers want to quit, and about half attempt to kick the habit at least once per year. But more than 90% are unable to stop smoking, partly because of the lack of assistance; fewer than 5% of smokers appear able to quit without support.

That's why Norris and others say that if federal officials truly want to improve public health, the law should prioritize anti-smoking efforts like counseling and medication for tobacco users. And the ACA does require new health insurance plans to offer smoking cessation products and therapy.

But as Ankita Rao writes at Kaiser Health News, the coverage of those measures thus far is spotty. Some plans leave out nasal sprays and inhalers; others shift costs to smokers, possibly deterring them from seeking treatment.

Some anti-smoking crusaders hope that states will step into the gap and ramp up cessation opportunities, such as by including cessation therapy as an essential health benefit.

"The federal government has missed several opportunities since the enactment of the ACA to grant smokers access to more cessation treatments," the American Lung Association warned in November. "Now, as states are beginning implementation of state exchanges and Medicaid expansions, state policymakers have the opportunity to stand up for smokers in their states who want to quit."

Source: Diamond, Dan. "The Premium Conundrum: Do Smokers Get a Fair Break Under Obamacare?" *California Healthline*, 23 Jan. 2013. Web. 31 May 2013.

How's Obamacare Turning Out? Great If You Live in a Blue State, and "Screw You" If You Have a Republican Governor

by Steve Rosenfeld

Alternet 25 May 2013

Obamacare implementation is becoming the latest dividing line between blue- and red-state America, with Democrat-led states making progress to expand healthcare to the uninsured and the poor—and Republican-led states saying "screw you" to millions of their most vulnerable and needy residents.

The latest sign of the Republican Party's increasingly secessionist tendencies comes as Obamacare passed a major milestone in California, which late last week announced lower-than-expected healthcare premiums for its 5.3 million uninsured, less than many small businesses now pay in group plans.

"Covered California's Silver Plan... offers premiums that can be 29 percent lower than comparable plans provided on today's small group market," the state's new insurance exchange announced Thursday, referring to the least-expensive option of four state-administered plans and posting this price comparison chart.

In contrast, the refusal by red-state America to create these health exchanges, which would be more local control—a supposed Republican value—and to accept federal funds to expand state-run Medicaid programs for the poor, means that about half the states are turning their backs on their residents, especially millions of the poorest people.

The federal government plans to step in later this summer and offer uninsured people in recalcitrant red states the option of buying plans via federally run health care exchanges. But the poorest people can't afford that, meaning the refusal to expand Medicaid programs will leave them in the cold. They will see ads selling new federal healthcare options that will be unaffordable for them.

The *New York Times* reports that local healthcare advocates in red states are predicting a backlash once Obamacare is rolled out and the poor realize that they cannot take advantage of it because Republicans are blocking it. However, that does not change the bottom line in state-run Medicaid programs: the GOP is again penalizing the poor.

Progress in Blue States

Meanwhile, in blue states, there have been surprising developments in the cost of Obamacare for those people who currently are uninsured. There, the bottom line is insurance premiums are hundreds of dollars a month lower than what employers are now paying for their workers under existing group plans.

California, with 5.3 million uninsured adults, is the biggest state to release cost estimates for Obamacare. Its lower-than-expected estimates are in line with announcements in Washington, Oregon, Maryland and Vermont. The actual prices will be known after insurers file rate documents in coming weeks.

Source: Rosenfeld, Steven. "How's Obamacare Turning Out? Great If You Live in a Blue State, and 'Screw You' If You Have a Republican Governor." *Alternet*, 25 May 2013. Web. 31 May 2013.

All three sources are relevant to both assignments, but are they useful? To answer that question, first determine whether each source is trustworthy by addressing the three main aspects of trustworthiness described in this chapter:

- Is the source credible?
- Is the source reliable?
- What is the bias of the source?

Is the Source Credible?

As we saw earlier (see pages 213–215), the credibility of a source depends on several important factors: the author, the nature of the publication, the purpose of the publication, and the date. Review each source accordingly:

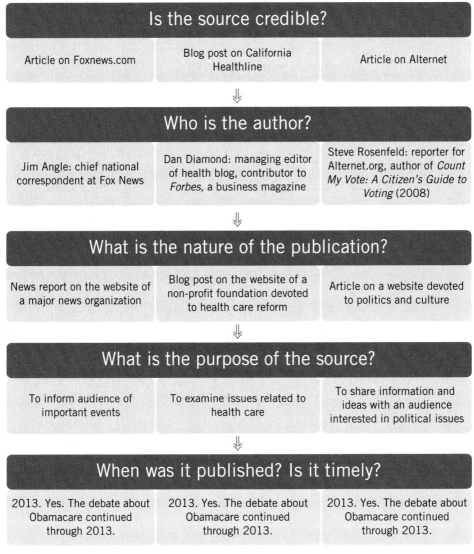

Addressing these questions will help you develop a better sense of the nature of each source, which will help you determine its credibility. Evaluating these sources in comparison to each other also reveals some important differences among them. For example, Fox News and Alternet cover all kinds of newsworthy topics, whereas California Healthline focuses only on health issues and can therefore be assumed to have more in-depth and expert coverage of issues like the Affordable Care Act.

If necessary, you can find more information to answer each of these questions about these sources. For example, you can look for more information about each author. Visiting a website like Amazon.com or Alibris.com might enable you to learn more about Steven Rosenfeld's book *Count My Vote*, which could give you insight into his background and his perspective on political issues. Similarly, you could find more information about the sponsor of California Healthline to determine whether the site could be considered a credible source of information.

As noted earlier in this chapter, credibility can also be a function of a writer's tone, fairness, and general approach to the subject. With those criteria in mind, you might note that the general tone of the Fox News article toward the Affordable Care Act is negative, and the language of the Alternet article is explicitly dismissive and disrespectful of a conservative viewpoint. These characteristics should make you a bit more skeptical about these two sources. Nevertheless, both sources seem to have accurate information about the topic of health care reform, even though they present that information from a decidedly partisan perspective.

Let's say that after examining each source in this example, you have determined that all three sources can be considered credible, despite your reservations about the Alternet and Fox News articles. Next, try to decide whether the source is reliable.

Is the Source Reliable?

Reliability generally has to do with your confidence that a source has established a record for accuracy and credibility. In this example, both Fox News and Alternet represent perspectives that are consistent over time. Both sources are respected by their constituencies. You are aware of their respective political leanings, and you can judge the reliability of information from each site in the context of those perspectives. For example, you expect Fox News to be skeptical about the Affordable Care Act because of Fox's generally conservative perspective on large government programs; by contrast, you expect articles on Alternet to be supportive of the ACA and critical of conservative resistance to it. Neither article is surprising in this regard. In other words, each site is reliable in terms of its political perspective and generally reliable in the kinds of information it presents.

The reliability of the blog post from California Healthline is less clear, mostly because it is a less well-known and more specialized source. To gain a better sense of its reliability, you should investigate further. For one thing, you can check the "About" page on its website. Here's what you would find:

> *California Healthline* is a free, daily digest of health care news, policy and opinion. It is designed to meet the information needs of busy health care professionals and decision makers. *California Healthline* is part of the California HealthCare Foundation's commitment to important issues affecting health care policy, delivery, and financing.

The Advisory Board Company is a leader in national health care research and publishing. It independently publishes *California Healthline* for the California HealthCare Foundation and is responsible for the editorial content of the publication. *California Healthline* editors review more than 300 newspapers, journals, and trade publications to produce daily news summaries.

Source: "About California Healthline." *California Healthline*, 2013. Web. 3 June 2013.

This description provides the important information that California Healthline is sponsored by an organization called California Healthcare Foundation but is published independently by a national health care research and publishing organization. That information lends credibility to the site because it suggests that the publication is non-partisan and lacks a particular political or ideological agenda. The site also indicates that it has been in operation since 1998, which gives you confidence in its reliability as a source for information about health care issues. Finally, the author of the blog post seems to be an established observer of health care and business matters (he writes for *Forbes* magazine, a leading and well-respected business publication). All these facts can give you confidence that this is a reliable source for information about health care issues.

This analysis enables you to conclude that all three of these sources can be considered reliable.

What Is the Bias of the Source?

You have established your sources as credible and reliable, but their usefulness to you will also depend on the extent to which they are biased.

You have already determined that Fox News and Alternet reflect conservative and left-leaning political biases, respectively. What about California Healthline? Your review of its "About" page led you to conclude that it is credible, reliable, and probably politically non-partisan, but even if it does not reflect a political bias, it might reflect other kinds of bias. It makes sense to look more closely at this source.

The "About" page indicates California Healthline is sponsored by a non-profit organization called California Health Care Foundation. Here's how the organization describes itself on its website:

CHCF is a nonprofit grantmaking philanthropy based in Oakland, California. Founded in 1996, the staff of about 50 people issues around $40 million in grants each year from an endowment of $700 million. CHCF does not participate in lobbying or fundraising.

Source: "About CHCF." *California Health Care Foundation*, 2013. Web. 3 June 2013.

This explanation tells you that the foundation is not a political group and supports health care reform by providing grants rather than by lobbying on behalf of specific reforms or political interests. But on the same web page you also find the following statement:

The passage of the federal Affordable Care Act creates an extraordinary opportunity to provide health coverage to millions of Californians. Its success will depend on how the law is implemented by the states. This initiative focuses on elements of health reform that have the greatest potential to affect California.

From this passage you could reasonably conclude that the organization is generally supportive of the Affordable Care Act. That conclusion doesn't necessarily call into question the information on the California Healthline site, but it does suggest that the site is likely to cover the Affordable Care Act closely and is not likely to be consistently critical of it. In other words, articles and blog posts on the site are likely to reflect a bias in favor of expanded and effective health care reform, including the ACA.

You can examine the biases of your three sources in more depth by addressing the four sets of questions listed on page 218:

To what extent is the source biased?

| Article on Foxnews.com | Blog post on California Healthline | Article on Alternet |

Does the source reflect a particular viewpoint or perspective?

| Yes, a generally conservative viewpoint | No obvious political or ideological perspective | Yes, a left-leaning political point of view |

Does the source represent a specific group or organization?

| Yes, website is part of the Fox News organization. | Yes, sponsored by a non-profit foundation that supports health care reform. | No, the site is an independent, non-profit news entity. |

Does the source have an agenda regarding the subject?

| Yes, generally opposed to federal health care reform initiative | Yes, supports health care reform | Yes, generally supportive of the presidential administration's reform efforts |

To what extent is the bias of the source evident?

| The critical stance toward the ACA is noticeable. | Bias in favor of health care reform is implicit. | Overt bias in favor of presidential administration and against its conservative opponents. |

8

At this point, you should have a good sense of the biases of your three sources.

Now that you have carefully evaluated your sources, examine their usefulness for your rhetorical purposes. Recall that both your hypothetical assignments—the analysis and the argument—are about health care reform in the United States, but their purposes and intended audiences differ, which will influence your decisions about whether and how to use the sources you have evaluated.

Let's imagine that your analysis is an effort to answer this question:

Why is the debate about the Affordable Care Act in the United States so intense and confrontational?

You want to understand some of the reasons for the vitriolic nature of this debate and what it might reveal about public debates in general. You are writing your analysis primarily for your instructor and other students in your class. For your argument, let's imagine that you want to make the case that the intense debates about the Affordable Care Act are relevant to college students. For this piece, your audience is broader than for your analysis: students and faculty who read your campus newspaper. We can sum up the rhetorical situations for these two pieces of writing as follows:

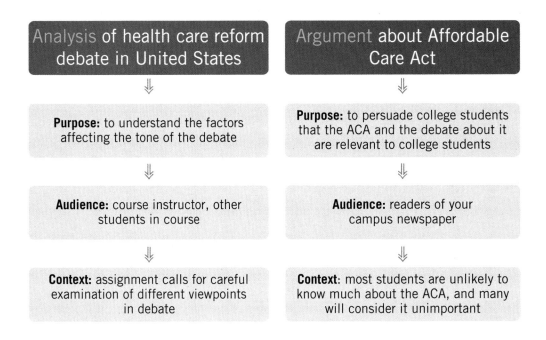

With these factors in mind, you can examine how each of the three sources you found might fit into these two assignments.

For your analysis of the debate about the Affordable Care Act, you might use the articles from Fox News and Alternet as examples of more extreme political positions in the debate. In this case, you don't need to worry much about the accuracy or reliability of the sources because you would be using them as examples of how conservative and left-leaning viewpoints emerge in the debate about health care reform. Your analysis would require you to identify clearly the political perspectives represented by each source and how those perspectives influence the way each source represents the Affordable Care Act. For example, you might examine the quotations from experts that are included in the Fox News article to show that the author cites only experts who are critical of the ACA. Similarly, you might evaluate the specific language used in the Alternet article to refer to Republican or conservative positions—for example, "secessionist" and "recalcitrant"—and the unsupported claim that "the GOP is again penalizing the poor." For your purposes, it would not be necessary to decide how accurate the information in each source is; you are simply analyzing *how* the sources present the information, not the information itself, so the overt biases of the sources is not a problem.

For your argument, by contrast, you would likely need to present accurate information about the Affordable Care Act and the problems it is intended to address, especially in terms of how it might affect college students. You want to convince your audience that the debate about health care reform is one they should pay attention to. In this case, some of the information from the California Healthline blog post is likely to be useful in arguing that the debate matters to college students. For example, the author notes that the new law is "designed to ensure that every American obtains health coverage or pays a fine for choosing to go uninsured." That fact should be important to college students, many of whom will lose their health care insurance once they graduate. If you include that quotation in your argument, you will need to be confident that it is accurate. Your evaluation of this source should give you that confidence, but you can also look for other sources that could corroborate it. At the same time, the information included in the Fox News and Alternet articles might also be useful, but given your rhetorical purpose, you would have to take into account the clear political biases of those sources as you decide whether to use specific information. For instance, the author of the Alternet article identifies differences in how individual states will enact the Affordable Care Act. Those differences could be important to college students because they could affect the kind of health insurance that is available to them in one state or another. However, you might be more skeptical of the author's claim that "Republican-led states [are] saying 'screw you' to millions of their most vulnerable and needy residents." Given the author's political perspective, which makes him more likely to be critical of Republican policies, it would be sensible to verify such a claim before using it in your own argument. Moreover, you would want to avoid undermining your argument by relying on sources whose political views might alienate some of your intended readers.

These examples illustrate how the rhetorical situation can influence your decisions about how to use the source material you find in your research. Obviously, you should evaluate *all* source material in terms of credibility, reliability, and bias. But how your evaluation will affect your decisions about using source material will ultimately depend upon the rhetorical goals you hope to achieve with your intended audience.

8

Using Source Material

9

STUDENT WRITERS sometimes have less trouble finding the source material they need for their projects than they do using that material effectively in their own writing. The challenge for many students is resisting the tendency to rely too heavily on source material so that it doesn't take over the student's own writing. Using source materials effectively, then, is partly a matter of keeping in mind the purpose and main point of the project. The most important guideline to follow when using any source material is to focus on your own ideas and the point *you* are making. The source material you cite should support *your* thinking and should not become the focus of your writing. (See Core Concept #4: "A writer must have something to say.") So it is important to be able to *integrate* source material into your writing rather than simply reproduce information from a source. This chapter describes some basic strategies for using your source material strategically and maintaining control of your own writing.

Quoting from Sources

In academic writing, there are three main ways to integrate source material into your own prose:

- summarizing
- paraphrasing
- quoting

Summarizing and paraphrasing are discussed in Chapter 5 (see pages 127–131). In this section, we will examine how to quote sources appropriately.

To integrate source material smoothly into your writing, **follow these basic guidelines:**

- Quote only what you need and when necessary.
- Reproduce the original text accurately.
- Be concise.
- Make it fit.

Quote Only What You Need and When Necessary

Writers quote from a source when the rhetorical situation dictates that it is important to include information or ideas *as stated in the original language of the source.* If you are consulting a source for specific information and don't need the exact language of the source, summarize or paraphrase the source passage. (See Chapter 5 for advice about summarizing and paraphrasing.) Sometimes, however, the original wording of the source is necessary to make or emphasize a point. In such cases, quoting can enhance your writing.

For example, imagine that you are writing an analysis of the debate about what should be done to address global climate change. One of your sources is *Field Notes from a Catastrophe*, in which author Elizabeth Kolbert reviews scientific data indicating that climate change is an increasingly serious problem. Here are two passages that you consider important and want to include in your analysis:

> All told, the Greenland ice sheet holds enough water to raise sea levels worldwide by twenty-three feet. Scientists at NASA have calculated that throughout the 1990s the ice sheet, despite some thickening at the center, was shrinking by twelve cubic miles per year. (52)

> As the effects of global warming become more and more difficult to ignore, will we react by finally fashioning a global response? Or will we retreat into ever narrower and more destructive forms of self-interest? It may seem impossible to imagine that a technologically advanced society could choose, in essence, to destroy itself, but that is what we are now in the process of doing. (189)

Source: Kolbert, Elizabeth. *Field Notes from a Catastrophe*. New York: Bloomsbury Press, 2006. Print.

The first passage contains important information about shrinking glaciers, which scientists consider a sign of climate change that could have a significant impact on coastal communities. The second passage is taken from Kolbert's conclusion, where she makes a plea for action to address climate change. Here's how you might use these passages in your analysis:

> Scientists have documented the decline of glaciers and arctic sea ice over the past several decades. For example, the Greenland ice sheet, which contains enough water to increase global sea levels by 23 feet, is shrinking by 12 cubic miles per year (Kolbert 52). To many scientists, the loss of glacial and sea ice is one of the most worrisome indicators that climate change is accelerating, and some argue that humans must act now to avoid potentially catastrophic impacts on human communities in the coming decades. Elizabeth Kolbert expresses the concerns of many experts: "As the effects of global warming become more and more difficult to ignore, will we react by finally fashioning a global response? Or will we retreat into ever narrower and more destructive forms of self-interest? It may seem impossible to imagine that a technologically advanced society could choose, in essence, to destroy itself, but that is what we are now in the process of doing" (189).

Notice that the first passage from the source text (p. 52) is cited but not quoted. Although the information in that passage is important, the wording of the source text is not. The second passage (p.189), however, is quoted, because Kolbert's wording conveys her point more effectively than a summary or paraphrase would.

This example illustrates the need to be judicious in deciding whether to quote or summarize and cite your source. In making that decision, always consider the purpose of your project and the impact you wish to have on your audience.

Reproduce the Original Text Accurately

Quotation marks indicate to a reader that everything inside the quotation marks is exactly as it appears in the source text. So whenever you are using a quotation, make sure that you have reproduced the passage you are quoting accurately. Although this advice might seem obvious, misquoting is a common problem in student writing that can lead to misleading or inaccurate statements. For example, here's a statement from an article reporting the results of a study of the link between childhood obesity and cancer:

> Those whose Body Mass Index placed them in the range of obesity in adolescence had a 1.42% greater chance of developing urothelial or colorectal cancers in adulthood.

A misplaced quotation mark or incomplete quotation could significantly change the meaning of this statement:

> According to a recent study, "Those whose Body Mass Index placed them in the range of obesity in adolescence had a 1.42% greater chance of developing urothelial or colorectal cancers."

In this example, the writer failed to include the phrase "in adulthood" at the end of the quoted statement. Although everything else included in the quotation marks is accurate, the quoted statement is now misleading. The original study indicates that obese adolescents have a 1.42% greater chance of developing two specific kinds of cancer *in adulthood*. Because the quotation in this example omits that phrase, a reader could misinterpret the results of the study to mean that obese adolescents have a greater chance of developing specific cancers at any time in their lives, even before adulthood, which is not what the study found.

As this example indicates, even a minor mistake in quoting from a source could result in erroneous or misleading statements.

Be Concise

One of the most common problems students have when quoting from a source is wordiness. Often, students use unnecessary words to introduce a quotation. Here's an example:

> In the article "New Teachers" by Neil Postman and Charles Weingarten, the authors state, "One of the largest obstacles to the establishment of a sound learning environment is the desire of teachers to get something they think they know into the heads of people who don't know it" (138).

Technically, there is nothing wrong with this sentence, but the writer could introduce the quotation more smoothly with fewer words:

> In "New Teachers," Neil Postman and Charles Weingarten state, "One of the largest obstacles to the establishment of a sound learning environment is the desire of teachers to get something they think they know into the heads of people who don't know it" (138).

9

In their article, Neil Postman and Charles Weingarten state, "One of the largest obstacles to the establishment of a sound learning environment is the desire of teachers to get something they think they know into the heads of people who don't know it" (138).

Neil Postman and Charles Weingarten state, "One of the largest obstacles to the establishment of a sound learning environment is the desire of teachers to get something they think they know into the heads of people who don't know it" ("New Teachers" 138).

Here are a few more examples:

Wordy: Janet Emig, in her work "Writing as a Mode of Learning," argues that "writing serves learning uniquely because writing as process-and-product possesses a cluster of attributes that correspond uniquely to certain powerful learning strategies" (122).

Better: According to Janet Emig, "Writing serves learning uniquely because writing as process-and-product possesses a cluster of attributes that correspond uniquely to certain powerful learning strategies" ("Writing as a Mode of Learning" 122).

Wordy: "Nobody Mean More to Me than You and the Future Life of Willie Jordan" is an essay written by June Jordan that analyzes Black English as a language "system constructed by people constantly needing to insist that we exist, that we are present" (460).

Better: In "Nobody Mean More to Me than You and the Future Life of Willie Jordan," June Jordan analyzes Black English as a language "system constructed by people constantly needing to insist that we exist, that we are present" (460).

The rule of thumb is to be concise and include only the necessary information about the source. If you're not sure how to introduce a quotation, use one of the standard approaches to introducing a quotation. (See "Four Common Ways to Introduce Quotations in Academic Writing.") Keep in mind that if you have a bibliography or works cited page (which you should if you are using sources), you need to give your readers only enough information in your text to be able to find the citation in your bibliography or works cited page.

FOCUS | **Four Common Ways to Introduce Quotations in Academic Writing**

If you pay attention as you read scholarly writing in books and journals, you will notice four common patterns that writers use to introduce quotations from source materials. You can use these patterns to make your own use of source material more effective and help give your own prose a more scholarly "sound":

1. In [title of source], [name of author] states (argues, asserts, claims, suggests), "[insert quotation]."

   In *Contemporary Philosophy of Social Science*, Brian Fay argues, "Knowledge of what we are experiencing always involves an interpretation of these experiences" (19).

2. According to [name of author], "[insert quotation]."

   According to Brian Fay, "Knowledge of what we are experiencing always involves an interpretation of these experiences" (19).

3. [Name of author] states (argues, asserts, claims, suggests), "[insert quotation]."

   Brian Fay argues, "Knowledge of what we are experiencing always involves an interpretation of these experiences" (19).

4. "[Beginning of quotation]," according to [name of author], "[rest of quotation]."

   "Knowledge of what we are experiencing," according to Brian Fay, "always involves an interpretation of these experiences" (19).

You can use all four patterns to vary the way you introduce quotations and therefore avoid making your prose sound repetitive.

Make It Fit

Core Concept #9 ("There is always a voice in writing, even when there isn't an I") underscores the importance of voice in academic writing, no matter what the specific writing task might be. Many students weaken their voices by failing to integrate quotations and source material smoothly into their writing.

For example, in the following passage, the student discusses ideas for education reform proposed by the authors of a source text:

> In the article "New Teachers" by Postman and Weingartner, there are several explanations as to why change is not an option for some teachers. The biggest problem is, "Where do we get the new teachers necessary to translate the new education into action? Obviously, it will be very difficult to get many of them from the old education. Most of these have a commitment to existing metaphors, procedures, and goals that would preclude their accepting a 'new education'" (133). Older teachers have no use for the "new education." This article focuses mainly on how teachers can be trained to translate this "new education" to their students.

In this example, the student relies too heavily on the source and does not allow her own voice to emerge. Part of the problem is wordiness, but also notice that the quotations from the source text tend to overpower the student's own writing style. Compare this passage to the following one, in which a student also writes about the possibility of education reform and draws on the work of a well-known education theorist. Unlike the previous example, in this case the student

9

effectively integrates references to and quotations from the source text while maintaining her own voice:

> One of a teacher's main objectives in the classroom should be to equip students with cognitive and metacognitive skills so that they are mindful of the world around them. This process of critical thinking is an essential practice that students must not only understand but also be able to utilize in order to become knowledgeable, empowered individuals. In "The Banking Concept of Education," a chapter from *Pedagogy of the Oppressed*, however, Paulo Freire discusses something *more* than providing students with critical thinking skills in school. He encourages teachers to raise students' awareness about themselves and society, so that they are able to work towards the broader idea of social change; this is what he calls "critical consciousness" (35). According to Freire, it is the responsibility of the teacher to instill in his/her students a sense of agency, fostering the potential and possibility for change. Without knowing that they have the capacity to transform society, Freire argues, students will become passive members of society; change, therefore, will never be possible. With this argument, Freire places great responsibility on the shoulders of those who work within the education system. But can educators really take on this role?

In this passage, the student maintains control of the material. The paragraph includes summary, paraphrase, and quotations from the source text, but the main point of the paragraph is the student's own. (See "A Strategy for Integrating Source Material into Your Writing.") Moreover, the voice of the source never takes over, and the student's voice remains strong.

As you work with source material, remember that even when your assignment calls for a review or critique of a source text, the analysis and conclusions about that text are yours. So work the source material into your own writing—not the other way around.

FOCUS   A Strategy for Integrating Source Material into Your Writing

Chapter 5 provides advice for writing clear, cohesive paragraphs. Sometimes paragraphs become incoherent because the student loses control of the source material. Use the advice in this chapter to avoid that problem. You can also follow a basic structure for your paragraphs when you are integrating source material into a paragraph:

1. **Topic statement.** Introduce the subject of the paragraph and provide context for the source material to follow.

2. **Source material.** Summarize, paraphrase, or quote from the source.

3. **Takeaway.** Comment on the source material to connect it to your topic statement.

Be sure to cite the source using MLA or APA format (see Chapters 10 and 11).

The sample paragraph on page 238 illustrates this structure:

One of a teacher's main objectives in the classroom should be to equip students with cognitive and metacognitive skills so that they are mindful of the world around them. This process of critical thinking is an essential practice that students must not only understand but also be able to utilize in order to become knowledgeable, empowered individuals. In "The Banking Concept of Education," a chapter from *Pedagogy of the Oppressed*, however, Paulo Freire discusses something *more* than providing students with critical thinking skills in school. He encourages teachers to raise students' awareness about themselves and society, so that they are able to work towards the broader idea of social change; this is what he calls "critical consciousness" (35). According to Freire, it is the responsibility of the teacher to instill in his/her students a sense of agency, fostering the potential and possibility for change. Without knowing that they have the capacity to transform society, Freire argues, students will become passive members of society; change, therefore, will never be possible. With this argument, Freire places great responsibility on the shoulders of those who work within the education system. But can educators really take on this role?

Topic Statement: The student establishes the focus of the paragraph and provides context for the source material.

Source Material: The student paraphrases and quotes from the source.

Citation: Using MLA format, the student properly cites the source of the quoted phrase.

Takeaway: The student connects the source material to the topic statement and poses a question about the material to provide a transition to the next paragraph.

Additional Guidelines

Punctuate Complete Quotations Correctly

When including a complete quotation from a source in your writing, use quotation marks and final punctuation marks as follows:

Direct Quotation:

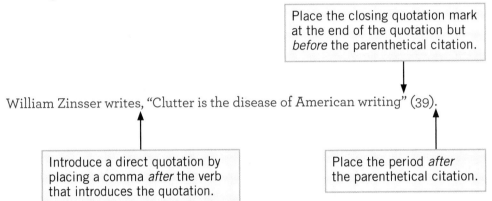

Place the closing quotation mark at the end of the quotation but *before* the parenthetical citation.

William Zinsser writes, "Clutter is the disease of American writing" (39).

Introduce a direct quotation by placing a comma *after* the verb that introduces the quotation.

Place the period *after* the parenthetical citation.

Direct Quotation Following *that*:

When the word "that" follows the verb introducing the quotation, there is *no* comma after "that."

William Zinsser believes that "[c]lutter is the disease of American writing" (39).

The capital *C* is made lowercase because the quotation is a continuation of the sentence. (If the first word of the quotation is a word that is always capitalized, such as a name or proper noun, then it is capitalized here.) The brackets indicate that the letter *C* is capitalized in the original.

You can also introduce a quotation with a colon:

Zinsser makes a provocative point: "Clutter is the disease of American writing" (39).

Insert Phrases When You Don't Need an Entire Statement

Sometimes you only want to quote a word or phrase from a source rather than an entire sentence or passage. In such cases, integrate the phrase into your sentence, using quotation marks to indicate the quoted words and citing the source properly with a parenthetical citation:

> The economist E. F. Schumacher argued that "work and leisure are complementary parts of the same living process" and therefore should not be considered separate from one another (55).

In this example, there is no need for commas around the quoted phrase because it is used as part of the sentence.

This sentence requires a comma after the quoted phrase because of the coordinating conjunction *but*.

> The economist E. F. Schumacher argued that "work and leisure are complementary parts of the same living process," but he also acknowledged that few people in industrialized societies understand work and leisure in this way (55).

Use Ellipses to Indicate Missing Words from a Quotation

If you quote a passage from a source but omit part of that passage, you can indicate that something is missing by using ellipses—that is, three periods, each followed by a space:

Original Passage from Source:

> To my mind, voyaging through wildernesses, be they full of woods or waves, is essential to the growth and maturity of the human spirit.

Quotation with Missing Words:

> Despite his ordeal at sea, in which he survived alone in a life raft for 76 days, Steven Callahan still believed in the value of wilderness experiences. "To my mind," he writes, "voyaging through wildernesses . . . is essential to the growth and maturity of the human spirit" (234).

In this case, the writer decided that the phrase *be they full of woods or waves* was unnecessary and therefore omitted it; the ellipses indicate to a reader that words are missing at that point in the quoted passage.

9

Use Brackets to Indicate a Modified Quotation

If you have to modify a quotation in order to fit it into your sentence, use brackets to indicate changes you have made to the source material:

Original Passage from Source:

> I have focused on two people, one familiar, the other less so: Plymouth governor William Bradford and Benjamin Church, a carpenter turned Indian fighter whose maternal grandfather had sailed on the *Mayflower*.

Modified Passage in Quotation:

> In his provocative history of the Pilgrims, Nathaniel Philbrick "focuse[s] on two people, one familiar, the other less so: Plymouth governor William Bradford and Benjamin Church, a carpenter turned Indian fighter whose maternal grandfather had sailed on the *Mayflower*" (xvii).

In this example, the writer has changed the original verb *focused* to *focuses* so it fits into the passage. The brackets indicate to a reader that the *s* at the end of *focuses* is not in the original text.

Avoiding Plagiarism

Plagiarism is the use of others' words or ideas without giving credit or presenting someone else's words or ideas as your own. It is tantamount to intellectual theft. It goes without saying that plagiarism is unethical. It is dishonest as well as unfair to your classmates, your instructor, and the plagiarized source. It is also a squandering of an opportunity to learn or make something new and useful through your academic work.

Because plagiarism is such a serious breach of ethical standards, it can have serious consequences. In the most extreme cases, plagiarism can result in lawsuits, penalties, or fines. Most colleges and universities have strict codes of student conduct that often include severe sanctions for students caught plagiarizing, including failing an assignment, failing a course, and even expulsion from school.

Plagiarism can range from failing to cite a source to submitting someone else's work as your own (which includes purchasing a paper online from a so-called "paper mill" and submitting it to your instructor as if you wrote it yourself). But students sometimes plagiarize unintentionally—often because they misunderstand the nature of academic research or rely too heavily on source material instead of using sources to support or extend their own ideas. The best way to avoid plagiarism is to apply the Ten Core Concepts in your writing and follow the advice presented in Chapters 7, 8, and 9 for finding and using source material. If you focus on what you have to say in your writing, you are much less likely to plagiarize. Also, review the advice for summarizing and paraphrasing in Chapter 5. Sometimes students inadvertently plagiarize by borrowing too heavily from a source because they don't sufficiently understand the functions of summary and paraphrase.

To avoid plagiarizing inadvertently, follow these guidelines:

- **Use sources to support or extend your own ideas.** As noted earlier, if you focus on making and supporting your main point (Core Concepts #4 and #5), you are less likely to fall victim to unnecessarily borrowing from a source or unintentionally presenting ideas from a source as your own.

- **Integrate source material into your own writing.** Following the advice in this chapter will help you present source material appropriately. Learn to use summary and paraphrase effectively. Apply the strategies for quoting from sources described in this chapter to make it clear to your readers when the material you are presenting is taken from a source.

- **Credit your sources.** Follow the conventions for citing sources that are explained in Chapters 10 and 11. Use APA or MLA format correctly (or use another format approved by your instructor). Be sure to cite sources correctly so that there is no confusion about whether the material you are presenting is yours or taken from a source.

- **Take careful notes.** When you are researching a topic, keep accurate notes about the sources you have consulted so that you know where you found the material you are using and have the correct information for citing the sources. If you are using online sources, it is a good idea to bookmark the pages from which you have taken information.

9

Citing Sources Using MLA Style 10

THE PURPOSE OF CITING SOURCES is to be as clear as possible in showing where your information comes from. Citing your sources according to established style guides not only enables you to give credit to the source for the material you are using but also provides your readers with sufficient bibliographic information to judge or even find your sources for themselves. In general, you must document the source of

- a direct quotation
- an idea or opinion that is not your own
- visual materials, such as photographs, maps, or graphs, that you did not create
- multimedia content, such as videos or audios, that you did not create
- information (a fact or statistic) that is not general knowledge

In most academic writing today, writers use the Modern Language Association (MLA) style guide when they are writing in the humanities: literature, languages, performing and visual arts, history, classics, philosophy, and religion. This chapter explains how to cite sources using MLA style. (APA style, which tends to be used in the social sciences—psychology, sociology, education, economics, anthropology, geography, and political science—is explained in Chapter 11.) The guidelines in this chapter are based on the *MLA Handbook for Writers of Research Papers,* 7th ed., and the *MLA Style Manual and Guide to Scholarly Publishing,* 3rd ed.

Two Main Components in MLA Style

MLA style uses in-text parenthetical citations to document sources. There are **two main components to in-text parenthetical citation systems:**

1. **In-text citations.** Parenthetical citations, which appear in the body of your writing, indicate to a reader that information you are presenting is taken from another source.

2. **A Works Cited list.** The Works Cited list is a separate section at the end of your document that includes bibliographic information for every source you cited in your document.

Let's imagine you are writing an essay about the cultural significance of heavy metal music and you want to refer to a specific analysis of so-called death metal music in a book by Natalie J. Purcell titled *Death Metal Music: The Passion and Politics of a Subculture.* On page 188 of that book,

Purcell makes a point about the philosophical function of death metal music that you want to include in your essay. Using MLA style, you would cite your source as follows:

> Death metal music performs a genuine philosophical function by examining the dark side of human nature (Purcell 188).

If you mention the author's name in your sentence, you do not need to include it in the parenthetical citation:

> Critic Natalie Purcell considers death metal a "philosophical response, whether conscious or subconscious, to terrifying questions about nebulous human nature"(188).

The information in parentheses indicates to readers that the idea about the philosophical function of death metal is taken from page 188 of a work by Purcell. Readers can then consult your Works Cited page, where they will find the following entry:

> Purcell, Natalie J. *Death Metal Music: The Passion and Politics of a Subculture*. Jefferson: McFarland, 2003. Print.

Each in-text citation in your document must have a corresponding Works Cited entry to give your readers the means to find and read the original source themselves.

FOCUS | **Footnotes, Endnotes, and Content Notes**

Traditionally, footnotes or endnotes were used to document sources. Strictly speaking, a **footnote** appears at the foot of the page and an **endnote** appears at the end of the paper. However, the MLA now recommends that writers use parenthetical, or in-text, citations of the kind described in this chapter. Traditional footnotes are used not for documenting sources but for additional explanation or discussion of a point in the main text. These notes are called **content notes**.

Creating In-Text Citations in MLA Style

MLA style, which reflects the conventions of the humanities, emphasizes the author and the author's work and places less emphasis on the date of publication. When citing a work parenthetically, the author's last name is followed by a page number or range of pages. There are particular situations in which somewhat different information is given in parentheses, but *the general rule is to provide enough information to enable a reader to find the source in your Works Cited list*. You do not need to include inside the parentheses information you have already provided in the text. For instance, if you start the sentence with the author's name, you do not need to include the author's name in the parentheses.

A. Work by one author

If you were citing information taken from page 82 of a book called *The Printing Revolution in Early Modern Europe* by Elizabeth L. Eisenstein, the parenthetical citation would look like this:

> The widespread adoption of the printing press in the 16th century helped standardize the major European languages (Eisenstein 82).

If you used Eisenstein's name in your sentence, the citation would include only the page reference:

> Elizabeth Eisenstein examines how the widespread adoption of the printing press in the 16th century helped standardize the major European languages (82).

There is no punctuation between the author's name and the page number. Note that the parentheses are placed *inside* the period at the end of the sentence. Also, the abbreviation *p.* or *pp.* is not used before the page reference in MLA style.

B. Work by multiple authors

When citing a work by two or three authors, include all the authors' names in the citation (or in your sentence). For example, if you wanted to quote from page 2 of *Undead TV: Essays on Buffy the Vampire Slayer*, by Elana Levine and Lisa Parks, you could do so as follows:

> We might consider how the hit television series *Buffy the Vampire Slayer* "dramatizes the travails of its title character but uses its metaphorical representations of life and

death, good and evil, comedy and tragedy to speak about the power struggles inherent in many people's everyday lives in the Western world" (Levine and Parks 2).

or

Elana Levine and Lisa Parks assert that *"Buffy the Vampire Slayer* dramatizes the travails of its title character but uses its metaphorical representations of life and death, good and evil, comedy and tragedy to speak about the power struggles inherent in many people's everyday lives in the Western world" (2).

If you are referring to a work by more than three authors, list only the first author's name followed by the Latin phrase *et al.* (which means "and others"). For example, if you were citing information from page 79 of a journal article titled "Empirical Foundations for Writing in Prevention and Psychotherapy," by Brian A. Esterling, Luciano L'Abate, Edward J. Murray, and James W. Pennebaker, the parenthetical citation would look like this

Studies have shown that writing has therapeutic benefits for some patients (Esterling et al. 79).

Note that there is no comma after the name of the author.

C. Work by a corporate author

A "corporate author" is an organization, committee, or agency (rather than an individual or group of individually named authors). When citing a corporate author, use the same format as for a single author. For example, if you were citing a study by the Center for Research on Educational Outcomes, you would do so as follows:

According to the Center for Research on Educational Outcomes, in 37 percent of charter schools, students had math scores that were lower than their public school peers (3).

You could also include the corporate author in the parentheses; omit any initial article:

In one recent study, 37 percent of charter schools had student math scores that were lower than in public schools (Center for Research on Educational Outcomes 3.).

D. More than one work by the same author

If you cite more than one work by the same author, you need to distinguish among the works by using a shortened form of the title of each work you cite. For example, if you were quoting from two different books by Paulo Freire, *Pedagogy of Hope* and *Letters to Cristina*, your parenthetical citations might look like this:

Freire emphasizes the crucial role of hope in the struggle for change. Acknowledging that hope "seldom exists apart from the reverses of fate" (*Letters* 14), Freire argues that the "dream of humanization . . . is always a process" (*Pedagogy* 99).

The shortened titles (*Letters* and *Pedagogy*) enable a reader to find the specific references in the Works Cited list. Also note that because it is clear from the context that both works cited are by the same author, the author's name does not need to be placed inside the parentheses. If the author's name is not included in the text itself, include it inside the parenthetical citation:

> Hope is a crucial element in the struggle for change. We should acknowledge that hope "seldom exists apart from the reverses of fate" (Freire, *Letters* 14) and remember that the "dream of humanization . . . is always a process" (Freire, *Pedagogy* 99).

Note that a comma separates the author's name from the shortened title, but no comma appears between the title and the page number.

E. Work without an author listed

If you cite a work without an author listed, include a brief version of the title in parentheses. For example, if you cited information from page 27 of an article from *The Economist* titled "Carrying the Torch," you would do so as follows:

> The sports management industry in Great Britain received a significant boost in business as a result of the 2012 Olympic Games in London ("Carrying" 27).

F. Entire work

When you refer to an entire work, include only the author's name, either in your sentence or in parentheses. No page numbers are needed.

> Cheryl Sandberg discusses the reasons women are still not adequately represented in leadership positions.

G. Quotation within a cited work

When using a quotation from one source that you have found in another source, you must show that the quotation was acquired "secondhand" and was not taken directly from the original source. In such cases, use the abbreviation *qtd. in* (for "quoted in") to indicate that you are taking the quotation from a second source rather than from the original text. For example, let's say you were reading a book titled *Literary Theory* by Terry Eagleton that included a quotation by Sigmund Freud. If you wanted to use Freud's quotation in your essay, you would cite it as follows:

> Even Freud acknowledged the central importance of economics in human relations, famously stating, "The motive of human society is in the last resort an economic one" (qtd. in Eagleton 151).

In this instance, you are signaling to readers that you read Freud's statement in the book by Terry Eagleton. Your Works Cited list will contain an entry for Eagleton's book but not Freud's original text.

H. Work in an anthology

Name the author of the particular work, not the editor of the entire anthology, in your citation. For example, if you were citing a story by Nathan Englander that appears in the anthology *The*

Best American Short Stories 2012, edited by Tom Perrotta and Heidi Pitlor, you would not need to mention the editors of the anthology:

> Nathan Englander plays off Raymond Carver's famous story title in his short work "What We Talk About When We Talk About Anne Frank."

The entry in your Works Cited list would include the editors' names.

I. Electronic sources

When citing electronic sources, follow the same principles you would use when citing other sources. However, there are many different kinds of electronic sources, which might not include the same kinds of information that are available for a print book or journal article. For example, online sources, such as websites, often do not have page numbers. In such cases, if possible provide the number of the paragraph in which you found the information or quotation you are citing:

> (Martinez, par. 8)

Note that a comma is placed after the author's name.

If page numbers are not available, include sufficient information for readers to find the source you are citing, such as the author's last name or a brief title:

> (Martinez)

J. Long quotations

In MLA style, a long prose quotation is defined as one that takes more than four lines in your paper. Quotations of more than three lines of poetry are considered long, and any amount of quoted dialogue from a play is treated as a block quotation. These quotations should be indented one inch from the left as a block quotation—*without* quotation marks. The entire block should be double-spaced, and no additional space should be used above or below the block quotation. In this example, the writer introduces a long quotation from an author named Sharon Crowley:

> Sharon Crowley offers contemporary composition a radical inspiration from ancient times:
>
> > I can see no reason why contemporary teachers cannot develop theories of composition that are fully as rich as those developed in ancient times. Much thinking remains to be done, and I do not doubt that enterprising teachers of composition will do it—because there is a place for composition in the university, and that place does not depend on Freshman English. (265)

The page number for the quotation is included in parentheses at the end of the block quotation. Notice that the parenthetical citation is placed *after* the final period of the block quotation. If the author's name does not appear in the main text, include it in the parentheses.

K. Work in more than one volume

If you use more than one volume from a multivolume work in your paper, indicate the volume and page number in each citation. The volume number is followed by a colon. In this example, page 236 in volume 3 of a work by Trieste is cited:

(Trieste 3: 236)

If you cite only one volume, however, you can provide the page number only. In your Works Cited entry, list the volume number.

Creating a Works Cited List in MLA Style

Each source you cite in your text must correspond to an entry in your Works Cited list. Your list of Works Cited should appear at the end of your project, beginning with a new page. Organize the Works Cited list alphabetically according to the authors' last names (or, if the work includes no author, the first main word of the title). In MLA style, follow these rules:

- Capitalize the first word, the last word, and every important word in titles and subtitles. Do not capitalize prepositions (such as *on* and *to*), coordinating conjunctions (such as *and* and *but*), or articles (*a, an, the*) unless they begin the title or subtitle.
- Italicize the titles of long works such as books and periodicals.
- Place the titles of shorter works, such as articles, stories, and poems, in quotation marks.
- Indicate the medium of publication for every entry (e.g. Print, Web, DVD), but do not include the URL for websites or other online sources.
- Double-space citations but do not skip spaces between entries.
- Using hanging indents for entries in the Works Cited list.

FOCUS **Find the Works Cited Citation Model You Need**

Books (Print and Online)

1. Book with one author (page 253)

2. Book with two or more authors (page 253)

3. Two or more books by the same author (page 254)

4. Anthology with an editor (page 254)

5. Work(s) in an anthology (page 254)

6. Book with an author and an editor (page 254)

7. Book with a translator (page 254)

8. Book by a corporate author or without an author listed (page 255)

(Continued)

Note: The list of in-text citation models appears on page 247.

Books

Here is the general format for an entry for a book in the Works Cited list:

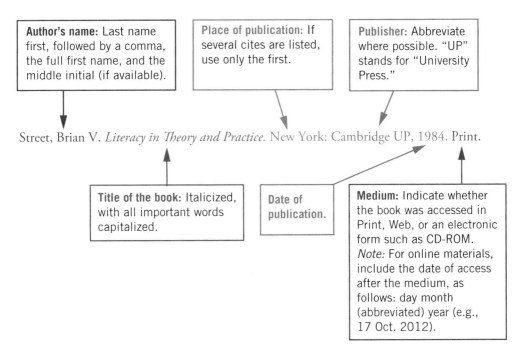

Author's name: Last name first, followed by a comma, the full first name, and the middle initial (if available).

Place of publication: If several cites are listed, use only the first.

Publisher: Abbreviate where possible. "UP" stands for "University Press."

Street, Brian V. *Literacy in Theory and Practice.* New York: Cambridge UP, 1984. Print.

Title of the book: Italicized, with all important words capitalized.

Date of publication.

Medium: Indicate whether the book was accessed in Print, Web, or an electronic form such as CD-ROM. *Note:* For online materials, include the date of access after the medium, as follows: day month (abbreviated) year (e.g., 17 Oct. 2012).

1. Book with one author

> Fineman, Howard. *The Thirteen American Arguments: Enduring Debates That Define and Inspire Our Country.* New York: Random, 2008. Print.

> Lockhart, Charles. *Gaining Ground: Tailoring Social Programs to American Values.* Berkeley: U of California P, 1989. Web. 20 Aug. 2012.

In the second example, the date of access is included at the end of the citation because the work was accessed online.

2. Book with two or more authors

> Stewart, David W., Prem N. Shamdasani, and Dennis W. Rook. *Focus Groups: Theory and Practice.* Thousand Oaks: Sage, 2007. Print.

If there are two or three authors, list all the authors' names. Notice that only the first author is listed with the last name first.

For books with four or more authors, use the abbreviation *et al.*:

> Wysocki, Anne Frances et al. *Writing New Media: Theory and Applications for Expanding the Teaching of Composition.* Logan: Utah State UP, 2004. Print.

3. Two or more books by the same author

When you are listing two or more books by the same author, you do not repeat the author's name for each entry. Instead, use three hyphens and a period in place of the author's name for the second, third, and subsequent entries by the same author. Also, list the entries in alphabetical order by the book title.

> Freire, Paulo. *Letters to Cristina: Reflections on My Life and Work*. New York: Routledge, 1996. Print.
>
> ---. *Pedagogy of Hope: Reliving Pedagogy of the Oppressed*. New York: Continuum, 2004. Print.
>
> ---. *Pedagogy of the Oppressed*. Trans. Myra Bergman Ramos. New York: Continuum, 1970. Print.

4. Anthology with an editor

> McComiskey, Bruce, ed. *English Studies: An Introduction to the Discipline(s)*. Urbana: NCTE, 2006. Print.
>
> Hill, Charles A., and Marguerite Helmers, eds. *Defining Visual Rhetorics*. Mahwah: Erlbaum, 2004. Print.

Use the abbreviation *ed.* for a single editor and *eds.* for multiple editors. Place the abbreviation after the editor's name, which is followed by a comma.

5. Work(s) in an anthology

> Dittrich, Luke. "The Brain That Changed Everything." *The Best American Science and Nature Writing*. Ed. Mary Roach. Boston: Houghton, 2011. 46–68. Print.

Notice that the page numbers for the article are provided. Also, the abbreviation *Ed.* appears *before* the editor's name (Mary Roach).

If you cite two or more articles (or other short works) from the same anthology, use a shortened form of the citation for each one, and then cite the entire anthology according to example 4 above:

> Bhattacharjee. "The Organ Dealer." Roach 1–14.
>
> Dittrich, Luke. "The Brain That Changed Everything." Roach 46–68.

6. Book with an author and an editor

> Thoreau, Henry David. *Walden*. Ed. Jeffrey S. Cramer. New Haven: Yale UP, 2004. Print.

The author's name is placed first. The editor's name is placed after the title, preceded by the abbreviation *Ed.*

7. Book with a translator

> Tsunetomo, Yamamoto. *Hagakure: The Book of the Samurai*. Trans. William Scott Wilson. Tokyo: Kadansha Intl., 1979. Print.

The abbreviation *Trans.* appears before the translator's name (William Scott Wilson).

8. Book by a corporate author or without an author listed

> ACT. *The Condition of College and Career Readiness 2011.* Iowa City: ACT, 2011. Web.
>   17 Sept. 2012.

If no author or organization is listed, omit the author and begin the entry with the title of the book.

9. Introduction, preface, foreword, or afterword written by someone other than the author of the work

> Zelazny, Roger. Introduction. *Do Androids Dream of Electric Sheep?* By Philip K. Dick.
>   New York: Del Ray, 1968. vii–x. Print.

In this example, Roger Zelazny wrote the introduction to the book *Do Androids Dream of Electric Sheep?* by Philip K. Dick. Include the page numbers of the introduction after the date of publication.

10. Subsequent editions of a book

> Creswell, John W., ed. *Qualitative Research and Design: Choosing Among Five
>   Approaches.* 2nd ed. Thousand Oaks: Sage, 2007. Print.

Use the abbreviation *ed.* for "edition."

11. Work in more than one volume

> Milton, John. *The Prose Works of John Milton.* 2 vols. Philadelphia: Moore, 1847. Print.

12. Book in a series

> Pedersen, Isabel. *Ready to Wear: A Rhetoric of Wearable Computers and Reality-Shifting
>   Media.* Anderson: Parlor, 2013. Print. New Media Theory.

The series name ("New Media Theory") is placed after the medium of publication (which is "Print" in this example).

13. Encyclopedia article

The format for entries for encyclopedia articles is similar to articles in anthologies or edited collections.

> Sockett, Hugh. "The Moral and Epistemic Purposes of Teacher Education." *Handbook
>   of Research on Teacher Education.* 3rd ed. Eds. Marilyn Cochran-Smith, Sharon
>   Feiman-Nemser, and D. John McIntyre. New York: Routledge, 2008. 45–66. Print.

This example shows an article written by Hugh Sockett that appeared in the third edition of an encyclopedia called the *Handbook of Research on Teacher Education* edited by Marilyn Cochran-Smith, Sharon Feiman-Nemser, and D. John McIntyre. If no author is listed, begin with the title of the article. The rest of the citation is the same.

If you accessed the encyclopedia article through an online database, include the name of the database (in italics, placed after the date of publication) followed by the medium and date of access:

Lacey, Alan. "The Meaning of Life." *The Oxford Companion to Philosophy*. Ed. Ted Honderich. New York: Oxford UP, 1995. *Oxford Reference Online*. Web. 19 Aug. 2012.

14. Sacred text

The King James Version Bible. New York: American Bible Society. 1980. Print.

Begin the entry with the name of the version you are using. Include names of editors or translators after the title.

FOCUS   Citing Wikipedia and Other Online References

Many instructors have policies regarding the use of *Wikipedia* and similar online references, so check with your instructor before using such resources in your research. In MLA style, if you cite information taken from such sources, the format is similar to the format for citing a web page (see example 21):

"Ultramarathon." *Wikipedia, The Free Encyclopedia*. Wikimedia Foundation, Inc. 16 Aug. 2012. Web. 21 Aug. 2012.

In this example, because there is no author, the entry begins with the title of the article, followed by the name of the website in italics (*Wikipedia, The Free Encyclopedia*), the sponsoring organization (Wikimedia Foundation, Inc.), the publication date, the medium, and the access date, all separated by periods.

Periodicals

Here is the general format for an article from a scholarly journal:

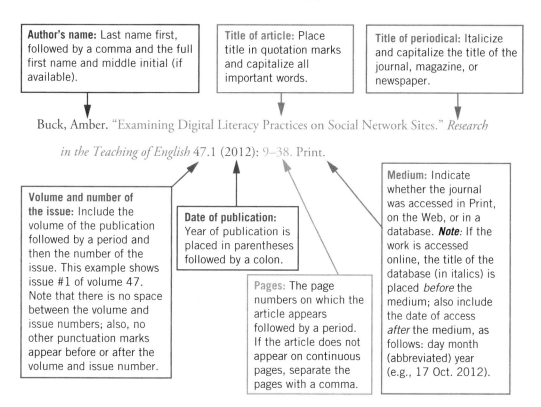

Author's name: Last name first, followed by a comma and the full first name and middle initial (if available).

Title of article: Place title in quotation marks and capitalize all important words.

Title of periodical: Italicize and capitalize the title of the journal, magazine, or newspaper.

Buck, Amber. "Examining Digital Literacy Practices on Social Network Sites." *Research in the Teaching of English* 47.1 (2012): 9–38. Print.

Volume and number of the issue: Include the volume of the publication followed by a period and then the number of the issue. This example shows issue #1 of volume 47. Note that there is no space between the volume and issue numbers; also, no other punctuation marks appear before or after the volume and issue number.

Date of publication: Year of publication is placed in parentheses followed by a colon.

Pages: The page numbers on which the article appears followed by a period. If the article does not appear on continuous pages, separate the pages with a comma.

Medium: Indicate whether the journal was accessed in Print, on the Web, or in a database. **Note**: If the work is accessed online, the title of the database (in italics) is placed *before* the medium; also include the date of access *after* the medium, as follows: day month (abbreviated) year (e.g., 17 Oct. 2012).

This example shows a scholarly journal. **For magazines and newspapers**:

- omit the volume and issue number
- eliminate the parentheses from the date of publication

15. Article from a scholarly journal

Mayers, Tim. "One Simple Word: From Creative Writing to Creative Writing Studies." *College English* 71.3 (2009): 217–228. Print.

If you accessed this article via the journal's website, the citation would appear like this:

Mayers, Tim. "One Simple Word: From Creative Writing to Creative Writing Studies." *College English* 71.3 (2009): 217–228. Web. 14 Jan. 2013.

Note that the date you accessed the article is placed *after* the medium.

If you accessed this article online via a database such as *JSTOR, LexisNexis, InfoTrac,* or *Academic Search Complete*, the citation would appear as follows:

> Mayers, Tim. "One Simple Word: From Creative Writing to Creative Writing Studies."
> *College English* 71.3 (2009): 217–228. *JSTOR*. Web. 14 Jan. 2013.

Note that the title of the database (*JSTOR* in this example) is placed in italics and appears *after* the page numbers but *before* the medium. The date of access appears last.

Be sure to place periods after the page numbers, the title of the database, and the medium.

16. Article from a weekly or monthly magazine

> Gover, Robert. "One Novel's Sojourn Through Culture Wars and Privacy." *The Writer's Chronicle* Sept. 2011: 50–57. Print.

If you accessed the article online through a database such as *Academic Search Complete*, include the italicized title of the database followed by the medium and date of access (all separated by periods):

> Gover, Robert. "One Novel's Sojourn Through Culture Wars and Privacy." *The Writer's Chronicle* Sept. 2011: 50–57. *Academic Search Complete*. Web. 8 Oct. 2012.

If you found the article through the magazine website, cite it as follows:

> Gover, Robert. "One Novel's Sojourn Through Culture Wars and Privacy." *The Writer's Chronicle* Sept. 2011: n. pag. Web. 12 Feb. 2012.

Note that the abbreviation *n. pag.* (for "no page numbers") replaces the page numbers. Also include the date you accessed the article (12 Feb. 2012, in this example).

17. Article from a daily newspaper

> Kepner, Tyler. "Grand Home of a Larger-Than-Life Team." *The New York Times* 21 Sept. 2008, natl ed.: N1. Print.

Note that the page number includes the section in which the article appeared—in this example, section N, page 1. Also, if available, include the edition (in this example, *natl. ed.* for "national edition") before the colon. (If there is no edition, place a colon after the year instead of a comma.)

If the article is accessed online through a database, include the italicized title of the database, followed by the medium and date of access—just as you would cite a magazine article:

> Kepner, Tyler. "Grand Home of a Larger-Than-Life Team." *The New York Times* 21 Sept. 2008, natl ed.: N1. *LexisNexis Academic*. Web. 3 June 2011.

If you accessed the article through the newspaper's website, cite it as follows:

> Kepner, Tyler. "Grand Home of a Larger-Than-Life Team." *The New York Times* 21 Sept. 2008, natl ed.: N1. Web. 3 June 2011.

If there is no page number, follow the date (and edition, if there is one) with a period instead of a colon.

18. Editorial

>Kayyem, Juliette. "A Rainy Day Fund Doesn't Work If It's Always Raining." Editorial. *Boston Globe* 23 May 2013. Web. 25 May 2013.

The term *Editorial* appears after the title of the article, followed by a period. In this example, there is no edition or page number.

19. Letter to the editor

>Goldberg, Anita. Letter. *New York Times* 22 May 2013. Web. 25 May 2013.

20. Review

>Uglow, Jenny. "The Saga of the Flaming Zucchini." Rev. of *Consider the Fork: A History of How We Cook and Eat,* by Bee Wilson. *New York Review of Books* 6 June 2013. Web. 24 June 2013.

Notice that the name of the author of the review is placed first. The name of the author of the work being reviewed follows the title of the work being reviewed, preceded by the word *by* (in this example, "by Bee Wilson").

If the review does not include a title, omit that part of the citation. For publication information, use the format for the kind of source you used.

For film reviews, include the name of the director of the film, placed after the title of the film and preceded by the abbreviation *dir.*:

>Sharkey, Betsy. "*Before Midnight* Finds Its Couple in a Dark Place." Rev. of *Before Midnight,* dir. Richard Linklater. *Los Angeles Times* 24 May 2013. Web. 17 June 2013.

Other Sources

21. Website

When citing an entire website, include the author, editor, or compiler of the site (if available), followed by the title of the site in italics, the name of the organization sponsoring the site, the publication date, the medium, and the date of access:

>*Swing Dance America.* Swing Dance America. N.d. Web. 15 May 2013.

In this example, there is no author, so the entry begins with the title of the website (*Swing Dance America*). Because there is no date on the website, the abbreviation *N.d.* is used.

22. Web page

For a web page, include the name of the author (if available), the title of the page in quotation marks followed by the italicized title of the website, the name of the sponsoring organization (if available), the date of publication, the medium, and the date of access:

>Pollan, Michael. "Sustainable Eating and Nutrition: FAQs and Useful Links." *Michael Pollan.* N.p. 2010. Web. 23 July 2012.

The title of the web page is placed in quotation marks. If there is no sponsoring organization, use the abbreviation *N.p.* (for "no publisher"). If you can't find a date of publication, use the abbreviation *n.d.* (for "no date").

The citation for a web page by a corporate author (such as an organization or business) is similar in format:

> People for the Ethical Treatment of Animals. "Turned Away: A Closer Look at 'No-Kill.'" *PETA*. People for the Ethical Treatment of Animals, n.d. Web. 15 May 2013.

Notice that the name of the agency or organization appears in place of an author's name.

For a web page without an author, the citation appears like this:

> "How to Anchor Securely." *West Marine West Advisor*. West Marine. N.d. Web. 23 July 2012.

In this example, the title of the web page ("How to Anchor Securely") appears first, followed by the italicized title of the website (*West Marine West Advisor*) and the name of the sponsoring organization (West Marine).

23. Blog

> Schoenkopf, Rebecca. "Breitbart's Ghost: Obama Exploited Catholics by Being Endorsed by Them." *Wonkette*. Wonkette Media, LLC. 6 Apr. 2012. Web. 9 Apr. 2012.

Note that the title of the blog (*Wonkette*) is italicized and appears *after* the title of the blog entry ("Breitbart's Ghost: Obama Exploited Catholics by Being Endorsed by Them"). Follow the title of the blog with the sponsor (Wonkette Media, LLC), the date of the blog entry, the medium, and finally the date of access—all separated by periods.

24. Podcast

> Gross, Terry. "Do Voter ID Laws Prevent Fraud, or Dampen Turnout?" *Fresh Air*. Natl. Public Radio. 15 Aug. 2012. Web. 25 Aug. 2012.

Begin with the performer's or author's name, followed by the title of the podcast, the italicized name of the program on which the podcast was broadcast, the sponsor of the program, and the date of the original broadcast. Also include the medium of publication (Web) and the date you accessed the podcast.

25. Interview

For an interview that you conduct, indicate whether the interview was conducted via email, by telephone, or in person.

> Gallehr, Don. Telephone interview. 19 Apr. 2010.

For a published or broadcast interview, include the title, if available. Add the name of the interviewer if pertinent to your use. Be sure to include the medium (as well as the date of access if you accessed the interview online).

> Pollan, Michael. "A Coffee Date with Michael Pollan." Interview by Keane Amdahl. *City Pages*. City Pages, 7 May 2013. Web. 15 May 2013.

26. CD-ROM

For a nonperiodical published on CD-ROM, start with information from the most relevant example from 1 to 8 (pages 253–259). Add the edition or release number, if there is one, and the medium. If the publication information for a printed source is provided, start with that information.

> *Flower Designs and Motifs.* New York: Dover Publications, 2005. CD-ROM.

> Reid, T. R. "The New Europe." *National Geographic* Jan. 2002: 32+. *The Complete National Geographic.* Washington: The National Geographic Society, 2010. CD-ROM. Disk 6.

For material from a periodically published database and for periodicals such as journals, magazines, and newspapers that are published in both print and on CD-ROM, provide the print information first, then the medium of publication, the title of the database, the name of the vendor, and the publication date of the database. (See the third item in example 15.)

27. Film, video, DVD

> *The Great Gatsby.* Dir. Baz Luhrmann. Perf. Leonardo DiCaprio, Joel Edgerton, Tobey Maguire, and Carey Mulligan. Warner, 2013. Film.

Begin with the name of the director or performer if you are citing that person's contribution. For videos, DVDs, and filmstrips, use the same format. Place the medium at the end of the citation, followed by a period.

28. Television or radio program

> "Second Sons." Dir. Michelle MacLaren. *Game of Thrones.* HBO. 19 May 2013. Television.

Begin with the title of the episode. If you include additional information about the episode, place it after the episode title; however, if the added information pertains to the series, place it after the series title. Insert the call letters and city of the local station and broadcast date (if any) after the name of the network. Place the medium at the end of the citation, followed by a period.

29. Sound recording

> Rollins, Sonny. *Saxophone Colossus.* Prestige, 1987. CD.

Begin with the name of the artists, followed by the title of the recording, manufacturer, and year of issue. Indicate the medium (CD, Mp3, LP, Audiocassette) after the date, followed by a period.
To cite a specific song, include the song title, in quotation marks, after the name of the artist.

> Rollins, Sonny. "You Don't Know What Love Is." *Saxophone Colossus.* Prestige, 1987. CD.

30. Advertisement

> Nike. Advertisement. *Adweek.* 27 Mar. 2013. Web. 28 May 2013.

31. Art

> Cave, Nick. *Soundsuit.* 2011. Found objects, knit head and bodysuit, and mannequin. Museum of Mod. Art, New York.

Cite the artist first and then the title of the work. Describe the medium, and then indicate where the art is housed. If you found the art in a print source, follow the appropriate format for publication details.

32. Government publication

> United States. Dept. of Transportation. *Bridge Management*. Washington: GPO, 2012.
>   Print.

For government documents, the name of the nation or state appears first, followed by the agency (Department of Transportation, in this example) and the title of the publication (*Bridge Management*). Also include the place of publication (Washington), the publisher (Government Printing Office, abbreviated as GPO by MLA), date of publication (2012), and medium (Print).

> If you accessed the publication online, indicate the medium and date of access:

> United States. Dept. of Transportation. *Bridge Management*. Washington: GPO, 2012.
>   Web. 25 April 2012.

Sample MLA-Style Research Paper

The following essay by Matt Searle, written for the "Evolution of Expression" class he took as a freshman at Emerson College, follows MLA guidelines for formatting a research paper. Matt's essay is a causal analysis that explores the potential impact of digital technologies on literacy and cognition. Matt addresses the question, What effects are the rapidly growing uses of digital technologies having on how we read and think? As you read, notice how Matt examines this question from various angles, taking into account what different experts think and what research has shown. Notice, too, how Matt carefully documents his sources using MLA style.

For research papers, MLA recommends placing your name, the title of your paper, and other relevant information (such as the date, the course number, and the instructor's name) on the first page, as Matt has done, rather than on a separate title page. If you are required to use a title page, center this information on the page.

When formatting a paper in MLA style, remember to

- use one-inch margins
- double-space the text throughout the document (including the title and Works Cited list)
- double-space between the heading and the title and between the title and the main text on the first page
- indent paragraphs one-half inch
- number all pages, including the first page, in the upper-right-hand corner
- place your last name before the page number on each page (if you are using a program such as Microsoft Word, you can use the header function to create a running head that includes your name and the page number on each page)
- include the Works Cited list on a separate page at the end of the document

Matt Searle

Dr. John Dennis Anderson

Evolution of Expression

20 October 2011

Anxieties Over Electracy

Over the course of the past decade, technology has shaped the way society accesses and absorbs information. In *Internet Invention: From Literacy to Electracy*, Gregory L. Ulmer argues that our culture is transitioning from traditional literacy to a type of "electracy" afforded by the digital age. However, this transition has been met with resistance by those who fear the changes it will bring. Concerns involving the superficiality of Internet reading, loss of memory, and depletion of traditional literary skills have been brought to the forefront of the debate between literacy and electracy. As the Internet continues to rewire our brains and becomes a ubiquitous presence in our world, we must take the time to fully understand its impact.

One of the primary criticisms of electracy, defined by Ulmer as being to digital media what literacy is to print, is that it causes superficial understanding (Ulmer, *Internet* xii). Just as Johann Gutenberg's invention of the printing press increased freedom of thought and public expression, the advent of the Internet has increased the availability of information. Those who welcome this influx of data subscribe to a philosophy that Adam Gopnik has coined "Never Better-ism," a belief in the Internet's potential to create a new utopia (Gopnik). However, there are others who are as skeptical as the "Never-Betters" are optimistic. In a well-known article titled "Is Google Making Us Stupid?," writer Nicholas Carr expresses the belief that digital literacy leads to a depletion of textual analysis and cognition. Citing his own inability to read lengthy articles without skimming and an increasing lack of patience with text, Carr claims that the Internet leads to ADD-like behavior. He contends that we are no longer "scuba divers" of information—that is, we no longer critically assess what we read (Carr 57). Furthermore, Internet users often feel the need to hop around to various sites rather than focus on one in particular. Though some believe this habit of "power browsing" stimulates creativity, Internet critics such as Carr worry that our culture will be permanently unable to perform in-depth analysis (59). With newspapers such as *The New York Times* attracting readers by adding abstracts for every three pages and online journalists peppering their articles with hyperlinks, the medium is gradually adjusting to our changing behavior (61).

 While the criticisms lodged by Carr and others towards electracy may seem extreme, some research suggests that the Internet is shaping the way we think. Human brains are extremely malleable as neurons often break old connections and form new ones. Just as reading Chinese text from right to left is not a natural talent, electrate reading is very much a learned skill. Rather than following the typical linear progression of alphabetic literacy, numerous hyperlinks and a virtual cornucopia of information encourage a "zigzag" approach to reading (Rich A27). Thus, the question is not whether the Internet is affecting the way we think, but whether it is modifying the brain in a positive fashion. It is possible that our neurological transition to electrate thinking is a natural progression in our mental development, but anxiety still exists over electracy's permanent effects. For example, studies have shown that the Internet can have a serious impact on memory (Johnson).

Because websites such as Google easily provide the answers to our questions, some consider it no longer necessary to attempt to memorize information. In this way, we as a culture tend to "outsource" our memories to electronics rather than use our brains for retention (Johnson A7). In one study, three thousand people were asked to remember the birthdate of a relative; only forty percent of people under thirty years old were able to answer correctly as compared to eighty-seven percent of people over the age of fifty (Thompson). Even more staggering was the fact that fully a third of youths were able to recite their phone number only after checking the phone itself (Thompson).

This loss of recall seems to be directly linked to electracy, as further studies have shown that people are more likely to remember information that they believe will be deleted. According to neuroscientist Gary Small, "We're . . . [u]sing the World Wide Web as an external hard drive to augment our biological memory stores" (Johnson A7). However, as with any neurobiological development, there are some psychological benefits. With less of our brain used for memory storage, we can free up our grey matter to be used for brainstorming and daydreaming. Some experts promote the idea that intelligence is not truly about knowing information, but instead knowing where to find it. University of Pittsburgh psychology professor Richard Moreland has labeled the perceived need to retain all information "maladaptive" (Johnson A7). Thus, skeptics of electracy must consider both the positive and negative aspects of the transition.

The question of whether electracy will supersede traditional literacy has also become an issue in recent years. Children between the ages of eight and eighteen have increased their Internet usage from an average of forty-six minutes per day in 1984 to an hour and forty-one minutes per day in the present (Rich A16). At the same time, only one-fifth of seventeen-year-olds read for fun every day, a statistic that some critics argue seems to correlate with a drastic drop on critical reading test scores (Rich A16). Proponents of Internet reading claim that it is simply a new type of literacy that allows its users to create their own beginnings, middles, and ends. Reading online can also allow those who have learning disabilities such as dyslexia to read in a more comfortable environment and format (Rich A17).

Another argument against electrate skepticism is that the Internet encourages reading amongst those who would not normally read otherwise. For example, giving Internet access to low-income families who may struggle to buy books has been shown to increase overall reading time (Rich A16). With ninety percent of employers listing reading comprehension as very important (Rich A16), it is essential that future generations be able to comprehend the information they take in. This means that while electracy may have a place in our culture, where it belongs is still unclear. Groups such as the Organization for Economic Cooperation and Development plan to add electronic reading sections to aptitude tests, but these actions have been scoffed at by many (Rich A17). The experts that fear our transition from literacy to electracy are aware that only the reading of traditional literate texts has been proven to cause higher comprehension and performance levels (Rich A16). Therefore, electracy opponents do not necessarily want to dissolve the medium, but simply do not want it to replace what is currently known as reading.

Ulmer does not see the Internet as destroying our literate abilities, but rather building on them in what he calls a "society of the spectacle" (*Internet* xiii). In Ulmer's vision, imagination and visualization can be used in combination with critical thinking in order to solve problems: "What literacy is to the analytical mind, electracy is to the affective body: a prosthesis that enhances and augments a natural or organic human potential" ("Gregory Ulmer"). For Ulmer, electracy is an apparatus that is to be used for future generations, which is why he labels *Internet Invention* as a new generation textbook (*Internet* xiii). Ulmer's convictions are reflected by others who support the movement towards electracy. These thinkers point out that when literacy first began, it also caused cynicism, but it ultimately became the widely accepted norm. Indeed, it seems that the advent of new technologies has always made people uneasy and stirred fears that the capacities of the human brain may either be replaced or diminished. However, as Ulmer sees the situation, technological progression is both a natural and welcome development. We may no longer be able to think in a purely literate and literal sense, but as Michigan State University professor Rand J. Spiro puts it, "[T]he world doesn't go in a line" (Rich A16). If we as a culture can harness the potential of the Internet, perhaps Ulmer's vision can come to fruition.

The world is constantly evolving as new technologies and philosophies begin to dominate the cultural landscape. With the Internet a ubiquitous presence in the lives of almost all human beings, becoming fluent in what Greg Ulmer has dubbed electracy is integral. Fears that the Internet causes superficiality, rewires our brains, and decreases literacy have been corroborated by studies, but that does not mean that the Internet is without benefits. By understanding its effects and using electracy to build off our literate knowledge, we can determine where this skill fits within our society.

Works Cited

Carr, Nicholas. "Is Google Making Us Stupid?" *Atlantic Monthly* Jul./Aug.
    2008: 56–63. Print.

Gopnik, Adam. "The Information: How the Internet Gets Inside Us." *The
    New Yorker* 14 Feb. 2011. Web. 16 Oct. 2011.

Johnson, Carolyn Y. "Memory Slips Caught in the Net." *Boston Globe*
    15 July 2011: A1+. Print.

Rich, Motoko. "Literacy Debate: Online, R U Really Reading?" *New York
    Times* 27 July 2008,
    late ed.: A1+. Print.

Thompson, Clive. "Your Outboard Brain Knows It All." *Wired.com*. Conde
    Nast, 25 Sept. 2007. Web. 16 Oct. 2011.

Ulmer, Gregory L. "Gregory Ulmer–Quotes." European Graduate School
    Faculty. 2011. Web. 16 Oct. 2011.

---. *Internet Invention: From Literacy to Electracy*. New York: Longman, 2002.
    Print.

Citing Sources Using APA Style

11

THE PURPOSE of citing sources is to be as clear as possible in showing where your information comes from. Citing your sources according to established style guides not only enables you to give credit to the source for the material you are using but also provides your readers with sufficient bibliographic information to judge or even find your sources for themselves. In general, you must document the source of the following:

- direct quotations
- ideas or opinions that are not your own
- visual materials, such as photographs, maps, or graphs, that you did not create
- multimedia content, such as videos or audios, that you did not create
- information (a fact or statistic) that is not general knowledge

In most academic writing today, writers use the American Psychological Association (APA) style guide when they are writing in the social sciences: psychology, sociology, education, economics, anthropology, geography, and political science. This chapter explains how to cite sources using APA style. (MLA style, which tends to be used in the humanities—literature, languages, performing and visual arts, history, classics, philosophy, and religion—is explained in Chapter 10.) The guidelines in this chapter are based on the *Publication Manual of the American Psychological Association*, 6th edition (2009).

Two Main Components in APA Style

APA style uses in-text parenthetical citations to document sources. There are **two main components to in-text parenthetical citation systems:**

1. **In-text citations.** Parenthetical citations, which appear in the body of your writing, indicate to a reader that information you are presenting is taken from another source.

2. **A References list.** The References list, sometimes referred to as a bibliography, is a separate section at the end of your document that includes bibliographic information for every source you cited in your document.

Let's imagine you are writing an essay about the cultural significance of heavy metal music and you want to refer to a specific analysis of so-called death metal music in a book titled *Death Metal*

Music: The Passion and Politics of a Subculture, by Natalie J. Purcell. On page 188 of that book, Purcell makes a point about the philosophical function of death metal music that you want to include in your essay. If you were using APA style, you would cite the source as follows:

> Death metal music performs a genuine philosophical function by examining the dark side of human nature (Purcell, 2003, p. 188).

or

> Critic Natalie Purcell (2003) considers death metal a "philosophical response, whether conscious or subconscious, to terrifying questions about nebulous human nature" (p. 188).

The entry in the References list would look like this:

> Purcell, N. J. (2003). *Death metal music: The passion and politics of a subculture*. Jefferson, NC: McFarland.

Each in-text citation in your paper must have a corresponding entry on the References page, which enables your readers to consult the original source themselves.

FOCUS   Content Notes

The American Psychological Association recommends that writers use parenthetical, or in-text, citations of the kind described in this chapter when documenting sources (rather than traditional footnotes or endnotes). Writers can also use **content notes** for additional explanation or discussion of a point in the main text. APA discourages the use of such notes unless they are essential to the discussion. If you do use content notes, APA format requires them to be placed on a separate page titled "Footnotes" that appears at the end of the document. Indicate the presence of a content note in your main text by using a superscript number. For example, if you wanted to include a content note related to the following sentence in your main text, place the superscript number at the end of the sentence:

> Some research suggests a correlation between literacy and higher-order cognitive skills.[1]

The corresponding footnote would appear at the end of your main document on the Footnotes page:

---

[1] The correlation between literacy and cognition has been seriously questioned by many scholars, notably Sylvia Scribner and Michael Cole in their well-known study *The Psychology of Literacy*.

Creating In-Text Citations Using APA Style

APA style for citing sources reflects the conventions of empirical research. Because research tends to build on previously conducted studies and the relative currency of research is important, APA emphasizes the author's last name and year of publication in in-text citations. APA style also requires that in-text citations include page number(s) for material quoted directly from a source. However, direct quotation in APA style is not as common as paraphrase and summary.

FOCUS **Find the In-Text Citation Model You Need**

A. Work by one author (page 273)

B. Work by multiple authors (page 274)

C. Work by a corporate author (page 275)

D. More than one work by the same author (page 275)

E. Two or more works cited within one set of parentheses (page 275)

F. Authors with the same last name (page 275)

G. Work without an author listed (page 275)

H. Online source (page 276)

I. Quotation within a cited work (page 276)

J. Long quotations (page 276)

K. Work in more than one volume (page 277)

L. Personal communications (page 277)

Note: The list of References models appears on page 278.

A. Work by one author

If you were citing information taken from a book called *The Printing Revolution in Early Modern Europe* by Elizabeth L. Eisenstein, published in 1983, the parenthetical citation would look like this:

> The widespread adoption of the printing press in the 16th century helped standardize the major European languages (Eisenstein, 1983).

Note that there is a comma between the author's name and the year of publication. As always in APA style, you could use Eisenstein's name in your sentence and include only the year of publication in the parentheses immediately following the name:

> Eisenstein (1983) examines how the widespread adoption of the printing press in the 16th century helped standardize the major European languages.

B. Work by multiple authors

APA has several rules for citing works by multiple authors.

- **Work by two authors.** When citing a work by two authors, use both authors' names in the citation or in your sentence. If authors are named in parentheses, use an ampersand (&) to join them; however, if you name the authors in your sentence, use the word *and*. For example, if you wanted to quote from page 2 of the introduction to *Undead TV: Essays on Buffy the Vampire Slayer*, by Elana Levine and Lisa Parks, published in 2007, you could do so as follows:

   > We might consider how the hit television series *Buffy the Vampire Slayer* "uses its metaphorical representations of life and death, good and evil, comedy and tragedy to speak about the power struggles inherent in many people's everyday lives in the Western world" (Levine & Parks, 2007, p. 2).

   Note that a comma is placed after the second author's name and another comma is placed after the year of publication.

   If you use the authors' names in your sentence, cite the quotation like this:

   > Levine and Parks (2007) assert that *Buffy the Vampire Slayer* "uses its metaphorical representations of life and death, good and evil, comedy and tragedy to speak about the power struggles inherent in many people's everyday lives in the Western world" (p. 2).

   Place the date in parentheses immediately after the authors' names. The page reference should be placed in parentheses at the end of the sentence.

- **Work by three to five authors.** If you are referring to a work by three, four, or five authors, list all the authors' names the first time you cite the work. For example, if you were citing a journal article titled "Empirical Foundations for Writing in Prevention and Psychotherapy," by Brian A. Esterling, Luciano L'Abate, Edward J. Murray, and James W. Pennebaker, the parenthetical citation would look like this:

   > Studies have shown that writing has therapeutic benefits for some patients (Esterling, L'Abate, Murray, & Pennebaker, 1999).

   If you cite the same work again, list only the first author's name followed by the Latin phrase *et al.* (which means "and others"):

   > The therapeutic benefits of writing include lower blood pressure and higher self-esteem (Esterling et al., 1999).

   Note that there is no comma after the name of the author, but a comma is placed before the date of publication. Also note that there is no period after *et*, but there is a period after *al.*

- **Work by six or more authors.** When citing a work by six or more authors, use the first author's last name followed by the phrase *et al.* For example, if you cited a 2008 book co-written by Mark Smith and eight additional authors, the citation would appear as follows:

   > Researchers have found that many mammals mate for life (Smith et al., 2008).

If you included the name of the author in your sentence, the citation would look like this:

> Smith et al. (2008) found that many mammals mate for life.

C. Work by a corporate author

A "corporate author" is an organization, committee, association, or agency (rather than an individual or group of individually named authors). When citing a corporate author, use the same format as for a single author. For example, if you were citing a 2012 study by the Center for Research on Educational Outcomes, you would do so as follows:

> According to the Center for Research on Educational Outcomes (2012), 37 percent of charter schools had math scores that were lower than their public school peers.

You could also include the corporate author in the parentheses; omit any initial article:

> In one recent study, 37 percent of charter schools had math scores that were lower than their public school peers (Center for Research on Educational Outcomes, 2012).

D. More than one work by the same author

If you cite more than one work by the same author, you need to distinguish among the works by including the publication date of each work you cite. For example, if you were citing two different books by Paulo Freire—*Pedagogy of Hope*, published in 1994, and *Letters to Cristina*, published in 1996—your parenthetical citations might look like this:

> Some reformers emphasize the crucial role of hope in the struggle for change. They argue that hope is part of the process of improving human existence (Freire, 1994), but they also acknowledge that hope "seldom exists apart from the reverses of fate" (Freire, 1996, p. 14).

The dates enable a reader to find the specific works in the References list.

E. Two or more works cited within one set of parentheses

List the works alphabetically, separated by a semicolon, as they appear in your References list:

> (Harden, 2012; Raine, 2013)

F. Authors with the same last name

Include the author's first and middle initials (if given) in all in-text citations to avoid confusion.

> B. Brown (2013) and S. T. Brown (2011) found that weather patterns have changed significantly in the past decade.

G. Work without an author listed

If you cite a work without an author listed, include a brief version of the title, either in parentheses or in the signal phrase. Here the title "Carrying the Torch" is shortened to "Carrying":

> The sports management industry in Great Britain received a significant boost in business as a result of the 2012 Olympic Games in London ("Carrying," 2012).

In in-text parenthetical citations, titles of articles and web pages are placed in quotation marks; titles of books are italicized or underlined.

H. Online source

When citing online sources in in-text parenthetical citations, follow the same principles you would use when citing print sources. However, there are many different kinds of electronic sources, and they might not include the same kinds of information that are available for a print book or journal article. For example, websites don't usually have page numbers. In such cases, provide the number of the paragraph in which you found the information or quotation you are citing, using the abbreviation *para*.:

> (Martinez, 2000, para. 8)

If page numbers are not available or paragraph numbers are not feasible, include sufficient information for readers to find the source you are citing, such as the subheading or name of the section in which the source material appears:

> (Madoff, Bradley, & Rico, Results section).

If the heading is too lengthy to cite, then use a shortened title. For the long heading "Genetic Variations Link Found in Bipolar Twins Separately Adopted," you could use the first several words:

> (Bico & Marley, 2013, "Genetic Variations Link Found," para. 3).

According to APA style, if you do not have reliable page numbers or paragraph numbers, leave them out of the parenthetical citation:

> (Martinez, 2000)

I. Quotation within a cited work

When using a quotation from one source that you have found in another source, you have to show that the quotation was acquired "secondhand" and was not taken directly from the original source. In such cases, indicate the original source in your text and the secondary source in parentheses. For example, let's say you were reading a book called *Literary Theory* by Terry Eagleton that included a quotation by Sigmund Freud that you wanted to use in your essay. You would cite the Freud quotation as follows:

> Even Freud acknowledged the central important of economics in human relations, famously stating, "The motive of human society is in the last resort an economic one" (as cited in Eagleton, 1983, p. 151).

Note the phrase *as cited in* in the parenthetical citation. In this instance, you are signaling to readers that you read Freud's statement on page 151 of the book by Terry Eagleton.

J. Long quotations

In APA style, a long quotation is defined as one than contains more than 40 words. These quotations should be indented one inch from the left margin as a block quotation—*without* quotation marks.

> LeVine et al. (1994) describe the child care practices of the Gusii people of Kenya in regard to cultural assumptions:
>
> > Gusii mothers are devoted to the welfare and development of their infants, and their sense of what is best for them is framed in terms of indigenous cultural models that

assume high infant mortality, high fertility (but with protective birth-spacing), and a domestic age-hierarchy in which young children acquire useful skills and moral virtues through participation in household food production. (p. 2)

The page number for the quotation is included in parentheses at the end of the quotation. Include the abbreviation *p.* for "page." Notice that the parenthetical citation is placed *after* the final period of the block quotation. If the author's name does not appear in the main text, include it in the parentheses.

K. Work in more than one volume

If you use more than one volume from a multivolume work in your paper, indicate the years of publication in each citation.

(Trieste, 1999–2002)

If you cite only one volume, provide the year of its publication only. In your References entry, you will list the volume number.

L. Personal communication

Personal emails, letters, interviews, conversations, and other private communications are not retrievable by others and so are not listed in the References list. In the in-text citation, provide initials and last name for the correspondent, provide an exact date, and use the label "personal communication":

(L. L. Fothergill, personal communication, October 5, 2013)

Creating a References List in APA Style

Each source you cite in your text must correspond to an entry in your bibliography, which is called the References list in APA style. Your list of References should appear at the end of your document, beginning with a new page. Organize the References list alphabetically according to the authors' last names (or, if the work includes no author, the first main word of the title). In APA style, follow these rules:

- Capitalize only proper nouns and the first word in the titles and subtitles of books, chapters, and articles.
- Capitalize all important words in the names of journals, newspapers, and magazines.
- Italicize the titles of books and longer works.
- Do *not* italicize names of journals, newspapers, and magazines.
- For both print and electronic sources, provide the DOI if available. (See "What Is DOI?" on page 280.) If there is no DOI for an online source, include the URL.
- Double-space entries but do not skip spaces between entries.
- Using hanging indents of one-half inch for entries in the References list.

Books (Print and Online)

Periodicals (Print and Online)

Other Sources

24. Film, video, DVD (page 287)

25. Television or radio program (page 287)

26. Music recording (page 287)

27. Advertisement (page 287)

Note: The list of in-text citation models appears on page 273.

Books (Print and Online)

Here is the general format for an entry for a book in the References list:

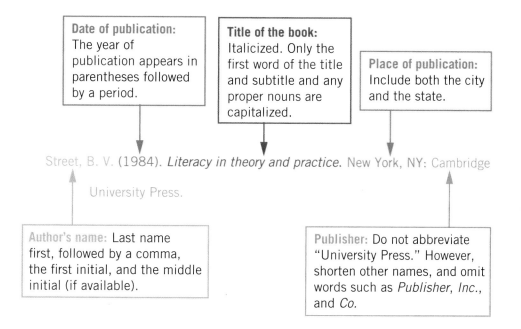

Date of publication: The year of publication appears in parentheses followed by a period.

Title of the book: Italicized. Only the first word of the title and subtitle and any proper nouns are capitalized.

Place of publication: Include both the city and the state.

Street, B. V. (1984). *Literacy in theory and practice.* New York, NY: Cambridge University Press.

Author's name: Last name first, followed by a comma, the first initial, and the middle initial (if available).

Publisher: Do not abbreviate "University Press." However, shorten other names, and omit words such as *Publisher, Inc.,* and *Co.*

However, for books that are accessed online, the publisher and place of publication are eliminated and replaced by the URL (web address) where the book was found:

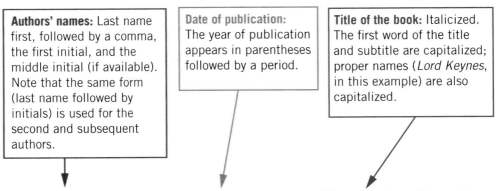

Authors' names: Last name first, followed by a comma, the first initial, and the middle initial (if available). Note that the same form (last name followed by initials) is used for the second and subsequent authors.

Date of publication: The year of publication appears in parentheses followed by a period.

Title of the book: Italicized. The first word of the title and subtitle are capitalized; proper names (*Lord Keynes*, in this example) are also capitalized.

Buchanan, J. M., and Wagner, R. E. (1977). *Democracy in deficit: The political legacy of*

Lord Keynes. Retrieved from

http://www.econlib.org/library/Buchanan/buchCv8.html

Online Location: Indicate that the work was accessed online with the phrase *Retrieved from*. Include the URL (web address) where the book was accessed online. If the publication has a DOI (see "What is DOI?"), replace the URL with the DOI and replace the phrase *Retrieved from* with *doi* in lowercase followed by a colon. Do not place a period after the URL or DOI number.

FOCUS   What Is DOI?

DOI stands for digital object identifier. A DOI is a unique string of numbers that identifies an electronic publication. It is more stable than a URL, which can change or be deleted. APA style requires that, when available, the DOI be included in an entry in the References list. Use the DOI in place of the URL.

Many scholarly journals now include DOIs for online publications. Usually, the DOI appears on the first page of the article, as in the example of an article published in the scholarly journal *School Effectiveness and School Improvement* on page 281; the DOI appears at the very bottom of the page. The entry in the References list would look like this:

Ross, J. A., and Gray, P. (2006). Transformational leadership and teacher commitment to organizational values: The mediating effects of collective teacher efficacy. *School Effectiveness and School Improvement,* 17(2), 179–199. doi: 10.1080/09243450600565795

School Effectiveness and School Improvement
Vol. 17, No. 2, June 2006, pp. 179–199

R Routledge
Taylor & Francis Group

Transformational Leadership and Teacher Commitment to Organizational Values: The mediating effects of collective teacher efficacy

John A. Ross* and Peter Gray

Ontario Institute for Studies in Education, University of Toronto, Ontario, Canada

Transformational leadership researchers have given little attention to teacher expectations that mediate between goals and actions. The most important of these expectations, teacher efficacy, refers to teacher beliefs that they will be able to bring about student learning. This study examined the mediating effects of teacher efficacy by comparing two models derived from Bandura's social-cognitive theory. Model A hypothesized that transformational leadership would contribute to teacher commitment to organizational values exclusively through collective teacher efficacy. Model B hypothesized that leadership would have direct effects on teacher commitment and indirect effects through teacher efficacy. Data from 3,074 teachers in 218 elementary schools in a cross-validation sample design provided greater support for Model B than Model A. Transformational leadership had an impact on the collective teacher efficacy of the school; teacher efficacy alone predicted teacher commitment to community partnerships; and transformational leadership had direct and indirect effects on teacher commitment to school mission and commitment to professional learning community.

Introduction

Previous research has demonstrated that transformational leadership contributes to valued teacher outcomes. For example, teachers in schools characterized by transformational principal behavior are more likely than teachers in other schools to express satisfaction with their principal, report that they exert extra effort, and be more committed to the organization and to improving it (Leithwood, Jantzi, & Steinbach, 1999). Few studies of the relationship between principal behavior and teacher outcomes have examined the mechanisms through which leadership impacts

*Corresponding author. OISE/University of Toronto, Trent Valley Centre, Box 719, Peterborough, Ontario, K9J 7A1, Canada. Email: jross@oise.utoronto.ca

ISSN 0924-3453 (print)/ISSN 1744-5124 (online)/06/020179–21
© 2006 Taylor & Francis
DOI: 10.1080/09243450600565795

1. Book with one author

Fineman, H. (2008). *The thirteen American arguments: Enduring debates that define and inspire our country*. New York, NY: Random House.

Cowles, J. T. (1937). *Food-tokens as incentives for learning by chimpanzees*. Baltimore, MD: The Johns Hopkins Press. doi: 10.1037/14268-000

2. Book with two or more authors

Stewart, D. W., Shamdasani, P. N., & Rook, D. W. (2007). *Focus groups: Theory and practice*. Thousand Oaks, CA: Sage.

Buchanan, J. M., & Wagner, R. E. (1977). *Democracy in deficit: The political legacy of Lord Keynes*. Retrieved from http://www.econlib.org/library/Buchanan/buchCv8.html

The second example shows a book accessed online. Eliminate the publisher and place of publication and include the URL where the work was accessed. If a DOI is available, use that instead of the URL (as shown in "What Is DOI?" on page 280).

Notice that an ampersand (&) is used in place of *and* before the name of the last author. If there are more than six authors, follow the sixth name with *et al.* (meaning "and others").

3. Two or more books by the same author

If you cite two books by the same author or by the same set of authors whose names are given in the same order in both books, arrange them by publication date in the References list. List the earlier work first.

Freire, P. (1970). *Pedagogy of the oppressed*. (M. B. Ramos, Trans.). New York, NY: Continuum.

Freire, P. (1996). *Letters to Cristina: Reflections on my life and work*. New York, NY: Routledge.

Freire, P. (2004). *Pedagogy of hope: Reliving* Pedagogy of the oppressed. New York, NY: Continuum.

If the works were both published in the same year, alphabetize the works by title, excluding *A* and *The*.

4. Anthology with an editor

Hill, C. A., & Helmers, M. (Eds.). (2004). *Defining visual rhetorics*. Mahwah, NJ: Erlbaum.

5. Work in an anthology

Olson, C. (1973). Projective verse. In D. M. Allen & W. Tallman (Eds.), *The poetics of the new American poetry* (pp. 147–158). New York, NY: Grove Press.

6. Introduction, preface, foreword, or afterword

Zelazny, R. (1968). Introduction. In P. K. Dick, *Do Androids Dream of Electric Sheep?* (pp. vii–x). New York, NY: Del Ray.

In this example, Roger Zelazny wrote the introduction to the book *Do Androids Dream of Electric Sheep?* by Philip K. Dick. Include the page numbers (in parentheses) of the introduction after the title of the book.

7. Work by a corporate author or without an author listed

Center for Research on Education Outcomes. (2009). *Multiple choice: Charter school performance in 16 states*. Stanford, CA: Stanford University.

If no author or organization is listed, begin the entry with the title of the book. Place the year after the title.

8. Translated book

Tsunetomo, Y. (1979). *Hagakure: The book of the samurai*. (W. S. Wilson, Trans.). Tokyo, Japan: Kadansha International.

Place the name of the translator and the abbreviation *Trans.* (for "translator") in parentheses, separated by a comma. Note that the abbreviation is capitalized. Also, the name of the translator appears with the first and middle initials first, followed by the last name.

9. Subsequent editions of a book

Creswell, J. W. (Ed.). (2007). *Qualitative research and design: Choosing among five approaches* (Rev. ed.). Thousand Oaks, CA: Sage.

10. Work in more than one volume

Milton, J. (1847). *The prose works of John Milton* (Vols. 1–2). Philadelphia, PA: John W. Moore. Retrieved from http://app.libraryofliberty.org/

11. Encyclopedia article

The format for entries for encyclopedia articles is similar to articles in anthologies.

Sockett, H. (2008). The moral and epistemic purposes of teacher education. In M. Cochran-Smith, S. Feiman-Nemser, & D. J. McIntyre (Eds.), *Handbook of Research on Teacher Education* (3rd ed., pp. 309–330). New York, NY: Routledge.

If no author is listed, begin with the title of the article. The rest of the citation is the same. (See also "Citing Wikipedia and Other Online References" on page 256.)

12. Government publication

United States Department of Transportation. (2012). *Bridge management*. Washington, DC: Government Printing Office.

For government documents, the name of the nation or state appears first combined with the agency (Department of Transportation, in this example). If you accessed the publication online, indicate the URL:

U. S. Department of Transportation. (2011). *National evaluation of the Safe Trip-21 initiative*. Washington, DC: Government Printing Office. Retrieved from http://ntl.bts.gov/lib/38000/38500/38510/safetrip_cfr.pdf

Periodicals (Print and Online)

Here is the general format for an article from a scholarly journal:

Title of article: Only the first word of the title and subtitle (if there is one) and proper names should be capitalized. Do *not* place titles of articles in quotation marks.

Author's name: Last name, followed by a comma, the first initial, and middle initial (if available).

Title of periodical: Italicize and capitalize the title of the journal, magazine, or newspaper. Place a comma after the title.

Buck, A. (2012). Examining digital literacy practices on social network sites. *Research in the Teaching of English, 47*(1), 9–38. Retrieved from http://www.ncte.org.libproxy.albany.edu/library/NCTEFiles/Resources/Journals/RTE/0471-aug2012/RTE0471Examining.pdf

Date of publication: Year of publication appears in parentheses followed by a period. For newspapers and magazines, place a comma after the year and include the month as follows: (2012, April).

Volume and issue number: Include the volume of the publication in italics followed by the issue number in parentheses. This example shows issue #1 of volume 47. Place a comma after the closing parenthesis.

Pages: The page numbers on which the article appears followed by a period. If the article does not appear on continuous pages, separate the page numbers with a comma.

Source: If you found the article in print, end the citation with the page numbers. If you found the article on a website or through an online database, indicate that by including "Retrieved from" followed by the URL (web address). If there is a DOI, use that in place of the URL and replace the phrase "Retrieved from" with "doi" in lowercase followed by a colon. Do not place a period after the URL or the DOI.

13. Journal article with one author

> Mayers, T. (2009). One simple word: From creative writing to creative writing studies. *College English, 71*(3), 217–228.

If you accessed this article via the journal's website or from another online resource, the citation would look like this:

> Mayers, T. (2009). One simple word: From creative writing to creative writing studies. *College English, 71*(3), 217–228. Retrieved from http://www.ncte.org/journals/ce/issues/v71-3

If a DOI is available, include it in place of the URL:

> Desimone, L. M. (2009). Improving impact studies of teachers' professional development: Toward better conceptualizations and measures. *Educational Researcher, 38* (3): 181–199. doi: 10.3102/0013189X08331140

The abbreviation *doi* is in lowercase and followed by a colon. Do not place a period after the DOI number.

Note: APA style does not require that you include the name of the database if you accessed the work through an online database such as *Academic Search Complete*.

14. Journal article with multiple authors

For a work with two authors:

> Bowles, S., & Gintis, H. (2002). *Schooling in Capitalist America* revisited. *Sociology of Education, 75* (1): 1–18.

In this example, part of the article title is capitalized and italicized because it includes the title of a book (*Schooling in Capitalist America*).

For a work with three to seven authors:

> Esterling, B. A., L'Abate, L., Murray, E. J., & Pennebaker, J. W. (1999). Empirical foundations for writing in prevention and psychotherapy: Mental and physical health outcomes. *Clinical Psychology Review, 19* (1): 79–96.

Note: For a work by more than seven authors, include the first six authors' names, as in the previous example, and use an ellipsis in place of the remaining author names. Include the final author's name after the ellipsis.

15. Magazine article

> Gover, R. (2011, September). One novel's sojourn through culture wars & privacy. *The Writer's Chronicle, 44,* 50–57.

If you found the article through the magazine website or other online resource, cite it as follows:

> Gover, R. (2011, September). One novel's sojourn through culture wars & privacy. *The Writer's Chronicle, 44,* 50–57. Retrieved from https://www.awpwriter.org/library/writers_chronicle_overview

Note: If the magazine is published weekly or biweekly, include the day in the parentheses: (2011, September 15).

16. Newspaper article

> Kepner, T. (2008, September 21). Grand home of a larger-than-life team. *The New York Times*, p. N1.

Include both the day and month of publication for daily newspapers. Note that the page number includes the section in which the article appeared (in this example, section N, page 1). Also, for newspapers, include the abbreviation *p.* (for "page") before the page number.

If you accessed the article through the newspaper's website, cite it as follows:

> Kepner, T. (2008, September 21). Grand home of a larger-than-life team. *The New York Times*, p. N1. Retrieved from http://www.nytimes.com

17. Editorial

> Fighting "Patent Trolls." [Editorial]. (2013, June 6). *The New York Times*, p. A22.

Notice that the word *Editorial* is capitalized, placed in brackets, and followed by a period. It is *not* italicized.

18. Letter to the editor

> Griffey, D. (2013, July). The price is wrong. [Letter to the editor]. *Money*, 10.

19. Review

> Krugman, P. (2013, June 6). How the case for austerity has crumbled. [Review of the books *The alchemists: Three central bankers and a world on fire; Austerity: The history of a dangerous idea;* and *The great deformation: The corruption of capitalism in America*]. *The New York Review of Books*. Retrieved from http://www.nybooks.com/articles/archives/2013/jun/06/how-case-austerity-has-crumbled/

Other Sources

20. Web page

Cite a web page as you would an article from a journal, including the following information, if available: author's name, the title of the document or page, the date of publication, and the online location:

> Pollan, M. (2010). Sustainable eating & nutrition: FAQs and useful links. Retrieved from http://michaelpollan.com/resources/sustainable-eating-nutrition/

If you can't find a date of publication, use the abbreviation *n.d.* (for "no date").

The citation for a web page by a corporate author (such as a government agency or business) is similar in format:

> U.S. Department of the Interior. (2011, April 23). Climate change. Retrieved from http://www.doi.gov/index.cfm

Notice that the name of the agency or organization appears in place of an author's name. For a web page without an author, the citation appears like this:

> How to anchor securely. (2012, July 23). Retrieved from http://www.westmarine.com/webapp/wcs/stores/servlet/TopCategories1_11151_10001_-1

21. Blog

> Schoenkopf, R. (2012, April 6). Breitbart's ghost: Obama exploited Catholics by being endorsed by them [Web log comment]. Retrieved from http://wonkette.com/

22. Podcast

> Gross, T. (Executive Producer). (2012, August 15). Do voter ID laws prevent fraud, or dampen turnout? [Audio podcast]. *Fresh Air Podcast*. Retrieved from www.npr.org

Begin with the name of the most relevant contributor. The contributor's title—*director, host,* or (as in this example) *executive producer*—appears next, capitalized and in parentheses, followed by a period.

23. Interview

Personal, telephone, and email interviews are cited only within the text because they are not retrievable by other researchers.

24. Film, video, DVD

> Luhrmann, B. (Director). (2013). *The Great Gatsby* [Motion picture]. United States: Warner.

For videos, DVDs, filmstrips, and similar media, use this same format, noting the medium in brackets.

25. Television or radio program

> MacLaren, M. (Director). (2013, May 19). Second sons. *Game of Thrones* [Television broadcast]. New York, NY: HBO.

Note that the episode title ("Second Sons" in this example) precedes the name of the program (*Game of Thrones*).

26. Music recording

> Kuhn, J. (2013). *All this happiness* [CD]. New York, NY: PS Classics.

27. Advertisement

> Nike [Advertisement]. (2013, March). *Adweek*, 14.

In this example, the page number (14) appears after the title of the publication (*Adweek*).

Sample APA-Style Research Paper

In the following essay, which was written for an introductory writing class at Emerson College, Duncan Gelder follows APA guidelines for formatting a research paper. Duncan examines differences between the generations, focusing on the ways in which different generations use new technologies and how those technologies relate to the way people think. He makes an argument that the differences between generations are not caused by technology but are a function of the values of each generation. Duncan's essay is a good example of an argument to inquire. His goal is not to "win" an argument about why generations think differently; rather, he makes his argument as a way to understand this complex question and share that understanding with his audience.

Duncan adheres to the APA guidelines in formatting his paper. First, he includes a title page with the title and his name centered on the page. APA does not require information on the title page other than the title, author's name, and institutional affiliation, but if the course instructor requires his or her name, the course name, and a date, omit the institutional affiliation and replace it with the information required by the instructor, as Duncan has done. Notice that the title page is numbered and includes the same running head ("Generations") as the rest of the paper.

Second, Duncan includes an abstract, which is a summary of his paper. According to APA style, abstracts should not exceed 250 words. Notice that the word "Abstract" is centered one inch from the top of the page.

When formatting a paper in APA style, remember to

- double-space the entire document

- use one-inch margins

- indent paragraphs one-half inch

- include the title at the start of the paper (on the third page, after the abstract), centered above the main text

- use running head with a shortened version of the title, in capital letters, on the left side of the page and the page number on the right side (include the running head on every page of the document)

Running Head: THE GENERATIONS THAT INFLUENCE TECHNOLOGY   1

The Generations That Influence Technology

Duncan Gelder

Professor Betsy Milarcik

WR 101 14 Introduction to College Writing

November 26, 2012

Abstract

Some experts believe we are witnessing a shift in cognitive styles between the Baby Boomer generation and younger generations as a result of the emergence of new technologies and the growing role of media in the lives of young people. However, in the past century, it has not been the technology and appliances that separate one generation from another; instead, the generation's needs and values at the time determine what innovations are prevalent for them.

The Generations That Influence Technology

How often does a person hear someone use the cliché phrase "back in my day…" followed by a long-winded explanation of how things used to be? Differences in generations is a common theme through much of the discussion about today's technology. According to N. Katherine Hayles (2007), "we are in the midst of a generational shift in cognitive styles" (p. 187). She believes that an "obvious explanation for the shift… is the increasing role of media in the everyday environments of young people" (189). However, in the past century, it has not been the technology and appliances that separate one generation from another; instead, the generation's needs and values at the time determine what innovations are prevalent for them.

A look back to the beginnings of the idea of "modern" technology, the Industrial Revolution in the 19th century, reveals that there are correlations between the ideas of that generation and the increase in technological innovations. The United States was going through major changes at the time. Increasing numbers of people who were willing to work quickly and for cheap were immigrating into the country. Owners of the factories and mills that dominated the era's industry wanted to ensure that this new surplus of workers were doing the work they were supposed to do. The capitalists who owned these businesses created the factory setting and the major technologies, such as the steam engine, that drove industrial growth (Backer, n.d.).

In a way, Hayles' (2007) idea of hyper attention comes into play during this era as well. Hayles (2007) describes hyper attention as being characterized partly by "switching focus rapidly between different tasks" (p. 187). The factories could take care of the steps of production from start to finish in one huge building. The technologies that were designed were, in a way, a mechanical form of hyper attention. This is really where our modern idea of capitalism began as well, with the wealthy starting businesses and buying out their competitors. Major monopolies became common during this generation because the upper class were not content with just owning one factory; they needed to own all of the factories and have the biggest hold on their sector of the industry, which is just another large-scale form of hyper attention among the wealthy. The attitudes, both of the workers being accountable for their work and the capitalists wanting to do as much as possible in a shorter amount of time, shaped what technology was prevalent and created the need for the innovations in the first place.

The way in which generational attitudes affected the technology of the era continued on as the industrial revolution began to fade. With two major world wars taking place, the country found itself in need of weapons and military technology. The unified attitude of the country forced these generations to come up with new innovations that would help protect our country. Aircraft and other forms of war transportation were made to be more efficient and able to withstand harsher conditions, bombs were perfected, and boots and uniforms were mass produced; the generations that were affected by these major wars fueled the need for new innovations that would help them succeed. The women, many of whom were not able to fight overseas, turned to other ways to assist the country; they began to build and assemble all of the parts needed by the soldiers. The first World War coincided with the women's suffrage movement, a major point in generational attitudes (National Women's History Museum, 2007). These women wanted to prove that they were equals to men, but not all of them were able to operate undercover overseas or as switchboard operators. So they turned to the factories and began to find new ways of creating wartime innovations that would prove to be instrumental in winning these two major wars.

When the Second World War ended, the generation known commonly as the "Baby Boomer" generation was born as soldiers were now coming home from war and families were complete once again. The country was now focused on family life. Children were born, couples were together again; the home was the most important value during this era. Because there was need for products to be tailored to the consumer again, instead of for the military, many companies found that they needed to create products for the home life. This was the generation of appliances and at-home technology. The housewives that women were now expected to be meant that the women who had been hard at work during the war were now faced with the need to find power and freedom. Here again the idea of hyper attention comes into play. Women, who were the ones who took care of the house and were unable to work due to social inequalities, were now faced with monotonous, time-consuming household tasks. They needed new and unique innovations to make housework faster, giving them less work to do. Thus came the major changes in appliances and at-home technology, with faster washing machines and stronger vacuums being invented and updated as quickly as they were released. The Baby Boomer generation, which focused on family life more than any other idea, influenced what technology and innovations were available and invented during this era. Women were not housewives because they had washing machines available; the washing machines were available because of the strong social inequalities that required women to find ways of coping with the new work they had at home. The invention of the birth control pill during this era was another example of an innovation being influenced by the ideas of the generation. Many women were looking for freedom from the household life. The birth control pill was invented to give them a chance to live their lives without being burdened by children (Walsh, 2010).

The same correlations between values and technology are evident. We live in a time when social equality is a common theme. Women have broken away from the housewife stereotype and are now working to try and break the glass ceiling in the workplace. The racism and prejudice towards people of color is being challenged, a change best symbolized by the election and reelection of our country's first African American president. Gays and lesbians are fighting to receive equal rights. The country is in the midst of a new emphasis on uniqueness and individual rights. And because of this emphasis, technology has adapted to become more customizable for each and every person. Netflix allows us to watch the shows we want to watch. Smart phones allow us to download any app we choose. The current generation is fueled by the need for individualism and customization, and our technology reflects that. Our "hyper attention" is not so much a product of technology; the human need to be entertained and to move forward influences the technology that is a major part of our day-to-day lives. Technology, in a way, is the result of hyper attention. It isn't the technology which influences us; it's us that influences the technology.

References

Backer, P. R. (n.d.). *The cause of the industrial revolution.* Retrieved from
   http://www.engr.sjsu.edu/pabacker/causeIR.htm

Hayles, N. K. (2007). Hyper and deep attention: The generational divide in
   cognitive modes. *Profession,* 187–199.

National Women's History Museum. (2007). *Clandestine Women: Spies
   in American History.* Retrieved from http://www.nwhm.org/online-
   exhibits/spies/12.htm

Walsh, K. T. (2010, March 12). The 1960s: A decade of change for women.
   U.S. News & World Report. Retrieved from http://www.usnews.com/
   news/articles/2010/03/12/the-1960s-a-decade-of-change-for-women

Avoiding Common Problems In Style, Grammar, and Usage

12

CORE CONCEPT #10—"Good writing means more than good grammar"—underscores a reality about writing that eludes many people: "good" writing and "correct" writing aren't necessarily the same thing. In fact, as noted elsewhere in this textbook, the complexity of writing and the importance of rhetorical context make it impossible to define "good" writing in a way that applies to all circumstances. What counts as good writing in one situation might look like poor writing in another. The same principle applies to the rules for "correct" writing. Rules that must be followed in one situation can be ignored in others. For example, using the first person ("I") is perfectly fine in an op-ed essay for the campus newspaper but inappropriate in a chemistry lab report.

At the same time, the widespread belief that good writing is also correct writing is powerful, both in academic settings and in American culture generally. Many people equate grammar with character, and they interpret errors in writing as signs of laziness, sloppy thinking, or, worse, ignorance and even stupidity. Of course, a punctuation error doesn't mean a student is lazy or stupid, and such attitudes about "good grammar" ignore the complexity and rhetorical nature of writing. Nevertheless, these common attitudes influence how readers respond to a writer's words. What that means for you is that it is important to follow the conventions of writing so that you avoid errors that can interfere with the clarity of your prose and weaken your credibility as a writer.

As every student writer knows, rules for usage, punctuation, and spelling can be confusing and often seem capricious. One teacher might take off points for an "error" that another teacher ignores. How can student writers produce clear, effective, "correct" writing when the rules often seem so vague and relative? This chapter is intended to help answer that question.

Despite the confusing nature of many rules for grammar and usage and despite the variability with which these rules are applied by teachers and others, there are some basic principles of grammar and usage that apply to most writing situations. Moreover, in academic writing, certain conventions for style and usage are widely followed. In addition, research has identified the kinds of errors students tend to make in their writing. The advice provided in this chapter is based on prevailing conventions of academic writing as well as research on writing quality and error.

This chapter is not a comprehensive guide to grammar and usage. Instead, it explains the most important principles of grammar and usage in academic writing and offers advice for avoiding the most common errors. If you follow this advice, chances are that your writing will have fewer errors. Moreover, the strategies described in this chapter should help you grasp important rules for writing and gain a better understanding of the conventions of writing.

Strategies for Avoiding Errors

Let's start with two important points.

- **You already know most of the important rules of grammar and usage.** If you've made it to college, you are already a competent writer, and you have a working knowledge of most of the basic rules of writing, including punctuation, spelling, verb tense, and so on. This is true even if you can't actually state the rules you apply in your writing. For example, you might know that a comma belongs in a certain place in a sentence without knowing exactly why a comma belongs there. The point is that you have a good foundation for strengthening your grasp of the conventions of writing. You can build on that foundation by identifying the rules you do know and learning the ones you should know—which this chapter will help you do.

- **You can't learn all the rules of grammar and usage.** Nobody can. I've been writing professionally for three decades, I've written textbooks (like this one) for writing courses, and I've been a consultant for various kinds of writing tests, yet I still need to check handbooks and style guides to clarify a rule or learn one that I didn't know. Sometimes I even find that I was mistaken about a rule I thought I knew. If someone who does this kind of thing for a living can't know all the rules, it makes little sense for student writers to expect to learn them. The fact is that you already know most of the important rules, and the ones you still need to clarify or learn are probably relatively few in number. Focus on identifying those.

These two points should help reduce your anxiety about grammar and usage. Students often tell me that they "have bad grammar" or that they know they "need better grammar." What they really need—what most student writers need—is to build on what they already know about grammar to increase their confidence as writers and determine what they should know in order to avoid the errors that might be weakening their writing.

To accomplish these goals, follow these three steps:

1. Identify the errors you make in your writing.

2. Learn the rules related to those errors.

3. Practice.

Identify the Errors You Make in Your Writing

What kinds of errors do you routinely make in your writing? What kinds of problems do your instructors point out in your writing? Once you pinpoint the specific errors you tend to make, you can begin to work on avoiding them. Although this approach might seem daunting, especially if you have often received papers back from instructors full of red ink, the challenge is probably not as great as you think. Research suggests that most students tend to make the same errors repeatedly in their writing. If they can identify and eliminate those errors, they will significantly improve their writing.

Learn the Rules Related to Those Errors

Once you have a sense of the errors you tend to make in your writing, use this chapter (perhaps in conjunction with a comprehensive grammar handbook) to understand the rules related to those errors. If you're like most students, most of the errors you make are probably minor, such as missing or misplaced commas or incorrect apostrophes. It's quite possible that you make those errors because you either misunderstand the appropriate rule or never learned the rule in the first place. In addition, college-level academic writing is governed by conventions that you might not have learned in high school, so you might need to learn some new rules. Understanding the principles of usage and the conventions that apply to the errors you make will help you avoid those errors.

Practice

The best way to improve as a writer is to practice writing. The same is true for learning to avoid errors. If you want to eliminate errors from your writing, you have to practice identifying and correcting those errors in your writing. You can do so in two general ways:

- **First, consult handbooks or style guides** that have exercises for applying the specific rules related to the errors you tend to make. Doing such exercises will sharpen your ability to identify and correct those errors and strengthen your knowledge of specific rules of usage and grammar.

- **Second, practice editing your own drafts** in a way that focuses specifically on the kinds of errors you tend to make. If you follow the procedure in Chapter 3 when you are working on a writing project, include in Step #10 an additional step that focuses on the specific errors you have identified as common in your own writing. If you make such a step a routine part of your practice as a writer, you will eventually begin to notice that fewer and fewer errors appear in your finished projects.

This rest of this chapter focuses on the problems that research indicates college students tend to make in their writing. The errors you commonly make in your own writing are probably on this "hit parade," and the usage and syntax problems that can make your sentences unclear are very likely the ones described here.

Coordination, Subordination, and Parallelism

The structure of a sentence—what teachers often call *syntax*—is more than a function of rules for usage and grammar. It is also a means of conveying relationships and emphasizing words, phrases, and ideas. The elements of a sentence must fit together syntactically, but the syntax should also match the intended meaning so that the structure of the sentence not only is grammatically correct but also helps convey the writer's ideas.

The many complexities and nuances of syntax are well beyond the scope of this chapter, but you can improve the clarity of your prose by avoiding common problems in three areas of syntax: coordination, subordination, and parallel structure.

Coordination

Coordination refers to the use of similar or equivalent grammatical constructions to link ideas or show relationships between generally equal ideas or information in a sentence. Writers use coordinating conjunctions (*and, but, so, yet, or*) to show coordinate relationships between elements of a sentence:

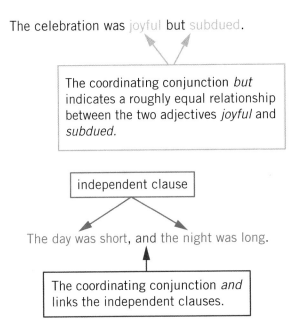

It is important to note here that using different coordinating conjunctions can change the relationships between the coordinate elements:

The day was short, but the night was long.

In this example, *but* changes the relationship between the first clause ("the day was short") and the second ("the night was long"). Although this point might seem obvious, using coordinating conjunctions strategically to convey specific or precise ideas about the relationships between elements of a sentence is a hallmark of effective academic writing. For example, consider how the choice of *and* or *but* in the following example affects the relationship between the first clause ("Life can be a constant struggle") and the second ("death is final"):

Life can be a constant struggle, and death is final.

Life can be a constant struggle, but death is final.

In both sentences, the clauses are still coordinate, but replacing *and* with *but* changes both the relationship between the clauses and the emphasis of the sentence—which is turn affects the meaning conveyed by the sentence. In the first sentence, the two clauses have equal emphasis and can be seen as two equal statements of the human condition. We might interpret the sentence as follows: Let's recognize the two important realities about human existence that life is hard and death is final. In the second sentence, however, the use of *but* shifts the emphasis to the second clause, which alters the meaning of the entire sentence. We might state the meaning this way: Yes, life is hard, but death is final. The implication might be something like this: Because death is final, live life to the fullest, no matter how hard it can be.

This example illustrates how the choice of a single coordinating conjunction, even in a seemingly straightforward sentence, can significantly affect the ideas conveyed by the sentence. In this sense, coordination can be a powerful tool for writers. Notice that greater emphasis is usually attached to the final element in a coordinate relationship.

Students commonly make two mistakes in using coordination in their writing: they use the wrong coordinating conjunction (usually *and* when *but* or *so* is more appropriate), and they use too much coordination:

Shifts in climate patterns have resulted in more frequent severe weather in many

regions, and local governments are struggling to develop more effective emergency

services.

| coordinating conjunction | | independent clause |

In this example, there is nothing grammatically incorrect about the sentence, but the conjunction *and* does not quite convey the correlation between the first and second clauses of the sentence. If the writer wanted to show that local governments are struggling to develop effective emergency services specifically as a result of changes in several weather patterns, *but* would be a better choice to link the two main clauses:

> Shifts in climate patterns have resulted in more frequent severe weather in many regions, but local governments are struggling to develop more effective emergency services.

As you revise your drafts for style, usage, and grammar, it is a good idea to pay attention to your use of coordinating conjunctions so that you can identify sentences in which the coordination does not convey the specific ideas or relationships you intend. If you notice that you are relying on *and* to link elements of a sentence—especially main clauses, as in this example—it is often a sign that you might need to adjust some of your sentences by using a different conjunction.

Subordination

Subordination refers to the use of elements in a sentence to show hierarchical relationships or relationships among ideas that are not equal. Subordination is indicated through the use of dependent clauses and is signaled by the use of *subordinating conjunctions*. The most common subordinating conjunctions are *if, although, because, before, after, since, whether, when, whereas, while, until,* and *unless*; writers also commonly use *than* and *that* to indicate subordination. Here are some examples.

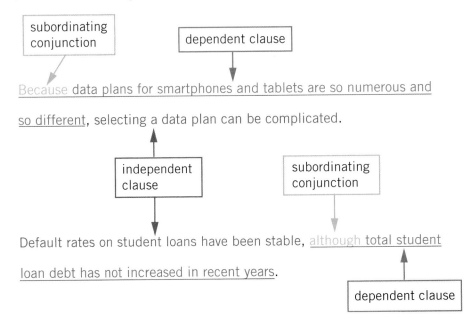

In these examples, the information in the dependent clauses is subordinated to the information in the main independent clause. Writers can use subordination to emphasize the ideas in the independent clause and to indicate the relationship between those ideas and the less important ideas in the dependent clause.

Notice that although the ideas in the independent clause receive emphasis, you can use the order of the clauses to adjust the relative emphasis of each clause. Consider how reversing the order of the clauses in the second example can change the emphasis on each clause and subtly influence the meaning of the sentence:

> Default rates on student loans have been stable, although total student loan debt has not increased in recent years.

> Although total student loan debt has not increased in recent years, default rates on student loans have been stable.

In both versions of this sentence, the main emphasis is on the independent clause; however, because the dependent clause comes last in the first version, there is slightly greater emphasis on the information in the dependent clause than in the second version. In this way, you can use subordination strategically to direct your readers' attention to specific ideas or convey a more precise sense of the relationship between the ideas in each clause.

Students often use coordination where subordination would be more effective. Consider this sentence:

> Genetically modified foods can have significant risks for farmers, but such foods can be less expensive for consumers.

The use of the coordinating conjunction (*but*) in this sentence results in equal emphasis on both independent clauses. Although the sentence is perfectly acceptable in this coordinate form, the writer can use subordination to emphasize one or the other independent clause:

> Although genetically modified foods can have significant risks for farmers, such foods can be less expensive for consumers.

> Although genetically modified foods can be less expensive for consumers, such foods can have significant risks for farmers.

In these two versions of the sentence, the emphasis is noticeably stronger on the ideas in the independent clause than in the coordinate version of the sentence, which gives more or less equal weight to the ideas in both clauses.

Parallel Structure

In general, sentences should be written so that words and phrases have the same grammatical form, especially if they are used in a series. Varying the form of words or phrases in a sentence can result in awkward prose:

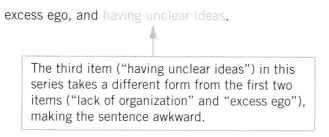

The protest movement was a failure for three reasons: lack of organization, excess ego, and having unclear ideas.

The third item ("having unclear ideas") in this series takes a different form from the first two items ("lack of organization" and "excess ego"), making the sentence awkward.

Make the series parallel by changing the form of the third item so that it is consistent with the form of the first two:

> The protest movement was a failure for three reasons: lack of organization, excess ego, and unclear ideas.

Sometimes two verb constructions in the same sentence take different forms and upset the parallelism of the sentence:

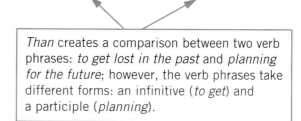

It is easier to get lost in the past than planning the future.

Than creates a comparison between two verb phrases: *to get lost in the past* and *planning for the future*; however, the verb phrases take different forms: an infinitive (*to get*) and a participle (*planning*).

Simply make the forms of the two verb phrases consistent:

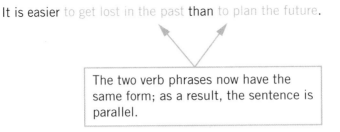

It is easier to get lost in the past **than** to plan the future.

The two verb phrases now have the same form; as a result, the sentence is parallel.

Common Sentence-Level Problems

Most student writers have a grasp of the basic rules of sentence structure, but sometimes writers stumble when trying to write academic prose. Usually, the sentence-level problems that result are of the three main types discussed here.

Run-on or Fused Sentences

A run-on occurs when two or more independent clauses are joined without proper punctuation or linking words:

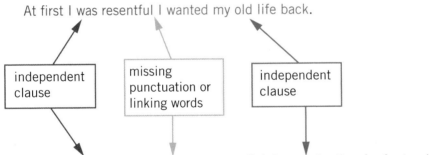

At first I was resentful I wanted my old life back.

| independent clause | missing punctuation or linking words | independent clause |

All this hate needs to disappear we've been fighting each other for far too long.

Often, the easiest solution is adding the proper punctuation mark (usually a period or semi-colon):

At first I was resentful. I wanted my old life back.

All this hate needs to disappear; we've been fighting each other for far too long.

Sometimes, adding linking words or rewriting the sentence is a better option:

At first I was resentful, and I wanted my old life back.

We've been fighting each other for far too long, so let's eliminate the hate.

In many cases, run-on sentences result from an effort to write a complex sentence that contains several ideas:

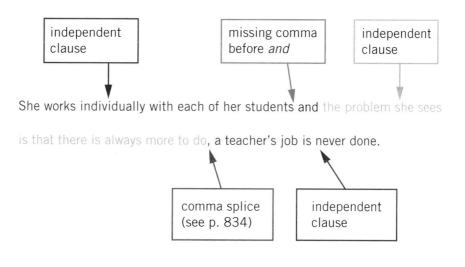

In this example, three independent clauses are fused without proper punctuation. To correct these errors, the writer has several options:

- **Insert correct punctuation:**

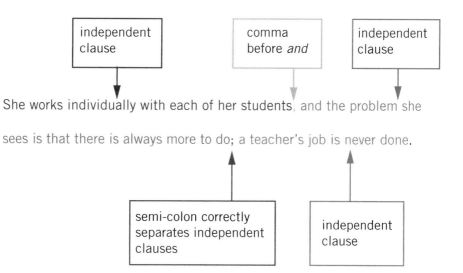

- **Break up the sentence into two or more shorter sentences:**

  She works individually with each of her students, and the problem she sees is that there is always more to do. A teacher's job is never done.

- **Rewrite the sentence:**

  Working individually with each of her students, she sees that there is always more to do and that a teacher's job is never done.

  Working individually with each student means that she always has more to do. A teacher's job is never done.

Which option is best depends on the context within which this sentence occurs and the effect you want to have on your audience.

Fragments

A sentence fragment is an incomplete sentence, often lacking either a subject or a main verb. Sentence fragments often occur when a period is placed incorrectly between a dependent clause or phrase and the main clause of the sentence:

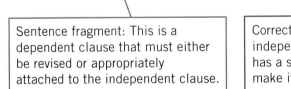

Her parents decided that there wouldn't be time to visit the last college on her list.

Although she was still very interested in applying to that school.

Sentence fragment: This is a dependent clause that must either be revised or appropriately attached to the independent clause.

Correct sentence: This independent clause correctly has a subject and verb to make it a complete sentence.

This error can be corrected by using the proper punctuation between the two clauses:

Her parents decided that there wouldn't be time to visit the last college on her list, although she was still very interested in applying to that school.

Replacing the period with a comma correctly attaches the dependent clause to the independent clause.

This error can be also corrected by rewriting the sentence fragment to make it an independent clause:

> Her parents decided that there wouldn't be time to visit the last college on her list. Still, she remained very interested in applying to that school.

Sometimes fragments occur when a phrase, such as a prepositional phrase or an appositive, is incorrectly set off from the main clause by a period:

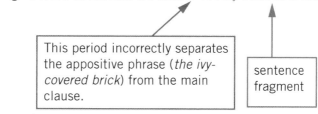

There was one thing he loved about that old house. The ivy-covered brick.

This period incorrectly separates the appositive phrase (*the ivy-covered brick*) from the main clause.

sentence fragment

In this case, the error can be corrected by using the proper punctuation (either a comma or a colon) or by rewriting the sentence slightly:

> There was one thing he loved about that old house: the ivy-covered brick.

> There was one thing he loved about that old house, the ivy-covered brick.

> The one thing he loved about that old house was the ivy-covered brick.

Faulty Sentence Structure

This category of common error is large. It includes a variety of problems that make sentences unclear, difficult to follow, or grammatically incorrect. Two of the most common types of this problem are dangling modifiers and a lack of parallel structure.

- **Misplaced and dangling modifiers.** In general, phrases and clauses that modify a word should be placed as close to that word as possible. Often, a sentence is written so that a clause or phrase modifies the wrong sentence element, as in this example:

When quoting the teachers at the working-class school, the tone is

negative and seems critical of teachers' efforts.

Grammatically, this clause modifies the subject of the main clause (*tone*). But the sentence doesn't make sense, because it is not the tone that is doing the quoting but the writer.

Address the problem by rewriting the sentence:

When quoting the teachers at the working-class school, the writer adopts a negative tone and seems critical of teachers' efforts.

In this revised sentence the modifying clause (*When quoting the teachers at the working-class school*) is placed close to the noun it modifies (*the writer*).

Sometimes, the problem is that the modifier is misplaced, which can change the meaning of the sentence:

Tad only played tennis on Wednesday.

With the adverb *only* placed here, the sentence means that the only thing Tad did on Wednesday was play tennis.

Simply move the modifier:

Tad played tennis only on Wednesday.

Moving the adverb *only* changes the meaning of the sentence. Now it means that Tad plays tennis only on Wednesdays rather than other days.

The same problem can occur when a modifying phrase is placed too far from the noun it modifies:

Chaz spent the rest of the night playing video games, having finally turned in his assignment.

Placed here, the phrase "having finally turned in his assignment" modifies the phrase "playing video games" rather than the subject of the sentence, "Chaz."

Clarify matters by moving the phrase closer to the word it modifies (*Chaz*):

Having finally turned in his assignment, Chaz spent the rest of the night playing video games.

Here is another very common version of the same problem; however, in this case, the intended subject of the main clause is replaced by an indefinite pronoun (*it*), which makes the sentence more awkward and confusing:

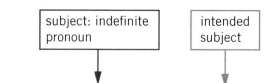

By using this research, it can help guide educators in developing teaching strategies to help adolescents become better readers.

Grammatically, the prepositional phrase ("By using this research") modifies the subject of the main clause ("it"), but *it* isn't using the research; "educators" are using the research. As written, the sentence is nonsensical.

There are two basic ways to address this kind of dangling modifier:

■ **Rewrite the sentence to make the intended subject the grammatical subject:**

By using this research, educators can develop curriculum and teaching strategies to help adolescents become better readers.

The pronoun *it* is deleted and the intended subject ("educators") is now the grammatical subject of the sentence.

■ **Change the modifying phrase into the subject of the sentence:**

The phrase "using this research" is now the subject of the sentence.

Using this research can help educators develop curriculum and teaching strategies to help adolescents become better readers.

Common Pronoun Errors

There are many different kinds of pronouns, which means that there are many opportunities for incorrectly using pronouns. However, most pronoun errors are of two kinds: (1) lack of agreement between the pronoun and its antecedent (that is, the word the pronoun refers to) and (2) a missing or vague antecedent for the pronoun.

There are three basic principles governing the uses of pronouns:

- The pronoun must be in the correct **case** corresponding to its function in the sentence.

- Every pronoun (except indefinite pronouns) must have an **antecedent**—that is, the noun to which the pronoun refers.

- The pronoun must agree with its antecedent in number and gender. (If the antecedent is singular, the pronoun must also be singular; if the antecedent is female, so must the pronoun be.)

If you apply these principles, you are unlikely to make the following common mistakes with pronouns.

Incorrect Pronoun Case

Case refers to the form of a pronoun that reflects its specific function in a sentence: subject, object, or possessive:

He is an excellent dancer. (The pronoun *He* is the subject of the sentence and is therefore correctly in the subjective case.)

Me and Jose went swimming yesterday. (*Me*, which is the objective case of the first-person pronoun *I*, is incorrect because it is being used as a subject. The correct form is *I* in this instance.)

The dance club gave **he** and **I** an award for best dancer. (The pronouns *he* and *I*, which are in the subjective case, are incorrect because they are being used as indirect objects of the verb *gave*. They should be in the objective case: *him* and *me*.)

He brought **his** dancing shoes. (The pronoun *his* is possessive and is therefore correctly in the possessive case.)

Most students are able to identify the proper case of pronouns. In academic writing, however, students sometimes lose track of the proper case when writing lengthy, complex sentences.

Lack of Pronoun-Antecedent Agreement

This error is usually easy to avoid if you identify the antecedent; however, this kind of pronoun error is common in part because the wrong pronoun often "sounds" right:

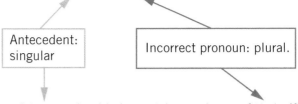

Every student has their own laptop.

Antecedent: singular

Incorrect pronoun: plural.

A hunter should always take good care of their rifle.

Correct these errors either by changing the pronoun or rewriting the sentence:

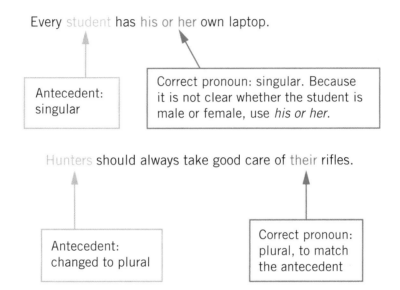

Every student has his or her own laptop.

Antecedent: singular

Correct pronoun: singular. Because it is not clear whether the student is male or female, use *his or her.*

Hunters should always take good care of their rifles.

Antecedent: changed to plural

Correct pronoun: plural, to match the antecedent

Making sure that the pronoun agrees with its antecedent can be tricky when the antecedent is an **indefinite pronoun** (e.g., everyone, anyone, anybody, someone):

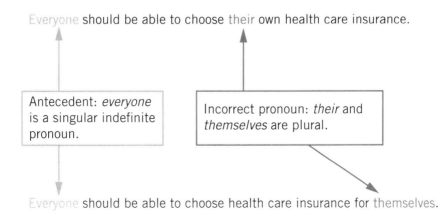

Everyone should be able to choose their own health care insurance.

Antecedent: *everyone* is a singular indefinite pronoun.

Incorrect pronoun: *their* and *themselves* are plural.

Everyone should be able to choose health care insurance for themselves.

Again, correct the errors by changing the pronoun or rewriting the sentence:

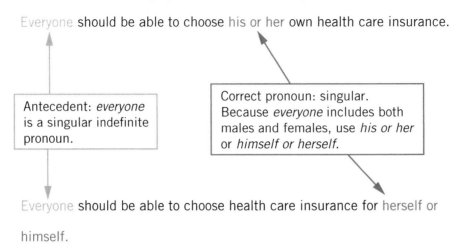

Everyone should be able to choose his or her own health care insurance.

Antecedent: *everyone* is a singular indefinite pronoun.

Correct pronoun: singular. Because *everyone* includes both males and females, use *his or her* or *himself or herself.*

Everyone should be able to choose health care insurance for herself or

himself.

Vague Pronoun Reference

Usually, the antecedent is the noun closest to the pronoun. Sometimes, however, the antecedent can seem to refer to more than one noun. In this example, technically the antecedent for the pronoun *he* should be *Steve*, because *Steve* is the closest noun to the pronoun. But a reader might assume that *he* refers instead to *Bob*.

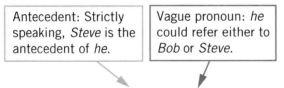

Antecedent: Strictly speaking, *Steve* is the antecedent of *he.*

Vague pronoun: *he* could refer either to *Bob* or *Steve.*

Bob explained to Steve that he wasn't a bad writer.

In such cases, rewrite the sentence to clarify the antecedent:

Bob explained to Steve that Steve wasn't a bad writer.

Bob said to Steve, "You're not a bad writer."

According to Bob, Steve wasn't a bad writer.

Word Choice and Style

An effective style in academic writing is partly a matter of careful and strategic selection of words, not only to craft clear sentences but also to meet the needs of the rhetorical situation. Sometimes that means using specialized terminology (often called "jargon") that is appropriate for the subject—say, economics or psychology. More often, though, writers must make choices among words that have slightly different shades of meaning to convey precisely what they want to say to their readers. Consider the differences in the following statements:

The audience was **interested** in the speaker's argument.

The audience was **engaged** by the speaker's argument.

The audience was **fascinated** by the speaker's argument.

The audience was **enthralled** by the speaker's argument.

Although all of these sentences generally mean that the audience listened intently to the speaker, each sentence conveys a different sense of the impact of the speaker's argument on the audience. Selecting the verb that conveys precisely what you want to convey about that impact is part of what it means to write effective prose.

Students tend to make three errors when it comes to word choice:

- making imprecise word choices
- using the wrong word
- confusing similar words

Imprecise Word Choices

The best word choice is always shaped by the rhetorical situation—especially the writer's sense of the audience's expectations and the appropriate style—as well as by the writer's own preferences. However, students sometimes rely too much on general words when more specialized or specific words would be more precise:

The mayor gave a **great** speech to the residents after their town was hit by the hurricane.

Words like *great, good, bad,* and *awesome* are overused and vague, even if their general meanings are clear. In this example, the writer conveys a positive sense of the mayor's speech but not much more than that. Consider these alternatives:

The mayor gave a **comforting** speech to the residents after their town was hit by the hurricane.

The mayor gave an **encouraging** speech to the residents after their town was hit by the hurricane.

The mayor gave an **emotional** speech to the residents after their town was hit by the hurricane.

Which of these choices is best will depend on the specific meaning you want to convey to your readers and the context of the text in which the sentence appears, but any of these choices conveys a clearer, more precise description of the mayor's speech than the original sentence. As this example shows, a single word can significantly improve a sentence.

Wrong Word

Studies show that one of the most common errors in student writing is the use of the wrong word or word form; however, those same studies do not identify specific words that students routinely misuse (other than the ones discussed in the next section). That might be because of the richness of the English language and the idiosyncrasies of each of us as writers. In other words, all writers sometimes use the wrong word, but we all make different versions of this error. You might have trouble remembering the correct form of a specific verb, while your classmate struggles with a different kind of word that you find easy to use. This variability does not allow us to make generalizations about specific errors in word choice that are common in student writing, and it underscores the need to become aware of the errors that you tend to make, as noted in the first section of this chapter.

Confusing Similar Words

Words that look and sound alike but have very different functions can sometimes confuse writers and lead to common errors. In such cases, the best approach is simply to learn the correct uses of these words and any rules related to their usage. Being aware that these words are often the source of errors is also important. You can be vigilant in using these words and focus on them when editing your drafts.

The three most commonly confused sets of words are *their, there,* and *they're; affect* and *effect;* and *then* and *than.*

■ **Their/there/they're.** Each of these words has a very different function:

Their is a plural possessive pronoun.

The players put on **their** uniforms.

Voters never seem to be able to make up **their** minds.

■ **There** is an adverb denoting place; it can also be used as a pronoun.

We don't want to go **there**. (adverb)

There are three reasons to support this candidate. (pronoun)

■ **They're** is a contraction for *they are.*

They told us that **they're** not going on the field trip.

Although the peaches are inexpensive, **they're** not very fresh.

A common mistake is using *their* in place of *they're*:

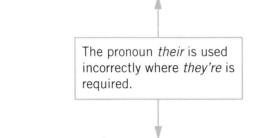

The students can't explain why their unhappy with the new class.

> The pronoun *their* is used incorrectly where *they're* is required.

Although the workers are tired, their planning to finish the job.

To avoid this mistake, replace the word (*their, there,* or *they're*) with the words *they are*. If the sentence makes sense, then you must use the word *they're*.

Another common mistake is using ***there*** in place of ***their***:

The children forgot to bring there towels to swimming class.

There can never be correctly used in place of the pronoun *their*.

When it began to rain, the workers covered up there tools with plastic tarps.

■ **Affect/effect.** Although both these words can be either nouns or verbs, *affect* is most often used as a verb meaning to act upon, whereas *effect* is most often used as a noun to mean an impact, result, or consequence:

The heavy rains will probably **affect** the harvest.

Seemingly, he was not **affected** by the long hours and lack of sleep.

The weather always **affects** our vacation plans.

Growing up in a small town had a big **effect** on me.

Historians have long debated the **effects** of the industrial revolution.

What is the **effect** of the new regulation?

The two most common errors involving these terms are using *effect* as a verb when *affect* is required and using *affect* as a noun when *effect* is required:

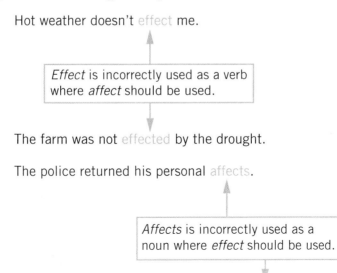

Hot weather doesn't effect me.

Effect is incorrectly used as a verb where *affect* should be used.

The farm was not effected by the drought.

The police returned his personal affects.

Affects is incorrectly used as a noun where *effect* should be used.

The economist could not anticipate the affects of the hurricanes.

Be aware that *affect* can be used as a noun and *effect* as a verb, although these uses are much less common than those explained above. As a noun, *affect* refers to an emotional state or feeling:

The patients lacked **affect** in their expressions.

The woman had a joyful **affect**.

The criminal displayed a disturbing **affect**.

When used as a verb, *effect* means to cause something to happen or to bring about:

The reformers sought to **effect** significant change in the way schools are run.

The farmers were successful in **effecting** an increase in commodity prices.

- **Then/than.** The easiest way to distinguish between these two common words is to remember that *then* refers to time, whereas *than* is always used in comparisons:

I'll go to the bank, and **then** I'll go to the grocery store.

The book's influence has been much greater **than** the author could ever have imagined.

We were much more optimistic back **then**.

She liked the green sweatshirt better **than** the blue one.

The most common mistake with these two words occurs when *then* is used in place of *than*:

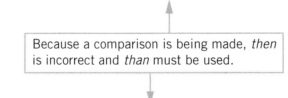

I have always been a better athlete then my sister.

Because a comparison is being made, *then* is incorrect and *than* must be used.

He wanted to visit Europe more then anything.

Here are some other commonly confused words.

- **Accept/except.** *Accept* is a verb meaning to receive something. *Except* is generally used as a preposition:

She was happy to **accept** the award.

Everyone **except** the boss received a raise.

- **Advice/advise.** The easiest way to avoid confusing these words is to remember that *advice* is a noun meaning guidance, whereas *advise* is a verb meaning to give guidance or advice:

My lawyer always provides me with good **advice** when I'm trying to make a decision involving legal matters.

The lawyer will **advise** a client about the best way to handle a legal problem.

- **Complement/compliment.** *Complement* can be used as a noun or a verb; it means to complete or add to. A *compliment* can also be a noun or verb; it means to praise.

The blue hat nicely **complemented** his tan suit.

I paid him a **compliment** on his blue hat.

- **Lie/lie/lay.** These often-confused words have very different meanings and functions. The irregular verb *lie* means to recline or place your body in a prone position and takes three forms: *lie, lay, have lain*. The regular verb *lie* (which takes the forms *lie, lied, and have lied*) means to tell a falsehood. The regular verb *lay* (which takes the forms *lay, laid, and have laid*) means to place something or put something down. Most often students use *lay* when they should use *lie*:

Incorrect: She likes to **lay** down on the sofa after lunch to take a nap.

Correct: She likes to **lie** down on the sofa after lunch to take a nap.

Incorrect: He **laid** down on the sofa to take a nap.

Correct: He **lay** down on the sofa to take a nap.

Incorrect: Before he finished his paper, he had **laid** down on the sofa to rest.

Correct: Before he finished his paper, he had **lain** down on the sofa to rest.

Incorrect: She commanded her dog to **lay** down.

Correct: She commanded her dog to **lie** down.

Incorrect: He **lied** the baby down in the crib. He lay the baby in the crib.

Correct: He **laid** the baby down in the crib.

- **Past/passed.** *Past* is a preposition meaning gone by or a noun meaning a time period before the present. *Passed* is the past tense of the verb *pass*, which means to go by.

He drove **past** the accident.

He **passed** by the accident.

The accident occurred in the **past**.

- **To/too/two.** These three words that sound similar have very different functions. *To* is a preposition. *Too* is an adverb. *Two* is a noun or adjective.

She ran **to** the finish line.

He gave his car **to** his friend.

She wanted a new car, **too**.

He, **too**, was interested in running the race.

There were **too** many runners in the race.

There were **two** runners who did not finish the race.

Two is better than one.

■ **Through/threw.** *Through* is used either as an adverb or preposition. *Threw* is the past tense of the verb *throw.*

He went **through** the tunnel.

She **threw** a rock into the tunnel.

Only **through** hard work can you succeed.

Common Punctuation Errors
Missing Commas

Missing commas where they are required are among the most common errors student writers make. This section reviews the rules for seven required uses of commas:

- before a coordinating conjunction
- after an introductory element
- before a quotation
- around nonessential elements
- in a series
- between coordinate adjectives
- to set off nouns of direct address, *yes* and *no,* interrogative tags, and interjections

If you become familiar with the rules for these seven uses of commas, you will avoid these common errors.

■ **Before a coordinating conjunction (for, and, nor, but, or, yet, so).** In most cases a comma should be placed *before* a coordinating conjunction (such as *for, and, nor, but, or, yet, so*) that connects two independent clauses:

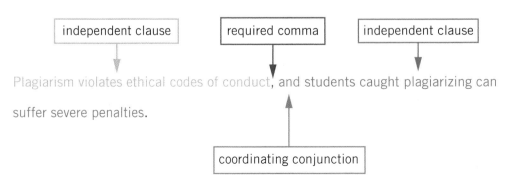

The weather promised to turn stormy later that afternoon, so we took along rain jackets.

Every student is potentially affected by tuition increases, but students who rely on loans might suffer the most because they will end up borrowing more money to pay for their educations.

One important exception to this rule: no comma is needed before a coordinating conjunction that joins two very short sentences:

I was tired but I slept well.

■ **After an introductory element.** A comma should be placed after an introductory word, phrase, or clause in a sentence:

When students are satisfied with their own writing, they are often eager to

share it with classmates.

■ **Introductory phrase:**

Worried about his car, Brian decided not to drive the long distance back to his apartment.

Despite her misgivings, she signed up for the backpacking trip.

■ **Introductory word:**

Furthermore, I was starting school that fall.

Ultimately, they found what they were seeking.

Traditionally, conservative teachers have never questioned the principle of school governance by part-time citizens.

Notice that in this last example, the comma changes the meaning of the sentence. Without the comma, the adverb "traditionally" modifies the adjective "conservative," which modifies the subject (teachers), and the sentence means that teachers who are traditionally conservative have never questioned the principle of school governance by part-time citizens. However, with the comma, "traditionally" modifies the main verb (questioned), and the sentence means that conservative teachers have traditionally not questioned the principle of school governance by part-time citizens.

■ **Before a quotation.** Direct quotations of complete sentences must be preceded by a comma:

John Lennon once said, "Life is what happens to you while you're busy making other plans."

Audre Lorde wrote, "It is not our differences that divide us. It is our inability to recognize, accept, and celebrate those differences."

- **Around nonessential elements.** Use commas to set off elements of a sentence that are not essential for understanding who or what is being discussed. Nonessential elements include appositives, modifying phrases or clauses, transitional words or phrases, or parenthetical words or phrases.

With appositives:

When my second brother was born, we switched rooms so that the boys could share the larger room and I, the only girl, could have the small room for myself.

In this sentence, the phrase "the only girl" is an appositive modifying the pronoun "I" and must be set off by commas.

Nonessential (non-restrictive) modifying phrases or clauses:

In the following sentences, the highlighted words are nonessential clauses or phrases that must be set off by commas. (In these cases, removing the highlighted words does not change the meaning of the main sentence, which is why they are called "nonessential.")

The car, which was brilliant red, was stuck on the side of the road.

David, who was wearing a blue rain jacket, quickly ran for shelter.

Hungry and cold, the stray cat hid under the back porch.

With transitional words or phrases:

What is interesting, though, is that they never realized what they were doing.

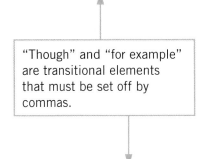

"Though" and "for example" are transitional elements that must be set off by commas.

Her most recent novel, for example, examines unconventional families.

With parenthetical words or phrases:

Parenthetical phrases or words are like "asides" or related but nonessential comments: They are not necessary, and removing them does not affect the meaning of the main sentence.

Jasmine heard the comment and, understandably, left the room.

> These parenthetical elements must be set off by commas.

Jerry believed that everyone, except maybe people with debilitating illnesses, should have to work.

- **In a series.** Place a comma after each item in a series, whether those items are words, phrases, or clauses. (In these examples, the different items in each series are shown in different colors.)

Students were told to bring a pencil, a paper, and an eraser.

The tired sailors found themselves struggling to stay on schedule, worried about the condition of their boat, and hoping for better weather.

The triathletes were wondering whether to emphasize swimming, running, or bicycling in their workouts.

Only a few days after the hurricane, power was restored, stores reopened, and people returned to their homes.

Note: The preceding sentences all contain **the Oxford Comma**, which is placed after the second-to-last item in a series and before the coordinating conjunction (and, or). The Oxford Comma is typically expected in academic writing; however, it is rarely used in popular writing. For college writing assignments, I recommend using the Oxford Comma unless instructed otherwise.

- **Between coordinate adjectives.** Coordinate adjectives are adjectives that are equal and reversible, so that their order does not affect the meaning of the phrase. Usually, if adjectives can be connected by "and," they are coordinate and should be separated by commas:

PJ Harvey's album *To Bring You My Love* is full of dirge-like, erotic vocals.

> These two adjectives (*dirge-like* and *erotic*), which modify the noun *vocals*, could be reversed without altering the meaning of the phrase or the sentence, so they must be separated by commas.

The juicy, ripe, sweet peach is one of the best tastes of summer.

> The adjectives modifying *peach* could be reversed without altering the meaning of the phrase or the sentence, so they must be separated by commas.

Compare the previous two examples with this one:

He bought seven red apples.

In this case, no comma separates the adjectives *seven* and *red* because the two are not equal. *Seven* modifies the entire phrase *red apples*. The adjectives *seven* and *red* are cumulative. They cannot be logically reordered or be connected with *and*: For example, we would not say, "seven and red apples" or "red seven apples." Commas should not be used to separate cumulative adjectives.

- **With nouns of direct address, the words *yes* and *no*, interrogative tags, and mild interjections.** Names and other terms used in direct address must be set off by commas:

Mike, turn it up. (direct address)

No, I won't turn it up.

You're not going to turn it up, are you? (The phrase "are you" is an interrogative tag.)

Look, take it easy. (The word "Look" is an interjection.)

Unnecessary Commas

Maybe because there are so many rules governing the uses of commas, students often place commas where they are not needed. Two kinds of unnecessary commas are among the most common punctuation errors: commas that incorrectly separate sentence elements and commas placed around essential (or restrictive) elements.

- **Separating sentence elements.** Commas should not be used to separate essential elements in a sentence, such as the subject and verb, compound words or phrases, and necessary phrases or clauses unless those essential elements are separated by other elements that must be set off by commas. Here are some examples of unnecessary commas:

> This comma incorrectly separates the two parts of a compound verb (*is* and *keeps*) with the same subject (*she*) and should be deleted.

She is meticulous, and keeps her equipment stored carefully in its original boxes.

If an element that must be set off by commas were included between the essential elements, then be sure to use commas:

> She is meticulous, almost to a fault, and keeps her equipment stored carefully in its original boxes.

> | This comma incorrectly separates the infinitive phrase (*to increase their power*) from the main clause of the sentence (*nations are taking land*). |

The European nations are taking land from weaker nations, to increase their power.

■ **With an essential (restrictive) element.** An element that is necessary for the intended meaning of a sentence should not be set off by commas. In many cases involving restrictive elements, the use of commas changes the meaning of the sentence.

| Because the relative clause ("who receives the most votes") indicates a specific candidate and affects the meaning of the sentence, it should not be set off by commas. These two commas should be deleted. |

The candidate, who receives the most votes, will win the election.

The Democratic Party supports quotas, which are consistent with the ideal of equality.

| This comma significantly changes the meaning of the sentence. With the comma, the sentence means that *all* quotas are consistent with the ideal of equality. Without the comma, the sentence means that the Democratic Party supports *only those quotas* that are consistent with the ideal of equality. |

Comma Splices

A comma splice, sometimes called a comma fault, occurs when a comma is incorrectly used to separate two independent clauses. The commas in the following sentences are incorrect:

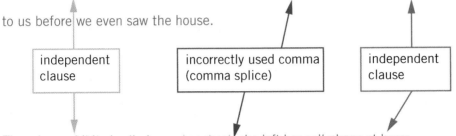

In many cases, there are several ways to correct a comma splice. Often, the simplest way is to replace the comma with a period or semi-colon:

> My brother and I raced up the stairs to our rooms. These rooms had been assigned to us before we even saw the house.

> The rules prohibited cell phones in school; she left her cell phone at home.

Sometimes, rewriting the sentence is a better option:

> My brother and I raced up the stairs to the rooms that had been assigned to us before we even saw the house.

> My brother and I raced up the stairs to our rooms, which had been assigned to us before we even saw the house.

> The rules prohibited cell phones in school, so she left her cell phone at home.

> Because the rules prohibited cell phones in school, she left her cell phone at home.

Incorrect Semi-colon

The semi-colon might well be the most misunderstood and misused punctuation mark. Learning a few basic rules can help you avoid misusing semi-colons and, more important, use them strategically to strengthen your writing.

The semi-colon has three main functions:

■ to separate two independent clauses whose subjects are closely linked, as in the following examples:

> With writing, the audience is usually absent; with talking, the listener is usually present.

> Apples in Des Moines supermarkets can be from China, even though there are apple farmers in Iowa; potatoes in Lima's supermarkets are from the United States, even though Peru boasts more varieties of potato than any other country.

Protecting the health of the environment is a prudent investment; it can avert scarcity, perpetuate abundance, and provide a solid basis for social development.

- to separate elements in a series when those elements include other punctuation marks, as in the following examples:

Present at the meeting were the board president, John Smith; April Jones, treasurer; Molly Harris, secretary; and Josh Jordan, who was filling in for an absent board member.

If you plan to hike in the mountains in winter, you should always carry proper clothing, especially dependable raingear; extra food and water; matches, a lighter, or a portable stove for cooking and for melting snow for water; and a tarp for shelter.

- to separate two independent clauses that are linked by a conjunctive adverb, such as *however, therefore, moreover, nevertheless,* and *consequently,* as in the following examples:

The students planned to attend the opening night of the play at the campus theater; however, when they arrived for the show, they learned that it was sold out.

Although many colleges do not use standardized test scores when evaluating applicants for admission, most colleges still require applicants to submit SAT or ACT scores; therefore, high school students who wish to attend college should plan to take either the SAT or the ACT or both.

There are other uses for the semi-colon, but if you learn to use the semi-colon in these three main ways, you will avoid the most common mistakes that student writers make with semi-colons.

- **Semi-colon instead of a colon.** One of the most common mistakes students make is using a semi-colon instead of a colon to introduce a sentence element, such as a series:

> The semi-colon should *never* be used to introduce a series. The correct punctuation mark here is a colon.

The mud was horrendous, and it got onto everything; our clothes, our skin, our hair.

He argued that the U.S. is too dependent on one kind of energy source; oil.

> In this example, either a colon or a comma would be correct, but a semi-colon is incorrect.

■ **Missing semi-colon.** Another very common error occurs when the writer neglects to use a semi-colon with a conjunctive adverb (e.g., *however, therefore, nevertheless, consequently*). When two independent clauses are joined by a conjunctive adverb, a semi-colon must precede the conjunctive adverb, which is followed by a comma. In such cases, a comma preceding the conjunctive adverb is incorrect:

The internal resistance of the battery was found to be lower than it was in

the other circuit, however, it still resulted in a significant difference in voltage.

| This comma is incorrect. A semi-colon must be used here. | The conjunctive adverb (*however*) should be followed by a comma. |

Incorrect Use of Apostrophe

Apostrophes can be confusing because they are used in several very different ways. The two main functions of apostrophes are

- to indicate possession
- to indicate omitted letters, especially in contractions

If you understand these functions, you will be able to avoid the most common mistakes student writers make in using apostrophes.

■ **Missing or incorrect apostrophe to indicate possession.** An apostrophe followed by the letter *s* indicates possession or ownership for most **singular nouns**:

John's car

the student's book

the government's role

Thomas Jefferson's signature

the musician's instrument

the tree's shadow

The most common violation of this rule occurs when a writer neglects to use an apostrophe where it is necessary to show possession:

She remembered to bring her husbands jacket when she left the house.

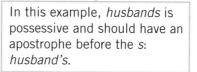

In this example, *husbands* is possessive and should have an apostrophe before the *s*: *husband's*.

In most cases, this rule also applies if the singular form of the noun ends in *s*:

New Orleans's mayor

the dress's hem

progress's risks

the witness's memory

Note that **possessive pronouns** (mine, yours, hers, his, theirs, ours, its) *do not* have an apostrophe:

If you don't have a bicycle, you can use **mine**.

The horse had a scar on **its** left foreleg.

To form **the possessive of a plural noun that already ends in s**, use an apostrophe at the end of the word *without* an additional *s*:

the birds' nests

the ships' destinations

the cowboys' horses

However, if the plural form of a noun does not end in *s*, use an apostrophe followed by an *s* to indicate possession:

the children's scarves

women's rights

the sheep's pen

Note that in these examples, the nouns are already in their plural forms, and the apostrophe does not make the nouns plural; rather, the apostrophe designates possession.

■ **Missing apostrophe in a contraction.** An apostrophe is required in a contraction, such as *isn't, can't, doesn't,* or *won't.* In contractions, the apostrophe stands for a missing letter or letters: *isn't* for *is not; can't* for *cannot; doesn't* for *does not; won't* for *will not.*

He couldnt see what was right in front of him.

Couldn't, the contraction for *could not*, requires an apostrophe between the letters *n* and *t*.

■ **Confusing *its* and *it's*.** *Its* and *it's* are two very different kinds of words: *its* is a possessive pronoun and *it's* is a contraction meaning *it is*. Students often confuse the two and, as a result, misuse them. To avoid this very common error, you need to **remember two rules**:

■ *its* is a possessive pronoun and therefore does not have an apostrophe

■ *it's* is the contraction for *it is* and therefore must always have an apostrophe

Use this simple strategy:

1. Replace *its* or *it's* with *it is* in the sentence.

2. If the sentence makes sense with *it is*, then *it's* is the correct word.

3. If the sentence doesn't make sense with *it is*, then *its* is the correct word.

Here's how it works:

Example 1

Sentence: The dog became extremely aggressive whenever anyone approached **it's** cage.

Strategy: Replace *it's* with *it is*: The dog became extremely aggressive whenever anyone approached **it is** cage.

Result: The sentence does not make sense with *it is*, so *it's* must be replaced with *its*: The dog became extremely aggressive whenever anyone approached **its** cage.

Example 2

Sentence: He is bringing a jacket on because **it's** very cold outside.

Strategy: Replace *it's* with *it is*: He is bringing a jacket on because **it is** very cold outside.

Result: The sentence make sense with *it is*, so *it's* is correct.

Example 3

Sentence: The sailboat was distinctive because of the loud color of **its** sails.

Strategy: Replace *it's* with *it is*: The sailboat was distinctive because of the loud color of **it is** sails.

Result: The sentence does not make sense with *it is*, so *its* is correct.

Incorrect Use of Colons

The colon is a kind of "pointing" mark of punctuation; it calls attention to the words that follow it. A colon is commonly used to introduce a list or series, a quotation, or an appositive.

To introduce a list or series

By the time she was twenty, my grandmother Virginia knew how to play several musical instruments: piano, fiddle, guitar, banjo, and mandolin.

The protest movement was a failure for three reasons: lack of organization, excess ego, and unclear ideas.

To introduce a quotation

Rainer Maria Rilke has unusual advice for young poets: "Love the questions themselves."

Among Thoreau's best-known statements is a line from *Walden*: "The mass of men lead lives of quiet desperation."

With appositives

As my father once told me, there is only one way to do things: the right way.

The gymnast had only one goal: a gold medal.

Notice that when a colon precedes a complete sentence, the first word after the colon *must* be capitalized; however, if the word or phrase following the colon does not make a complete sentence, the first word following the colon is *not* capitalized.

Index